TAINTED LOVE

Hope Daniels and Morag Livingstone

**SIMON &
SCHUSTER**

London · New York · Sydney · Toronto · New Delhi

A CBS COMPANY

First published in Great Britain by Simon & Schuster UK Ltd, 2014
A CBS Company

1 3 5 7 9 10 8 6 4 2

Simon & Schuster UK Ltd
1st Floor
222 Gray's Inn Road
London WC1X 8HB

www.simonandschuster.co.uk

Simon & Schuster Australia
Sydney

Simon & Schuster India
New Delhi

A CIP catalogue record for this book is available
from the British Library.

Paperback ISBN: 978-1-47112-988-9
Ebook ISBN: 978-1-47112-989-6

Typeset by Hewer Text UK Ltd, Edinburgh
Printed and Bound in Great Britain by CPI (UK) Ltd, Croydon, CR0 4YY

This story is based on real events and people that Hope Daniels has
met throughout her life, including those met during research in her
career as an advisor and lecturer. Many people in the book have kindly
given their stories in the knowledge that they would be incorporated
here. It is of course necessary to protect the identities of those people
and others with whom Hope has come into contact while growing
up. We have, with the exception of names and places in the public
domain, created composites of characters and situations, changed
names, ages, street names and altered some background details.

In memory of
all the care leavers who did not make it.

CONTENTS

Note   viii

Prologue   1
Part One – Home   9
Part Two – Tainted Love   55
Part Three – Secure   123
Part Four – Moving On   245
Epilogue   295

Postscript: Reflections From Hope   301
Authors' Notes and acknowledgements   305

Through *Hackney Child* I've been given an identity and
a voice where I felt none,
An inner sanctum of pain and self-hatred I did hide,
Oh, the many years I couldn't abide.
Whoosh the tears fall,
Allow the mask to install.
Must have been cathartic, they say,
Oh, there's now many an inner sunny day,
I am no longer a back seat driver,
Care Leavers are survivors.

Hope Daniels, 2014

People are always blaming their circumstances for what they are . . . the people who get on in this world are the people who look for the circumstances they want and, if they can't find them, make them.

George Bernard Shaw

PROLOGUE

Hope. 2013.

This can't be happening. This can't be happening. This isn't real.

I'm walking down the centre aisle of the great ballroom in the Grand Central Hotel, Glasgow, towards the stage, past hundreds of people who don't know who I am. Rows of people, 16 chairs in each row. A lot of rows.

Walking slowly, past the bowed heads of delegates, some examining the programme of events for the day, others whispering and catching up with old friends or colleagues, sharing, bonding. Some on their own, reading about what's to come.

He's reading my profile! Don't look up at me. Hope, you can do this, they want you here.

I look up at the stage; it still seems far away from where I am now.

This room's too big; it's so much bigger than I remember.

Even though I was here only yesterday for the first day of the conference, I made sure I sat at the front so I couldn't see how big the room was. Overnight it has grown bigger, in my head, than it was yesterday.

This room is huge, look at the lights, beautiful. Every seat is filled. Oh God, presentation, think presentation. I've prepared. Breathe. This can't be happening. But it is.

I look down at my own conference brochure, one of the many that the girls who are here with me from London and I have collected. My name is there in bold: Hope Daniels, Key Note Speaker, SIRCC National Conference, Glasgow.

I just didn't expect there to be so many people. I just didn't believe this could happen to me.

I look up at the chandeliers in the great ballroom, the scene of today's keynote speech, the opulence, the colours, the design, the richness. I love it all. So far, so far from that little girl who walked into a police station in Hackney, London, at nine years old with her two brothers and demanded to be taken into care; because care can be better than home. I move to the side, a quiet corner in this room full of people.

I wish my dad could see this. My husband, kids and friends are so proud and supportive, and I'm so happy for that. But you, too, Dad, are you? Can you see me, Dad? Me, about to speak to all these people, in a big, posh room like this? This is me, Hope, your little girl. It was tough to leave you, Dad, but I hope you can see now that I had no choice. I needed, deserved a better life. This is the result, here, now. Glasgow, speaking to the professionals, like those who raised me. Can you see? Being in care saved me. I hope you're proud . . . I love you, Dad.

There's a hand on my elbow, it's the conference organiser. She smiles in a way that she's smiled since we met three days ago, full of warmth and calm.

'Hope, everything's ready. Are you ready?'

'Yes. Thank you.'

Apart from my sweaty hands.

I don't take in what they say about me in the introduction but when people clap politely, I climb the steps to the stage and the podium. I look to the audience, my presentation on the big screen behind me.

Deep breath.

'Minister, Ladies and Gentlemen. My name is Hope Daniels and from the age of nine, I spent my life in the care system.'

I pause. I look out at the residential care workers. A sea of faces, full of warmth and love. I love people like this, what they do for people like me, for people whose life at home is shit. These people are my friends, people like this brought me up, and they're like my family.

I break the silence, change my voice so it's more like me, 'I feel like I'm with family, so . . . do you mind if I take off my shoes?'

The whole room erupts in laughter. I chuck off my shoes and, barefoot, I begin again.

There's a mass of people surrounding me, voices, comments and warmth. People shaking my hand, giving me hugs.

'There's never been a standing ovation at a conference before.'

'I thought it was going to be a sales pitch but, no, we really learnt from you.'

'Thank you so much.'

After the conference is over, and with success ringing in my ears, I need to go to a Narcotics Anonymous meeting before heading back to London. Recovery from my own addictions in the past few years has released me from a lot of pain and suffering, allowing me to move forward. Freedom.

Meetings, and the people at them, provide me with encouragement, love, support and understanding of a mutually shared disease. I put the details in my sat nav and head off to my sanctuary.

Oh no, I need petrol. It's okay, plenty of time.

The petrol pumping into my car is rhythmic, and I drift off again for a moment.

Scotland is wicked, the people are amazing, and so forward-thinking in their care approach to Looked-after Children. Maybe we can move here one day, buy a house, get out of the council house. All that mortgage debt, ha ha.

'Hope? Hope Daniels? Is that you?'

What? Who? No one knows me here.

The voice carries on. 'Hope Daniels, it is you; I am sure it is. We were in care at the same time. Do you remember? The laundry, we used to play with the laundry . . .'

'Jackie!'

Hope. 1984.

'Hope. Jackie. Come on, now, everything is dry.'

That call from Craig, one of the residential social workers at Chesterfields Children's Home, was enough to get us shifted from our rooms. Jackie, who is eight years old and I, almost two years older, meet each other at the top of the stairs, both with equal-sized Cheshire cat grins. This is our thing. Our special moment in the week.

Only she and I fully understand the meaning and get to share this together. Laughing. We reach out for each other's hands, leaning on each other as we run down the stairs.

'Careful, you two. Don't run.'

We don't listen to Craig. Our excitement takes over our legs and we zoom downstairs. A voice calls out from behind the kitchen door.

'I can hear you running – walk, please.'

In response to this call, we both slow down. Jackie's hand grasps mine a little tighter; she, too, is worried that we didn't stop running soon enough and that this treat shall be taken away.

Tentatively I push open the door of the kitchen, Jackie pushing in behind me.

'Don't rush, Jackie.'

I want to, but I like to savour the moment before it comes. Craig and Angela, the housekeeper, are sitting at the table finishing a mug of something, their grins matching ours. The smell of potatoes and slow-cooked stew on the stove distracts us only for a second. Right now, food isn't the priority. We know what's coming and Jackie is dancing foot to foot with excitement.

'Come on, then,' Angela says, the deepness of her friendly voice matching her big, motherly body. She pushes back her chair, stands and moves from her mug. I smell coffee.

'I don't know why you like this so much, you two. But wait there a second; I just need to check the dinner.'

While she goes over to the cooker, Jackie and I look at each other. I don't know exactly what she's remembering but I know from her expression that it's not so good. My memory takes me away from the kitchen, too. I know I'm standing in the kitchen of the children's home, but my body suddenly feels damp.

A smell of piss and damp and mould fills my nostrils. I'm in bed, about the age Jackie is now. I pull the sheets over me and a damp patch hits my arm. I move my body so it curls round a wet spot on the mattress, but as I curl my feet up, they hit another one. That one's from last night, when, to avoid the damp patches, I tried to sleep the other way round, with my head at the bottom and my feet at the top. But that didn't work, so I slept in wet and had an accident with my waterworks. Everything in my room's a bit grey. I don't know when the sheets, or my pyjamas, were last washed. They stink, they're wet and my brothers' beds are the same.

I can't sleep. It's too cold. Think of summer. Think of summer. Rub your feet together. Wrap your arms around yourself. Where's Mum tonight?

I roll over. I close my eyes and hold my nose to see if that stems the smell, but the mustiness of my bedclothes reaches through my fingers. I'm still cold in my wet and damp bed.

'Hope, don't get distracted.'

I come back from where I've been. I feel tired because, while I'm excited by what's to come, a little bit of the dampness seems to be hanging around and clinging to my skin.

'In you pop, girls.'

We both barge into the laundry room; it's hot, dry. Fresh smells welcome us.

'It smells of spring, even though it's just coming into autumn,' I announce.

Angela smiles. 'Are you both ready?'

'Yes!' we shout in unison, both of us now dancing from foot to foot.

Are we ever!

We stand in front of the industrial-sized dryer and she opens the door.

Immediately the tumble dryer smell hits the back of my throat and with it my spirits are lifted even further. All memories of my past life gone.

This feels safe. Secure.

Craig has now come into the room to help – we know we shall both get the same treatment at the same time as each other. I help Angela pull a warm sheet out of one side of the dryer. Jackie and Craig do the same on the other side. Even though the door is big, the sheets get stuck, so anxious are we to get them out.

'Hold on, girls,' Craig is laughing as he speaks. 'Take it slow.'

But I can't wait. I want to scream. This is the best thing ever.

Please, now. Please.

The sheets release themselves with a helping hand from the adults. Quickly they each turn and Angela wraps me from head to toe in the warm sheet. Craig does the same for Jackie. We bounce around, restricted in movement by the sheets but energised by their warmth.

'I love it,' shouts Jackie.

'Me, too,' I echo.

We all four are laughing, shrieking, playing with the warm sheets.

I want to eat the smell of the hot, freshly laundered sheets; carry it with me on bad days.

Craig and Angela are standing to the side of the laundry together. Laughing, smiling, occasionally stepping in to spin us around again in the sheets; watching our happy faces as we wrap ourselves up in sheet after sheet, as we laugh and they teach us what a childhood should be.

PART ONE

HOME

Hope. 1999.

The carpet of my living room is hidden by piles of paper. Big piles, little piles, any which way piles. It's been the same every night recently. Each night, when I'm sure my two kids are washed, their teeth brushed and they're safely asleep, I start sorting the paper from my files.

Files, my files. All mine.

With just my curiosity about my life in these, my social work files, my broken heart, and a glass of wine, each night I work, and work hard. It's like a military operation. I sit organising and reading this record of my family history, documented before and during my time as a ward of court, in care.

The files beckon me; they have been calling me since I first knew of their existence, more than fifteen years ago.

What's wrong with me? I know this is gonna hurt, but I can't stop.

I touch the top of the first file and feel the weight of my history haunting me, pushing upwards through the paper, calling me to revisit my past. In doing so, I'm searching for answers as to why my parents couldn't cope bringing us up, and answers about how to handle my own present, and my kids' future. How to make sure my kids know I love them and how to stop them going into care, too.

How do I make that happen? How do you love? The staff at the children's homes loved me and they were taken away from me. My social worker loved me, I think, and still she left.

The tears come before I even start.

I can't. I can. I am.

Walls of self-doubt try to block my concentration, my questions, but fail to distract me from my task.

Which file first? No, that's not right, that should be in that pile over there. Come on, Hope, you are never happy with the lay-out, stop avoiding this and start reading. What does this one say? What? How did they know that? I didn't even know that . . .

The papers are dog-eared with years of reading, marks where different fingers have searched, pulling the pages over from the top right-hand corner, so they, too, can learn about my family from other people's perceptions, judgments and prejudices.

What do you mean my dad is illiterate? He's not. Are you saying he's stupid? He isn't, he's my dad, leave him alone.

Even though the files have been in my house for months, they still smell of social work offices. A particular dusty dullness seeps through the paper from both the stress felt by social workers about doing the right thing and the stress of those they interview, people who hope they've done enough of the right things. The things that were asked of them at the last meeting.

Over a number of years, the happenings of these meetings are set out on paper by the social workers. The words are translated into a report, each completed and filed, in my case, under the heading 'Hackney Child'. Ready and waiting to hand over to the next responsible person who is placed in charge of my care, as I travel from my parents' home and then through various children's homes, from Hackney, to Essex, Croydon, Surrey and Kent.

I know I'm not meant to read these papers, because this time round I had to go to a solicitor to get them. They were never meant to be rescued from the deep, dark archives of a secret London location and presented to me. But here they are, all over my living room floor, where they shall remain until late into the evening, as I take notes in the notebook that never leaves my side. I take the notebook to work at the Citizens' Advice Bureau; I have it in my handbag to check at lunchtime.

Gives me something to do when I skip lunch to make sure the kids eat properly at night. One meal a day is enough for me; they need three. Free school meals for the kids stopped when I started work. God, am I happy about that!

I write the milestones passed at the back of my notebook:

Babies not removed at birth – check.

Babies free from sexualised behaviour – check.

Babies settled in school – check.

Babies pass ages we went into care – check.

When I think of normal parental milestones, I feel nothing. These are my milestones and no one's taking them away from me.

It broke my heart, having to take free school meals. Took me back to my own need for free food when I was a kid. My kids are not me. Remember that, Hope, remember that.

Why couldn't Mum and Dad cope? Am I gonna lose my kids to Care, too? Am I being a good mum? What is a good mum? They must think I'm a rubbish mum. How can I stop this thinking? I try my best. God, I'd do anything for my kids. How can I make Social Services see that? Shut up, Hope; Social Services are not in your kids' lives. And they ain't coming in neither. Over my dead body will my babies have files to read like this one day. Piles of Social Services files equals pain.

I feel a little sick inside as the names of the streets we lived in and selected shops that we stole from are mentioned in the files: Hamilton Road, where we lived; Church Street; Stoke Newington High Street; Manor Road – all roads that we played in, ran through, spent our Monday money in, and where later in the week we grabbed sandwiches kinder neighbours gave to us. Hackney in the 1970s and early 1980s was our backyard. We ran wild and free.

Because my parents were out of control.

Here's a piece of paper from Stoke Newington police station. I pick it up and feel it in my hands. Remember it being written. Now I smile.

Safe. Secure. This was the day I told them to take us into care. They listened; they saved us. This was the hour that I married off the policeman and the policewoman in my head. How many people have I married off over the years? Making happy families.

Mum and Dad must've caused some chaos. Social workers must've read these files again and again – each time we moved, every day we were living with Mum and Dad, the file got bigger. God, the social workers must've had a hard time with us. Did they hate us? Think we were scum? Detest us? We were known as a trouble family. Six kids removed. Reads like a horror story.

Shame rushes through me. I shiver. I frown when, however comprehensive the papers are, they miss a bit, and another, and another. I search and search through the papers but, somehow, I know even before reading them all, that they don't record the whole picture.

My dad loved me.

My dad loved me. As I roll these words round in my head, my mind goes back to when I was in care. There was an older boy there with me, Robert, told me I was lucky, 'cos he didn't know what it was like to have a Dad who loved him.

Robert. Aged four.

I wake up on the sofa in our front room. Me dad is cuddling me. Me head is resting sideways on the middle of his chest.

Nice.

Dad is watching Basil Fawlty on the telly. I can't quite see what's going on, his arm is covering my right eye as he strokes the top of my head, soothing where it hurts.

That's nice, Dad.

I snuggle further into his chest, my arm stretching round his tummy to give him a proper cuddle.

Ouch, my shoulder, that hurts. Don't cry, he won't like that. Don't swear, Mam won't like it.

A mixture of sweat, beer, cigarette smoke and ladies perfume fills my nose from his patterned shirt. Me dad is wearing the same shirt that he went out in yesterday afternoon, the one he bought with his benefits money yesterday morning; the money me mam calls 'the chat'. He spent it on the shirt instead of giving his money to us. I heard me dad speaking gently to me mam when he got home yesterday afternoon. I couldn't hear what he said, but from the stairs I could see him parading round the living room, all pleased with himself, while she looked on, her shoulders bent, pleading with him to stay in for once. As he shut the front door he called back, telling her not to worry. Mam sat at the table in the kitchen all night and I knew she was worrying, so I gave her a big cuddle before I went off to bed.

The next morning, she'd done her hair and she looked very pretty. It's not me mam's perfume on his shirt, but it never is when he's been out all night. Right now I don't care. Before he came home me mam and I were, as she said, relaxed, and now my dad is home I am relaxing with him, too.

This is the best bit, after he's done and I wake up. Me and him and the telly. Waking up to me and Dad, it's okay, it is. I like when he gives me his cuddles.

I feel my frown turn from upside down, into a small smile, like me mam says we have to when he's around. But this time I want to smile. I smile 'cos he's giving me a cuddle back.

This kind of time feels good, not quite as good as Leeds scoring a goal, but good. Me and me dad, just us two, curled up on the brown sofa in the front room with great big yellow flowers on the walls, his socks that match the sofa are settled on the purple carpet, which is the same colour as the curtains. I like those curtains when I'm warm in me dad's arms, 'cos they shut out the outside, where, today, it's raining.

My other eye can't see past the arm of the sofa, which is tattered at the end, as there's a can of Dad's beer sitting on it. I can hear Manuel protesting from inside 'the box' and me dad's other hand reaches out for his beer. As he lifts it up to his lips, I can see Basil chasing Manuel round the hall with a big fish. Dad is laughing. He puts the beer can back down and blocks my view again.

The wallpaper in this room, and all the rooms, is coming away from the top of the walls in the corners. As I can't see the telly, even though I feel tired and have a thump noise in my head, I lie on the sofa and try to work out if I can see more or less mould than the last time I checked.

Mam says our house just wasn't decorated properly by the council, but I heard Dad say it's 'cos the damp is coming in and, ever since I was very little, I have learnt he's always right.

I close my eyes. My head feels warm and safe against his chest; it feels nice that he's stroking my head. His chest rises up and down and he's giggling with laughter at what's on the telly. He reaches out for the can again, throws his head back, his chest pushing out and up as he moves the can, so it points straight up to the roof, then he drops it on the floor. As it lands I hear a clatter, so I know it's not the first beer he's had since he came home.

I must've been asleep for a while.

The rest of the house is quiet; I can feel it. I tense.

Where's me mam?

Dad feels I'm awake. 'Ah, there you are. Okay, lad, are ya? This is a great episode, shame you slept through it. Go get me another beer, pet, and get yoursel' some choco-late . . . Look out for your mam, she's in the kitchen.'

Me mam is on the floor. She's face up and still asleep. Her left leg is crooked and twisted over the right. Her arms are outstretched across the floor, above her head. Reaching for nothing in particular. To the right, our dinner is also on the floor. It's mixed in with one of the plates that has broken into three big pieces, and a clump of her hair. I remember the plate as it fell on the floor; she'd tried to use the table as a barrier, trying to delay, pleading with him not to do this again, same as she pleaded last time.

Why doesn't he listen?

The other two plates are okay, so I pick them up and put them on the side.

'Get out, Robert, get out.' I turn quickly, to where the words have come from.

'Shhh, Rooster, he'll hear you.'

But our budgie doesn't stop – Mam's words repeated in her accent, as he flaps about in his cage. Next to the cage, on the side of a cupboard door, a dark blob. Even from down here, I can see it's blood. Her blood. There's some more of her hair stuck to the underneath corner of the cupboard.

Her pretty, shiny hair is all over the place and I can see where the piece that's now on the floor mixed up with the squashed peas came from.

Oh, Mam! Your hair . . . Don't fret. Mam will know how to get a new hairstyle to hide the missing bit.

Her face is swollen, make-up unable to hide his late afternoon's work. I can't look at her properly, yet.

Focus. Dad needs a beer.

I try and pull her dress back down to nearer her knees; she's a dead weight and doesn't move, so the dress doesn't either. I clamber over her to open the fridge and she does move, just a bit.

I'm sad; not that she's alive, but that she's lying there at all.

I couldn't save her. I tried, but I couldn't stop him.

I felt guilty at being held off by him, not being the man he called on me to be.

'Come on, then, be a man and stop me,' he goaded, as he kicked her again and again. I moved forward, trying to get in between them.

I'll stop you. You have to get past me first. Don't hurt her. I can stop you.

My bravado egged me on, only to be met with the back of his left hand, full swing and force. At the same time his right boot expertly landed on target, in the middle of her stomach.

I woke up on the sofa, having a cuddle. I guess that's what she calls 'a mixed emotion'. Just like she explained when this happened four times ago and I asked, 'Mam, why can't we live somewhere else?'

'No, love, your dad and I aren't married, so no one would have us. It will be okay 'cos we've a roof over our heads here.'

Luckily, today she's fallen in such a way that I don't have to move her to get to the fridge door and his beer, like I had to the last time.

Don't look at her face. Get him his beer; that will keep him quiet while I help me mam and clean up this mess.

As I haul myself up to reach for the beers, she stirs. She opens her eyes, moves a hand to her face, feeling the damage. Her hand moves down towards her ribs. She starts to wriggle on the floor, in silence. I stare down at her, fixated as she moves herself slowly, painfully, from a twisted mess, back to looking a bit more normal. Lying on the kitchen floor, dried blood around her mouth, bruising on her legs, she stares blankly at the orange, bulb-shaped lampshade that hangs from the ceiling. She moves her neck back to look up at me. I turn away towards the fridge and grab a pack of four beers for me dad, turn back and step over her. I can't touch her, I just can't . . .

'It's okay, son. It's okay.'

'Shhh, shhh, Mam. I'll be back in a minute.'

Hope. 1999.

My notes from this evening's reading so far:

1978 – problems with neighbours – complaints of intimidation against my parents.

1979 – evicted.

How we hung onto that Silver Cross pram as Dad moved us. Mum wasn't there.

1979 – Princess Lodge, moved as was burnt down.

Mum did that.

1982 – Hamilton Road – getting worse at home.

Here we go, I'm back there – my brothers and I are running with the wind in our hair down Hamilton Road, Hackney. We turn sharp left through the school gates, spinning on the metal post. It's Jack's first week at school. We're all excited and my head is a little less worried than it was last week.

The worry I have for my two brothers still hangs around during term time, even though, with Jack starting school, all three of us will eat at least once a day until the next holiday. On Mondays, Mum and Dad leave us a fiver on the mantelpiece for the week's food and, as much as we try, it runs out way before the next Monday, leaving us to search or steal food, like my dad taught us, for the rest of the week.

At first, no one really takes any notice of us three in the school playground before the bell. We run around, the three of us together, following each other, making sure we all have sight of each other. I stop next to a group of girls who were in my class last year. I am out of breath from having run all the way from home to here and then round the playground twice without stopping. I smile half at the girls and half because my parents have managed a whole summer without being evicted or us moving and I'm at the same school I was before.

Harold and Jack carry on running past me, between the other kids, playing tag with me. I feel warm 'cos they're happy today. Then I hear a voice, a child's voice, and see a pointing finger.

She's pointing at me.

'UUUUHHHH Hope Daniels has nits! Look, look at her hair, it's crawling. You have nits, you have nits . . . And you smell of wee.'

I feel a lump in my throat. Water fills my eyes. I look at the ground; I want it to swallow me up. Why did I have to be here right now?

I look at her taunting face. Her words, her words. I run inside, leaving my brothers alone. The school bell rings as

I am running. Instead of going to class, I run into the down-stairs toilet, looking at my blonde hair, the knots, the matting. Checking to see if she's right.

Are there nits, are there? Oh no – there. There they are, right there.

Suddenly my head is itchy. My fingers go on to my scalp, scratch, scratching my head. I can't stop.

Got to get rid of them. Got to get rid of them.

I grab a bar of soap from the sink and run, run, run, panting, crying, away from school. I only stop when I reach our front door, breathless, the energy drained from me. I haul myself up the front steps.

Home.

Our front door, always on the latch, opens easily, but I am careful.

Don't want to be caught bunking off school.

When it's halfway open, I stick my head through the door to check if Mum and Dad are still up, or have gone to sleep. Elvis Presley greets me from the living room, which is on my right. He was playing when we got up this morn-ing and is still going round on repeat on our record player. Music like this at this time of the morning means one thing, that Mum and Dad have been up all night drinking. Male friends will have visited then left, leaving my mum depressed and in need of more drink, which my dad supplies using money from her night-time earnings.

As I creep though the front door and up the stairs, care-fully carrying my bar of school soap, the sounds of shout-ing and smashing plates join Elvis Presley in his morning chorus. Mum adds her voice, screaming at my poor dad, telling him he's useless and needs to pull his weight. Dad screams back, telling her he loves her and is doing the best he can.

Oh, Daddy, you are, Daddy. Mum, don't scream at him like that. Hope, ignore it, go and do your hair. They mustn't know you are home.

I take each stair as it comes, slowly sneaking upstairs, then right into the bedroom that I share with my parents. I grab Mum's hair comb to detangle and de-louse my hair, then I creep along the hall into the bathroom. There's no lock on the door, so I'll need to take my chances, but now I'm standing here, I realise I don't really know how to wash my hair properly.

Can't remember, I can't remember. Oh no, I'll never get the nits out if I can't remember. I should ask Mum. I can't ask Mum. It's not bath night, so even if she knew she wouldn't let me anyway. We've ten more sleeps before we can have a bath.

I stand in front of the bathroom sink, looking at myself in the mirror, rubbing soap on my dry hair, scratching my scalp at the same time. One hand trying to separate the knots in my hair while the other coats it with soap.

There's no lather. Shouldn't there be lather? Why can't I get any lather?

A voice calls me; it's my mum.

'Hope, is that you?'

Ignore her, she'll go away.

She doesn't. There are stockinged feet on the stairs. My mum is gentle, quiet, when in her stockinged feet. She calls out again; her voice is nearer, in the upstairs hallway.

'Hope?'

The bathroom door opens. Her blond head appears round the door. Her mascara's halfway down her face from a night of drinking and morning tears. Perfect, manicured red fingernails hold the door ajar. I am standing with soap in my hair, like wax, no lather and still full of nits.

'Hope! What are you doing? What's in your hair? Is that soap?'

'Someone at school said I had nits.'

My mum smells of Charlie perfume and booze. She's still drunk, her words are slightly slurred.

'Don't be stupid, Hope. Come down to the kitchen, we'll pour a pan of water over your head to get rid of that soap. Then you have to go back to school. We've got the social worker coming round in an hour and I want a kip before she comes. I don't want you to be here neither.'

The files those social workers made call me back to the present.

August 1983 – Mother prison, father disappeared, eldest brother out. Glass broken at house, vendetta the previous evening. Hope, aged nine, took herself and two younger brothers to the police station. Asked for her social worker and to be taken into care.

I shudder. Tears are rolling down my face and I don't care. The white wine is fresh and cold on my tongue. Another flashback.

We were just watching telly, me and my two little brothers. What right did they have? We were kids, all under nine years old. Jack's little face; he was so scared. Harold, frozen in shock. Me, scared. Running up and down the stairs. What to do? What to do? Open the door and say we're alone. Vigilantes. Hate them.

How dare they? We were kids. The first brick through the window, followed by so many other missiles. On and on. 'SLAG' spray-painted on the front door.

There's a bang outside my window. I jump.

Another sip.

That's enough. Check the kids are asleep. Put the files away, then go to bed, Hope.

I've had enough for this evening, emotionally beating myself up with family history and my own self-doubt. I tidy the files up again, away from inquisitive children; there are so many they fill two cupboards. My mask of 'don't care' returns.

They all knew. Why didn't they tell me they knew? God, I feel like shit – my chest hurts – fuck all this. Another glass of wine, another bottle of wine. Work in the morning. Huh, work, who do they think I am? I'm a fraud.

Have applied for a promotion. A big one. Imagine. 'Hi, I feel I'm suitable for the above role, supporting prisoners and their families. Oh, by the way, I come from an alcoholic, neglected, flea-infested shithole of a childhood, and please don't give me a man to interview me, cause they're all filth.'

The next day I walk into the interview. The lady who comes to collect me is a familiar face. Voices cry out at the same time.

'Hope! I thought it was you.'

'Debbie! Great to see you. What are you doing here?'

'I volunteer here one day a week – I teach the prisoners.'

Someone who knows, someone who understands about family history and bad men.

Debbie. Aged nine.

'Stay there until I come and get ya. Don't you two dare fuckin' move unless you want to confess. Little thievin' bastards.'

The bedroom door slams behind her and we're left alone, my older sister and I. We stand side by side, she aged eleven and me aged nine, all four hands pointing to the floor, both of us girls naked. I try to share a glance with her, asking with my eyes, 'Was it you?' But, as neither of us can see the other's face, and don't dare move a muscle, I don't know if it's my sister who is guilty, or if we've been set up by our step-dad, again.

I know Mum and the Dairylea tub that's missing one triangle of cheese are there outside the door, waiting for a confession. The smell of her lit cigarette creeps round the sides and underneath the door into our bedroom. It reaches inside my nostrils, making me sway a little.

Hate that smell. I feel sick. Stand straight. Stand still. Why does she do this? I'm so hungry.

We stand, we wait. She's waiting for us to disobey her orders, she's ready to pounce back into our room the second she thinks she hears a tiny movement from either of us. She's looking for an excuse to 'put the fear of God into us'. Since she first started using this method of extracting a confession, Mum has made it her own.

Whether she hears something or not, her speed at being back in here has been perfected over the years. She's so quick to open the bedroom door, be back in the middle of the room in a flash, hand already raised, ready to hit one of us if we've dared to move from the spot that she left us. She thinks we reflect about what she says one of us has done, when all we can really wonder about is how long it will last and how it is that hunger drives one child, then the other, to steal food from the person who is meant to care for us, our mum.

I hear the toilet door lock. She's moved away from the door.

'Was it you?' I hiss.

'Shhh, she'll hear ya.'

'It's OK, she's in the bathroom. Was it you?'

'No, it fuckin' wasn't. Was it you?'

'No. Your lips are going blue. Rub your hands together.'

'Shit. It's freezing in here.' My sister looks round to the open window. 'It's snowing. Shit.'

The toilet flushes.

'Shhh.'

We stand. We wait. Now it's been mentioned, the cold from the open window touches my skin. I start to shake.

Still. Be still. It's so cold. I'm hurting all over. My feet are numb. How long, how long? Can't do this much longer. Neither of us stole it. Fuckin' Step-dad, I bet ya it was him. Is it my turn to confess? Or hers? Shit, think it's mine. Mum's in a shit mood. Punishment gonna be bad. Just a bit longer before I confess, then.

It's easier to stand a little longer today than it was the first time Mum used this method to punish us, on my seventh birthday. I remember it 'cos it was when *Children in Need* came on the telly. Though I credit the 'nonce' babysitter with the idea, my sister tells me, while it's the first time for me, it isn't the first time she's been punished like this, by either the babysitter or Mum. The babysitter gets involved with punishing me because I steal his choco-late. He doesn't know it's me but when he goes to get the chocolate left out for him in the kitchen by my mum, it isn't there and there are only three of us in the house. He didn't eat it, so it must be me or my sister.

I remember this day as the day I get a card with a big number seven on it, a slap round the ear, and a telling that I need to be grateful that I've a roof over my head. It's my birthday, so I'm upset when Mum leaves us to go out with her new boyfriend on a first date. I steal the chocolate, eat it, enjoy it, and never intend to admit to it.

The babysitter uses this lack of telling him the truth as an excuse, as he has before, to make me and my sister stand naked in front of him, and we shall bloody well stay there until we give our confession. When we stand defiantly, he changes his mind. Instead of chucking me out of the room as he normally does at this point, today he keeps us both in the room, because he wants to take a present from us both in return for one of us stealing his chocolate. First me, then my sister. She doesn't seem surprised. Her reaction tells me this is kinda normal for her and so, too, will it become for me. She tells me to just do what he wants.

He tells her to watch as he holds me down and says he will take what he wants from us both. I feel numb. I try to think of nothing and just do as I'm told and follow my sister's advice.

When he finishes with me, he then starts and finishes with my sister. I think it's over, but he hasn't done. He makes us stand within arm's reach of him for a bit, then, once again, he makes my sister watch as he grabs out and moves back to where he started, with me.

Threats of things no worse than what's happening to us are being thrown around by him. We freeze, comply, stand naked, but neither of us moves away. We just do as we're told. When he grabs us round the neck and tells us he needs us to come here, for another go, we do without question, because this is what happens, has always happened, in this house, to my sister at least.

The living room door is locked, the key is on the top of the doorframe. I'm too frightened to do anything but watch when he's got my sister and move to where he tells me to, onto the sofa with him. I'm too sore, too scared, to cry.

Mum comes home within minutes of the living room door being unlocked to find us standing naked in front of the babysitter. He, now sitting watching the screen, has placed us to the left of the telly, facing him and the door when she comes in. She stands stock still for a minute, staring back at us. We dare not move as he's staring at us, too. The only thing that moves are his lips: 'One of them stole me chocolate, so I'm waiting for them to confess.'

She turns, leaves the room, and we hear her in the kitchen, rummaging in the drawer. He's looking at us with danger in his eyes, threatening us with silence. My instinct kicks in and, now she's here, I've a glimpse of a feeling.

Mum, this isn't normal. Go on, Mum, get the rolling pin and smash him over the head.

She returns, hands him some money, paying him his babysitting dues.

'Off you go, then. See ya. Same time next week.'

No, oh no, Mum, please no. Don't you know what he did? Please, Mum, no. No, not again.

Maybe it's normal?

'Sure thing, Mrs Peterson. Thanks.'

His head turns back towards us, 'Bye, girls, see you later.'

We both shudder as Mum follows him out to the front door. We hear it close. We relax. Heads fall back with exhaustion. My sister puts a hand on my shoulder, mumbles, 'Sorry, kid, thought you might've been okay for a bit longer. Welcome to the world.'

We start to move towards our clothes to get dressed when Mum comes back in.

'What the fuck are you two thevin' little shites thinking about? Stand where the fuck you are. Don't you dare fuckin' move 'til I tell ya.'

'But, Mum . . .'

My sister's bravery is met with a slap so hard that she stumbles to the right, then rights herself, and stands.

'That's it. Do as you're fuckin' told if you know what's good for ya.'

For hours we stand naked in front of Mum as she falls asleep with Terry Wogan, Sue Lawley and Esther Rantzen on BBC's *Children in Need*. We stand until Mum is woken up by the end credits and some charity seems to have rubbed off on my sister, who confesses that she did my crime.

Hope. 1999.

The living room is tidy and the kids' cereal and bowls are all laid out and ready to grab in the morning.

Learnt that in my first children's home.

I sit down on the sofa to read my notes.

I must go to bed. Just one more glass. That's empty. More in the fridge. What did the files say about Mum?

Age sixteen – psychiatric hospital for a year. Never told why she was there. Got a job as a cinema usherette – met an older man. Got pregnant. Put baby girl up for adoption.

She must've been so scared.

Met Dad – fifteen years older than her. Got pregnant. Had Phillip. Kept him. Had another girl two years later – she went for adoption. Two years later had Hope, then Harold, then baby Jack.

They kept me; things must've been getting a bit better. She would be in her thirties, my middle sister. Who is she? Who are they? Two kids, both girls, my sisters, given up . . . Why did they keep me? Does this explain why my mum couldn't bear me?

Mrs D – earned money from soliciting. Mr D served multiple prison sentences – living off immoral earnings. Evicted due to soliciting.

I pour myself some more wine. My obsession with my past is in full throttle; notes are scribbled down, fast and furious, barely legible.

I must learn, I must not turn into my mum. My poor mum. Why did my mum have to have such a sad life?

Why were we not supported to recover emotionally from our childhood? The trauma is with me today – it paralyses me and saddens me, deeply.

The man pops into my head. I'm eight years old, pouring him a drink.

The first time I ever opened the door of our house to him, his suit was one of the smartest I'd ever seen. Every time he visited after that, he made the same three sharp knocks on the door, 'cos the doorbell was always broken. He wore the same dark suit. I always noticed how clean he kept it. He'd first of all be welcomed by my dad on behalf of my mum. The man, like most of the men who visited her and were entertained in our house, would place a briefcase on the floor next to the bottom of the stairs. He, like many of the others, always brought a bottle of whisky with him, presenting it to Mum and Dad with a flourish, his wedding ring wrapped around his fat finger, his hand around the bottle. The bottle passed to my dad just before the man took off his coat, shaking it free of rain before he also placed these in my dad's care. Dad, in turn, placed the coat carefully on the end of the banister, admiring the material with words and touch before moving himself, the whisky and the man through to my mother. He'd try to get the man to forget his coat later – he could get a fiver for it down Ridley Road Market.

The man smoothed back his hair before walking down the hall to my mum, past the living room on his right, where we sometimes were, but not today. As he walked empty handed, he turned the wedding ring on his finger, just once, switching on a strange look in his eyes and smiling in such a way that made my skin crawl.

Die, you dirty old man. Die, you dirty old man.

I imagined he had a big job, that man, and that his wife took the suit to the dry-cleaners for him, not knowing he'd just been to see my mum. Dry-cleaners always smelt lovely. Dad had a deal going with the local one – he peddled the clothes that weren't collected. I loved that he called my dad 'Governor'.

The hairs on my skin stand on end as I serve him the same drink every week. I can't remember if I was cheeky to him or not, but I do remember him telling me, 'You will turn out nicely, just like your mother.'

Die, you dirty old man. Die, you dirty old man.

His briefcase stood to attention at the front door, and my urge to kick it increased every time he climbed the stairs with my mother. My dad sat downstairs in the kitchen, with its wooden cupboards and the sticky kitchen table rarely used for anything other than entertaining clients. In the daytime, when Mum had visitors, there he sat, ignoring us kids as we ran in and out; just staring, silently, into the bottom of his glass.

I take another sip of wine.

Be a shame not to finish the bottle.

Before I go to bed, even tho' I'm wobbling a bit, I pull my washing from the machine and think about what it is to be a mum. How I spend my life making sure my kids are safe and loved. How, even though my mum was around most of the time, she was unable to cope. While other kids I met in care just needed their mum to be there.

I don't understand how anyone can leave their kids on their own.

Jackie. Aged four.

When I wake up, the sun is out. I know this 'cos the curtains in my room don't quite shut properly and the sun creeps through the gap on sunny days to wake me up, too early. I listen to the flat. Mum isn't up yet, otherwise I'd hear her making a cup of tea. The china rattles when she's warming the pot and putting the cup on the saucer. I'm too young to help with this, but I can watch, so I know for when I'm older. She has proper china cups for tea and a teapot with flowers on that she got from the market. My mum likes tea and a good cup of tea can fix many a thing. I've my own room that I don't have to share with anyone. With my room and the tea, Mum says that we're doing okay. I don't know how they go together but they must 'cos she tells me this a lot.

The only sounds I can hear right now are outside on the landing, other people going out, doors shutting, sounds of 'Cheerio' and 'Have a good day,' then footsteps past my window and the sounds disappearing down the stairwell. I can't hear any birds singing. I only noticed there are no birds round here when I heard birds on the day we went to the countryside to try and visit Gran and Grandpa. They wouldn't see us. Mum tried to speak with this old man who is in a photo in our flat and said to him, 'Look, here is your granddaughter.' But Grandpa didn't look up. He just carried on with his gardening and, after we left, Mum cried on the bus home and said over and over, 'It doesn't matter. We can try another day,' while giving me a big squeeze. I noticed then that it's difficult to give her a hug back when your arms are straight down and she puts her arm round your shoulder and you are sitting side by side.

Another day hasn't come yet because we have never been to the countryside again to try and visit Gran and Grandpa. This morning, I can hear the sun is making people happier than they are when it's raining. I can hear neighbours saying hello cheerily to other neighbours. I don't know which voices belong to which person yet, but they sound happy. The people in the flats round us can get very loud, mainly at night when I'm trying to sleep. Mrs Nosey-Parker and her husband can be very loud when they have a big fight. Mum says I'm to steer clear of them 'cos they stick their noses in everywhere. I'm to be especially careful not to talk to them or have eye contact when Mum's away working.

I want to get up but I know I'm not allowed to get out of bed until the big hand on the clock points straight up and the little hand is on its way up from pointing down to the floor. I don't really understand when that is, but I worked out that when the little hand is pointing at Teddy's foot, it's the same thing, and I can get up.

Today I'm happy to stay in bed a bit longer as Mum changed the sheets last night before I went to bed, so it smells all fresh, like spring. Teddy is my friend. He stays with me all the time; wherever I go he holds my hand. I've to be careful not to drag him on the floor when I walk. Sometimes it's hard to remember this as I'm only four. But as my birthday was a lot of sleeps ago, I'm now nearly five. At night times, Teddy sits and watches me, making sure I'm safe, even when Mum isn't here. It doesn't matter that he doesn't have a name. He's still Teddy, and he's mine.

The clock is now pointing at Teddy's foot and the big hand is a little past pointing at the ceiling, so I can get up. But I'm not ready. It's warm and smells nice, and Mum is still not up.

Why is Mum not up? Mum?

Everything in my room is pink. Even the door. Mum painted it all when we first moved in here and she was happy. Now a lot of the time she seems to stay on the couch, staring into space and listening to the radio. We don't have a telly, even though I ask for one almost every day and, when she answers, she says I'm becoming annoying. Most of the time she doesn't answer, though. She just lies on the couch and stares at the wall.

Why isn't she up?

My door creaks when I open it; this is to let Mum know when I'm getting up in the night. If she fixed the squeak, she wouldn't hear me and wouldn't be able to come and check I'm okay.

Today, our flat seems normal, but something is saying it's not. I go to the kitchen and she isn't there. Just the table with its yellow and white cloth. Mum and I count the squares to learn my numbers; she calls the pattern 'gingham'. She laughs with me as I can't say it properly yet. Mum comes from a posh family and wants me to speak like her, not like some of the neighbours, who, Mum is sure, are very nice people but you need to change your accent, like Margaret Thatcher, the prime minister, the first woman prime minister, did, to get on in life, so I've to try and talk proper, properly. Then I can be anything I want.

The kettle is cold. She can't have got up yet.

Even before I open her bedroom door, I know she isn't there. It's too quiet. Even so, I go inside. Her dressing table is perfectly arranged but the perfume bottle and her powder are missing.

Maybe they're in the drawer.

Opening the make-up drawer there's a space where her blue eye shadow and red lipstick should be.

A girl shouldn't be without her lipstick.

I feel sad but, with nothing else to do, I sit down cross-legged on the floor, elbows on my knees and hands holding up my chin. Looking round the room, I see the bed isn't made and the top of the wardrobe is empty; her red leather case isn't there. A big sigh.

She's gone again. Has she gone for long? She took the case, but maybe she just took the case to carry some stuff for someone.

That will be it – she rushed out, taking some stuff to someone, and she'll be back tonight. But what stuff could she have taken?

If I make the bed, she'll be happy when she comes home.

I put my face into her pillow and breathe deeply. It smells of her. A combination of Charlie, Impulse and hairspray.

Mummy.

I make the bed, then unmake it again, to cuddle the pillow.

Mummy, where are you? Uh, oh. I need a wee. And I'm hungry.

There's no toothbrush in the bathroom, but there are tears. My tears. Quiet tears.

Don't make a noise when she's gone. She'll be back. When? Before the bread runs out.

Running into the kitchen, I see, there, on the counter, is the bread, white, just how I like it. But it's a whole loaf. My heart sinks into my tummy.

That's a lot of sleeps on my own. Don't cry. You gotta be quiet or they will come and take me away for ever. Mummy. Mummy. Mummy. Wait for Mummy.

Next to the bread, there's a jar full of 10ps and 50ps. There are so many I can't count them all. Mum must've been saving up those coins for a long while to leave me on my own, since at least before my birthday, and that seems like ages ago, 'cos now I'm almost five.

Hope. 1999.

The bus trundles to where I volunteer with the Citizens' Advice Bureau. My manager at the Bureau says there might be a place coming up at the national office soon. She says I should go for it, that she'll support me 'cos I work hard, am always on time, am honest with her, and that I support her.

Glen, the key worker who was allocated to look after me at Beaufort children's home, taught me these ethics.

My manager says she'll be sorry to lose me but a paid job is a paid job.

I hope so. I hate being broke.

As I sit on the bus, a memory comes back to me.

Me and my little brothers are standing at a bus stop in Mare Street, Hackney. I need to find something for the boys to do today. We were on our way to the park when it started raining so I've decided on the bus instead. Jumpin' on the bus and going to the end of the route and playin' hide-and-seek with the conductor is a good thing to do in the rain.

Mum has told us to 'Fuck off out the house' 'cos they've some people coming to visit. When Mum tells us to do this, my head goes in a spin, wondering who's comin' – the social worker or a dirty old man? I want to ask, but I get into trouble for askin' too many questions, so today I decide just to get me and my little brothers out of the house. I do ask one question, even though I know the answer; it's always worth a shot, 'Dad, have you any money?'

'No, Hope, but we'll have some by tonight and, when we do, we'll have Kentucky Fried Chicken!'

He spins me round by my arms and I dance on his feet. He winks at my mum. She looks towards the back door.

As we leave, Mum shouts after us, 'And don't you lot come back until late; we're entertaining.'

Dirty old man with a suit and a briefcase, then.

Die, you dirty old man. Die, you dirty old man.

The bus stop is busy, which should make our task easier.

'Harold, Jack – right, you know what to do?' I ask. My brothers' heads nod at the same time, their eyes half scared, half excited at the hide-and-seek game we play to get on the buses. 'Right, we all duck low, jump on the back of the bus and go upstairs; it's better if we're between other people gettin' on. Choose yer person before ya get on the bus . . . okay?'

'Yesss, Hope. We know, Hope. We've done it a thousand times before, Hope.'

I can hear Harold is slightly annoyed with me, so I reach out to ruffle his hair like Dad does, but he flicks his head away and frowns.

'Oh, come on, Harold; you know we can't get ourselves caught otherwise we can't go. Look, there's two women over there that Jack can get in between.'

'Yes, Hope.'

'Oh, Harold, don't be like that; I'm tryin' me best.'

'Did Dad give you any money? I'm hungry, Hope. It's been ages.'

'Nuh. But he said he'd have money tonight and he promised we'd have Kentucky Fried Chicken when we get home! We can try and get a snack when we get back to Hackney. That will keep us goin'. Come on, 'ere's the bus.'

As we jump on the bus, making our way between adults so the conductor does not see us, my head is overtaken by the thought of the man, or men, who will come to our house today.

I've seen and so I know the routine, even though I try not to think about it. It's better not to think as it hurts my head and we have to keep it secret if anyone asks. So many secrets in me head. But today I can't stop the thought of what's happening at home while we're on the bus. A man in bed with my mum, the cross of Jesus looking down at the man and my mum as he rocks back and forth.

Die, you dirty old man. Die, you dirty old man.

Ting. Ting. The conductor's bell brings me back to the bus. We're already on the move. The boys are at the back, upstairs, looking at me expectantly.

'A snack will be great when we get back, Hope, thank you.'

I love you two.

I smile. 'We're going to have the best day out. Now, will we go to the end of the route, which is Waterloo, and then turn round and come back again? Y'know what to do when the conductor comes?'

The boys jump up and down and scream in excitement.

A lady in a red coat turns and scowls at us. Jack sticks out his tongue. She looks away, shocked, unsure what to do.

'Jack!' I say, in the tone of voice the teacher does at school when I go and if I'm a bit cheeky.

The woman looks back, smiles and nods. Then turns away again.

I stick my middle finger up at her – stupid cow.

I grin at Jack. He grins back.

For the rest of the journey our faces are glued to the windows, there's no need to hide from the conductor as he smiles at me and turns back downstairs without asking us for any money. I smile back.

Even though we've done this route before, we all pretend it's the first time. I point out all the London landmarks to the boys that we can see and that I know. It stops raining by the time we get to St Paul's, which is their favourite and where Princess Diana is going to marry her prince soon, but I don't let the boys get off the bus as we need to stick together, and we all know that we still have to cross the river to get to the last stop at Waterloo, and crossing the river will be their next favourite.

When the bus gets to the end of the route, we all stay on, waiting for the bus to turn round and go back to Hackney again.

The boys don't ask or question why we don't get off; we just change seats to the upstairs front row and wait, quietly, so we don't get thrown off. I don't even need to tell them to shhh, we all know.

As soon as we pass Bethnal Green it starts raining again.

Shit. What do we do now? Can't stay out in the rain.

'I'm hungry, Hope.'

'All right, shhh, I'm thinking.'

The bus pulls up at Hackney Town Hall and I rush the boys off. The rain isn't too bad but still we run down Graham Road towards Ridley Road Indoor Market.

When we get there, I get the boys to stand where Dad normally positions me or my eldest brother Phillip as a lookout when Dad's peddlin' from his suitcase. I know the lookout has a good view in all directions.

'Stand 'ere, Harold. You look down there and, Jack, you look 'ere.' I point. 'An' don't either of ya move 'til I come back. And when I do, get ready to go quick, but not too quick. Keep an eye out for the coppers.'

Harold looks a little scared. 'Where you off to, Hope? I don't wanna be left on me own.'

I ruffle his hair, this time he doesn't flinch.

'It's okay, lovely. I'm off to try and get us some lunch. Shhh.'

They both smile.

'Okay, then, stay here, and shout if you see a copper. I won't be far.'

We three are sitting under the canopy of trees at Abney Park Cemetery, near where rhubarb will grow and where we will pick it and eat, later in the year. We've already eaten a can of spam that I stuffed up my jumper. When we got to our spot, I pulled it out and presented it to the boys like Paul Daniels the magician. I even did a 'Tadaaa!'

The can isn't so easy to open, as the key that came with the can doesn't turn properly, but we've a lot of time so we take things slowly. When we finally manage to get the spam open, we turn it upside down and use the lid as a plate.

Next time I shall get something easier. But in the shop I didn't think, I just grabbed whatever had an opener and stuffed it up me jumper.

On the way back to the boys, I grabbed some fruit and put that up my jumper with the spam, too.

Jack and I are now sharing an apple. Harold has an orange to himself and, even though he offers to share, Jack and I are happy with our apple. I haven't told them yet but we've a handful of stolen sweets in my pocket for pudding.

It's not dark yet and it's stopped raining, so we play here for a bit under the trees and among the graves, before we go home for Kentucky Fried Chicken.

A nice treat.

We open the door to the house and it's silent, which means Mum and Dad aren't here. The door is on the latch but when I try the switch there are no lights. It's dark.

I thought you were getting money. I thought you would've put 50p in the meter before going out.

Harold asks a question I don't know how to answer, 'Have Mum and Dad gone for Kentucky Fried Chicken?'

They never go and collect it; they always send us with the money.

My eyes adjust to the darkness and we move through to the kitchen where Dad keeps a torch.

When I switch it on, I see some lettuce sandwiches already made up for us on the table between a couple of empty bottles of whisky. This sandwich is a favourite of my dad's to make for us.

The mantelpiece!

I rush through to the living room, shine the torch on the spot where Mum and Dad leave us a fiver for food on Mondays before going out and spending the rest of their benefits money in the pub. There's nothing there. My head feels heavy. My heart sinks into a dark bowl of nothing.

What am I going to tell the boys? Where are you, Daddy? Did you go to the pub? Did you forget about Kentucky?

Back in the kitchen I don't need the lights to know how disappointed the boys are. We'd all been promised a hot meal, our favourite meal, finger-licking Kentucky Fried Chicken. We'd stayed out all day as Mum asked us to, as we wanted to win this reward.

Dad, you promised.

I shine the torch on the plate; the silence in the room is horrible. We all look at the white bread and green leaves sticking out the side. I try to be enthusiastic but my voice sounds all wrong when I speak, 'At least they left something for our dinner, boys. They can't of got as much money as Dad thought they would, otherwise he would've kept his promise. Come on, let's take them through to the front room, then we can . . .'

My voice trails off. The light from the moon shining into the kitchen shows me that both boys have let tears escape. I move to give them a hug. But they don't wait for my comfort; instead, they duck and dodge past me in unison and pick up a sandwich each.

A group of young girls get on the bus, passing by me as they head upstairs to the top deck. One of them reminds me of a childhood friend. She also had to steal food for herself and her brother.

Abby. Aged nine.
The cloakroom at school is empty of people; it's full of school bags, blazers, school uniforms and the packed lunches of kids who are lucky enough to have a mum that cares. I skulk around each row of pegs, shaking a blazer, listening for money. I know when there's enough money

that I can reduce it a bit without the owner wondering about the amount they have left.

If I only take 2p or 10p from each pocket, they might not notice. They'll think they dropped a coin.

When I first came up with this plan, I made a rule: never have all of the money, never all of the lunch from one person. A bit from each. It takes longer to gather the loot but it'll reduce the chance of kids reporting it. My hand is in a pocket which is heavy; I feel a lot of coins. I'm searching for a 10p.

What's that noise?

Quickly I remove my hand, which is still holding onto a coin. I know it isn't a 10p, but someone's coming, so I squeeze into the corner of the cloakroom between the lockers. A door opens, closes.

There's someone in the room. They walk across the room. Feet quiet. Adult feet.

Don't breathe. Be calm. Won't be caught if I stay still. When did they start patrolling the cloakroom? I only want some lunch. I'm starving. Go away, go away.

The person pauses. I can hear them breathing. Slow, calm, in control. The noise is coming from the other side of the room.

Are you over by the door? What are you doing? Go. Go. Go. GET OUT!

The door opens again and, with a click, announces its closure.

Wait. Wait. Might still be in here, fooling you. Like Mum does.

I stand stock still for a few minutes, listening, hearing nothing but the sounds from outside, of school children playing sport, kids from the year above me who will come into the cloakroom to find half a sandwich or maybe a packet of crisps or an apple gone, or maybe a few pence from their pockets missing. Never more than one piece of food taken from a lunch box; never money from the same pocket that I take food from.

Can't make others hungry to feed me.

The sandwich, apple or crisps rarely make it outside the cloakroom. When I'm done pilfering, I hide in the toilets and wait for Lee, my little brother, to come. He gets out of class by asking to go to the toilet. We eat our lunch until the class playing sports comes back and we wait until the bell goes. Then, we can leave our lunch spot in the toilet at the same time as the teachers would be expecting the other kids to leave.

We do this just in case they're waiting outside the door for the thief.

The evidence never leaves the cloakroom – the packaging and apple cores stuffed into sanitary bins. Some money in my pocket but not so much that, if caught, would arouse suspicion. An amount I can pass off as being given to me by my mum. But still enough for some food for me and my brother when we don't get fed at home for a day or so.

What's gonna happen to him when I go to senior school? How is Lee going to cope? Will he be able to get food for himself?

Lee. Aged seven.

I'm creeping through the hall towards the stairs. It's become a game; every day I try to sneak through the front door and up the stairs without her hearing. I never make it. The living room door is always open. However hard I try to be quiet, not to let her hear I've come in, I fail. I've even sat in her chair to work out how she does it, if she has some kind of secret way of spotting that I've come in the front door. But, nuh, she just knows . . .

'Lee, that you? Come here.'

Bugger.

'I'm tired, Mum. It was a long day at school. I just want to do my homework.'

I go into the living room. At least she's out of her dressing gown today, but her shit-coloured clothes show evidence of her sloppy eating at lunch, missing her mouth, not bothering to wipe down her clothes.

I bet she's been sitting there all day, doing nothing but watch daytime TV and stuffing her face. Lazy bitch. I'm so hungry.

'Want doesn't get. You can do it later. Do your chores first.'

'But, Mum, there are so many.'

Her voice turns stern, 'Do them. How many times do I have to say it? Every kid has fuckin' chores to do.'

Not this fuckin' many.

'Where's your chore book?'

'I'll get it.'

Going back into the hall, I pull my book out from behind the telephone. I turn, catching my face in the mirror.

Looking a bit pale there, mate.

My hand is outstretched, holding the book towards my mum. She quickly grabs it from me, creating a swoosh, drawing a battle line in the air between us. A flash of an advancing army comes to my mind. Over the brow of the hill they come, but when they see my mum sitting on the sofa, flapping the open book in my face, the army retreats, just as quickly, leaving me alone again. It's a battle she's already won.

'These are your chores. Look, today, Tuesday.'

There's a page for each day and then some monthly chores that need to be done at the weekends when I'm not at school, like cleaning the windows or washing the car. She thrusts the book back at me, pointing with dirty fingers at today's list.

'Read it out to me, so I know that fuckin' school is teaching you something.'

I look down the list and do as she says.

'The list for today says:

1. Clean dishes in kitchen from breakfast and Mum's lunch.
2. Downstairs bathroom: wash and polish everything in the bathroom until it shines.

This is most important – Mum has visitors on Wednesday so the bathroom needs to be shiny.

3. Sweep stairs – with the nail brush.
4. Hoover the hall and the living room, then fluff up the carpet with the comb.
5. Clean the front door – outside and in.
6. Polish everything in the hall.
7. Make sure anywhere visitors might see is spotless. Clean the corners of rooms with a damp cloth and, if not clean, use the old toothbrush to get into the corners. Be careful not to scratch the paintwork.

'That's it, Mum.'

She's vicious in her response. 'Right, so you don't have all night, why are you standing there looking at me? Get on with it.'

She lifts a hand, high, open palm.

Get away. Now!

She swipes, she misses. Another battle line drawn in the air. I run from it. Outside the door, in safety, I draw myself straight, stand to attention, salute myself in the mirror and retreat to the downstairs bathroom for 'cleaner duty'.

I'm on number four. My sister, Abby, will be home soon. Mum has a letter from the school next to her. I know Mum is mad about it but she's always mad. She doesn't like either of us very much. We get under her feet and are good-for-nothing pieces of shit.

Gotta get this right. Mum's watching. Corrie is on the box. Soon she'll be asleep. Should I wait to do the carpet, then? Nah, waking her will piss her off more. Maybe she'll fall asleep before Abby gets back. Will do it now. Quiet tho'.

I lie down flat on my tummy. Mum lifts her feet onto the sofa. She watches while I comb the carpet. This is the chore that I can pretend the most with. Turn it into a game in my head. I like to pretend that I'm a soldier in action, on a top-secret operation, mine-sweeping in the most dangerous parts of the world. Today I'm in the short grasses of the Falkland Isles. A soldier miles from home.

Miles from here.

I took my comb from the Operations Centre under the stairs and moved into the living room, low on the ground, from the door to the far corner in a flash. I work from there backwards, keeping my escape route, via the back of the chair that my mum doesn't sit on, open.

I work in lines corner to corner so I don't miss a bit, moving diagonally across the battlefield. First I clear the left half of the room, get to the centre and move operations to repeat the same job on the other side of the room.

This way, my work meets in the middle and I don't damage the places I've already been.

My comb is transformed into the latest technology. First of all it sweeps the carpet for crumbs. In my head these are dangerous parts of bombs and so I pick these up with tweezers and put them in the dustpan for careful disposal in the unit. Before I turned this into a game, it was just a comb and tweezers that my mum forced me to use to clean the house. It's still crap, and the unit isn't really a unit, it's really the outside bin, but I like to pretend. Sometimes, on a really bad day, I pretend all the dirt in the house is radio-active and I imagine I'm wearing a protective suit so no one and nothing can reach me.

Whatever the level of danger, I clean the carpet with the comb and the tweezers, and all the time I make-believe that I am somewhere else, saving British lives like my uncle did in the Falklands, even though he did not come back and my nan says the wind is howling over his patch of land, keeping him cold. I pretend I'm him when I'm combing the carpet for my mum. It's only number four on the list of chores so I can't spend too long playing. Number seven will be more difficult because, when I use the tooth-brush to clean things, I think I'm Private Benjamin from the movies. She's a girl and, even though she becomes a soldier in the end, it's difficult to image myself as a girl 'cos I'm not a girl, I'm a boy.

Number seven chore is the bit of pretending that I like the least. Cleaning the house with a toothbrush means that I'm almost done doing chores, but this is when I fill myself with worry. Once I've finished number seven, I have less pretend play to fill my head and I still have my homework to do for school. It's when I'm doing my homework that I start to feel hungry and then my eyes go a bit funny and I can't think.

Don't think about being hungry. Soldiers on patrol deal with this. Work with it. Maybe Abby will have completed her mission.

It was my older sister Abby's idea to pretend chores are soldier training. She also gives herself a new mission every day. Sometimes stealing from the fridge downstairs, which is super dangerous and, even though we scoff down what she can get as quick as we can, Mum always seems to know and gives us salt water to make us sick.

Other times Abby steals from school friends. She doesn't always manage it, but she tries every day to get something for us to eat. Yesterday she got me an apple and we kept back a digestive biscuit as Tuesdays are never a good day at school because there isn't any sports on the timetable so she has to sneak into classrooms at break time when they're empty to pilfer through people's desks. High risk Tuesday we call it 'cos if someone comes in and her hand is in another person's desk she'll be caught. Red-handed.

Try as she and I might, we can't find a good excuse to give if a teacher comes in and catches her. So when planning, we agree that she just can't get caught. If someone is around watching the classrooms, or if it's a little bit risky, she doesn't even try to do it.

I'm hungry. I wonder if she'll manage to get anything today. I hope she's careful. I hope she doesn't take too much from one person.

On the days with no food at all, we distract ourselves with getting ahead on our week's chores and going to bed so tired that we don't even think about being hungry. Then in the morning we watch the classroom clocks to get though to school lunchtime. Mum doesn't let us have school diners, but I just leave class a few minutes early to meet Abby in the toilet and she's always waiting. We meet in the gym toilets and grab a sandwich, and maybe share a packet of crisps or a piece of fruit.

When I've just about finished Tuesday's list of chores, I hear the key in the door; it's Abby.

Hope. 1999.
I'm sitting in my living room writing notes in my book.

Hope – exposed to her mother's work. Knew what was going on. Not protected.

I'm back there in the kitchen at home, shortly before I take myself and my brothers to the police station and demand they take us into care.

Enough of being scared, of being hungry.

There are three of us in the kitchen. Me, my mum and a man who I know will only be here for an hour or so.

Die, you dirty old man. Die, you dirty old man.

It's mid-afternoon and I stand looking out into our messy garden, standing, waiting by the back door. I'm looking at the rain, watching raindrops stick to the window. A heavier spell means they're bouncing on the yard slabs, watering the weeds. I'm waiting to see if Mum calls me to give the client another drink before they go upstairs. I steal a look.

I'm bored, wanna watch telly. But there's no money for the meter.

The whisky I served to the client and my mum has almost disappeared from both glasses, but the last drops and dirty glasses are being ignored.

The man is punching my mum really hard in the face. Really hard. Right hook into the face, throwing her head one way. A slap that throws her head the other and she falls onto the kitchen floor. She's crying out, the man spits in her face. I watch his saliva run slowly from her eye, over her cheek, moving much slower than the tears that are flowing down my cheeks. My body is shaking, tears, crying and crying. I push myself backwards into the corner between the door and the kitchen units.

What do I do? What do I do? Oh, Mum, I don't know what to do. Mum.

The man is holding her up by the neck of her blouse with one hand and raises his other fist once more. She's bent back and their eyes lock on to each other. There's nothing but hatred between them. They freeze in action for a moment. In the silence he lets her blouse go and she slumps back on the floor. He stands back, breathing heavily, hard, spits on her for a second time. He turns, grabs the whisky, finishes it in one, picks up the second glass and finishes her whisky, too. He grabs his coat and, without a word, without looking at me, without looking at the floor at the crumpled heap of leather skirt, red blouse and blonde hair that is my mum, he leaves.

I stare after him, unable to move from where I've edged myself into the corner. As he rushes out, he stands on the creaky floorboard in the corridor that Mum uses to warn us kids that she's taking a client upstairs. When we hear it, we know that we should get to sleep, or pretend we're asleep so she can entertain the clients in her room. The room I share with my parents.

Men are bastards.

The door slams, shaking the whole house. It shakes both my mum and me from our stillness.

Mum pushes herself up with her hands until she's sitting back against the cupboard door. She's crying, great big sobs and is mumbling to herself, but I can't hear what she's saying. Crying, sitting and crying. Hands over her face.

Mum is so small. Oh, Mum, why?

I kneel down in front of my mum. We're quiet. I take her hands, pull them forward and away from her face.

Mummy! That's a scary-looking bruise.

Mum's eye is already closed, black, with a lump the size of a golf ball, and tears coming out of the bottom of it.

I reach out. I move her blonde hair, tuck it behind her right ear. I stroke the side of her face, in a way she's never done with me or my brothers. She winces.

'Sorry, Mum, it's gonna be okay.'

Standing, I look around the mass of empty bottles and overflowing ashtrays, looking for something clean to wipe her face with.

There's a tea towel. I shake it to make sure nothing is stuck to it, I put the tap on, it comes out in a dribble. As best I can, I cover it in cold water.

It's not very cold. If only we had a fridge to get some ice.

'Hold that against your head, Mum. It's a big bruise. Needs some cooling down. We don't have any ice like they have in the *Rocky* films, but this should help.'

A hand with a broken red nail reaches out and grabs the tea towel. She presses it against her face.

'Fuck off, Hope. Leave me alone. And don't you go tellin' no one either.'

I close the file. Tears are streaming down my face. I reach for another sip of wine, wiping my tears away with my other hand as I do so.

PART TWO

TAINTED LOVE

Jackie. Aged four.

I don't feel well. My tummy hurts. I've been sick in the toilet and on the floor.

Must clean it up before it stinks.

The ham Mum left me in the fridge had a shiny film on it, like oil on a puddle, but I've eaten ham when it looked like that before and it was okay. But that time it tasted like ham; what I ate last night for tea tasted a bit funny, like it had a bit of vinegar on it. But I ate it anyway.

I am hungry all the time.

When I try to go to the shop I get scared and turn back, 'cos I'm on my own and there are some big boys hanging around on the stairs that go from the level my flat is on to the ground floor. It's scary 'cos I don't want them to get all the 50ps and 10ps that are in my pocket from the jar Mum left on the side. There are so many coins they're heavy and you can hear them tinkle in my pink anorak pocket.

Pink is me and my mum's favourite colour. Where are you, Mum? Mummy, when are you coming home?

The only person I'm allowed to give the coins to is Henry, the man at the corner shop. He's had the shop for a thousand years, wears a white coat and always smokes a cigar. He's tall and walks with bent shoulders, so it looks like he's been carrying too many stacks of potatoes. I don't steal anything from Henry, 'cos when Mum's not with me he always pops a bit extra into my bag. Last time it was an orange.

I wish I could tell Henry I'm on my own. But Mum says I'm not allowed to tell anyone when she's away, I'm just to do the best I can and she'll come back.

I want to eat all the bread on the first day she's not here, to make her come back quicker, but I can't 'cos I know that this isn't what she meant when she said it. I need to make the bread last a long time. The bread is beginning to taste funny, so I decide it's time to venture out for the first time since she went and go to the shop.

The stairs smell of piss and the boys don't move to let me past. So I've to try and squeeze through them until one of them says, 'Let her go.' I'm too scared to go on, so I run back to my flat and have to stand on my tip toes to put the key in the door.

Even though my hands are shaking I manage first time. When Mum isn't here, I keep the key on a string round my neck, all the time, even when I'm sleeping.

Back in the flat, I wait a little but when I look again they're still there, hanging about on the landing, so I can't go to get my milk and my fresh bread, and the Dairy Milk bar I was thinking of. I've to stay here instead and be safe.

For tea, I have the ham with bread like I've had every night. In the morning I'll have cornflakes. The milk has gone lumpy, so I'll have them with water instead, and for tea I'll have a ham sandwich with no butter.

There's less than half of the loaf left and Mum still isn't back. She says she'll be back before it runs out, so maybe if I go to bed then she'll be here when I wake up.

My bed isn't as clean as it was the day I woke up and she wasn't here. I spend most of the days and nights in my bed, or going from room to room in the flat. I don't go out unless I have to, like Mum says. I play with my dolls, pretending that my mum is home and I'm looking after them and she's looking after me. The dolls are my friends and so I share what I have to eat with them, including my biscuit before bed. We all go to bed at the same time, which is very early as I can't reach the switch to put the light on in my room. There's only one biscuit left as I ate more than one a day, even though I know Mum would have said no.

But she's not here.

I can reach the counter in the kitchen as the kitchen is small and there's a chair next to the counter. I can climb on the chair and crawl along the counter to get to the sink for some water, because I am nearly five. But as I am only four, I'm also too little to move the chair to be able to put the light on. The only light I have is the one in the hall as that's on all the time; Mummy must've left it that way when she left me.

I don't like going into her room 'cos it still smells of her, even though she hasn't been here for eleven sleeps now. When I feel really lonely, though, I curl up on her bed for a bit with her pillow. Her second pillow did smell of her but now it doesn't, 'cos I took that pillow through to my room and now that pillow smells musty, same as all my bedding.

When I stick my head out the door to check if the boys are still there, they are, and Mrs Nosey-Parker sees me and, even though I try not to look at her, she asks me where my mum is. I say she's sleeping and she looks at me funny, so I change my story and say she's busy at work and that I've to go to bed now.

Mrs Nosey-Parker has nice eyes and a smile that I imagine a gran would have. I really want to tell her that I'm on my own and now I really don't know what to do, as this morning the bread is getting green spots and I've not much of it left and the boys who hang out on the landing are back again, still stopping me going to the shop. Mum said not to eat the bread if it starts to go green, but to go to the shop and get another one. But she also said if she ever went away she would be home after not too long, so I don't know which one of those things she tells me is the true one.

Mum also said that when she goes away I'm not to tell anyone. So now the bread is going green and as it's daytime and not evening, I was thinking about just going to the shop like she told me, even with the boys there. That way I can get some more bread and some chocolate, but maybe I shouldn't spend the money on chocolate as I don't know how long she'll be gone for, and there's a few bits of bread left that are not spotted green, but there are more spotty than are not spotty.

Just scrape the green bits off.

I'm a little bit scared as the boys have moved from the end of the landing. I can hear them outside my window and I've just been sick and feel like crying. I should go to sleep.

If I cry, I'm to cry quietly so the people next door don't hear me. I don't know what I did to make Mum go away, but I must've done something.

Mummy come back now, I'll be good, I promise. I'm sorry, Mummy, come back.

Mrs Nosey-Parker is chasing the boys away.

'Go on, get outta here. Don't ya have homes to go to?'

Her husband is behind her, backing her up.

'Go on, get outta here.'

They're outside my window, Mrs Nosey-Parker and her husband.

'I don't know, George; I think she's gone and left her.'

Oh no! How do you know that?

I'm fully awake. I lie dead still in my bed. The walls are so thin, I can hear every word.

Go away, go away, Nosey-Parker, go away. Find me, look after me. Please?

'Who would do that? Don't be silly.'

'Let me just have a little look through the kitchen window.'

'Come on, don't be nosey, they're fine. The mum will just be sleeping. Come on, Anne.'

Mrs Nosey-Parker has a name! Anne. It's a nice name. Maybe if I tell her it won't be so bad. Maybe if I tell her she'll help me find my mum and tell Mum she has me, and Mum would come back and it would all be normal again.

'The boys have gone now. Anne – don't look! Come on. In!'

'All right, George, all right.'

The door to their flat shuts. I pull the covers around me. Half of me is glad I haven't been caught. The other part of me is sad 'cos her voice sounds friendly and Mum still isn't home. I drift in and out of sleep, waking up, being sick on the floor.

Come home, Mummy, I don't feel well. The bread is done. You must be coming home tomorrow.

What? What's going on? There are people outside my window. Oh, oh. Who are they? There's quite a few of them. Don't look out. Don't look out, they will see you.

I look at the clock, the hands are past the time I can get up.

I must've slept for a whole day. Tummy feels better. I'm thirsty.

The sun isn't shining through my curtains today and, as the people are down by the kitchen window, I can't see who is standing outside my house talking.

'I just couldn't rest yesterday, or sleep last night. All night I was pacing, wasn't I, George? I don't like to stick my nose into other people's business but I worry, don't I, George?'

I don't hear George but it must be him and Mrs Nosey-Parker, 'cos she's speaking to him.

Whew, it isn't the boys, then. But is there someone else with them?

'Then this morning, when I looked through the kitchen window, well, it's all such a mess. George told me I should leave well alone, but I just couldn't, up all night I was. I saw her yesterday, the little girl, and she was all grubby and didn't look like she'd had a wash in a long while. Hair all over the place. So I just couldn't rest myself. And look! Look! There's a gap in the curtains here. Dishes all over the place. Stuff spilt on the floor. Oh my, if anything has happened to that little girl, I'll never forgive myself. My. My. What a way to leave a child. Who would do such a thing? And if you look through the letter box, there are clothes and toys everywhere, and mouldy bread, right next to the dolls. Rats, that's what will happen next, rats!'

I hear the letter box lift up.

Oh no, hide, hide, don't look. Mum's not here, she'll be back soon, you can't find out . . .

'Now, Mrs Simpson . . .'

Who is Mrs Simpson?

'You did the right thing in calling us. We shall handle it from here.'

Who are you? Are you those boys back again? Oh no, oh no.

'Now, why don't you go inside with my colleague here and make us all a nice cup of tea? Mr Simpson, do you know the little girl's name?'

Colleague, what's a colleague? Who are you? Mummy, where's Mummy?

'Umm, no we don't, officer. We keep ourselves to ourselves, you know. They just moved here a few months back. The mum said her name was Mrs Brown. Anne – Mrs Simpson – didn't believe her, but I told her, we've no reason to disbelieve her and if she says her name is Mrs Brown then that's what we shall call her. But no, we don't really speak much, nor have much to do with them. So the long and the short of it is, we don't know the little girl's name, maybe we should . . .'

His voice fades so I can't hear him. Then a cough and the same voice comes back stronger again, 'Right, I shall leave you to it, officers . . . I'll go and help Anne with your cuppa.'

Silence. A radio. A man talking into a radio. I pull my covers up around me. The man stops talking and the letter box flap goes up again.

'Hello, hello. Anyone there? Mrs Brown? Are you in?'

There's banging on the door.

'Police. Mrs Brown, we're here to help. Is there anyone at home?'

I creep out of bed. My toes stand in something wet and cold. Goes through my toes. I look down. My own sick surrounds my feet and is coming out the top of my toes. I gag, retch, but there's nothing left in my tummy to come up.

Must be quiet, be quiet.

I creep towards the door of my room. Over the toys and clothes and crusts from my sandwich from the first day she wasn't here until I worked out she'd be away for longer than normal. After that I ate everything, even the crusts I don't like. I crouch down next to my wardrobe and put my hands round my knees. Tears come.

I don't know what to do.

There's more banging and voices saying they're here to help.

There's a woman's face with a police hat on top looking through the crack in my bedroom window. The woman is pointing and speaking in her radio at the same time.

I look round the room. For the first time I see it's messy. There's sick on the floor and in my feet.

I can't cope. I don't want to do this any more. I don't want to wait for Mum any more. I can't do this . . . What if she never comes back?

I scream.

'Right, that's it. We are going to break the door down. It's the police. Don't be scared.'

The front door goes on the first kick.

I hear it banging against the wall, then steps. Someone coughing. The police lady opens the door to my bedroom slowly, she's got her hand over her mouth, covering her nose. Other steps go past her into the other rooms. People coughing, gagging, saying to open a window to let fresh air in.

'It's all right, love, it's all right. Where's your mum? Do you know where your mum is?'

I can't move. I can't. I won't tell you.

'Are you hungry? Want an apple or some chocolate? What's your name, love?'

There's a man, another policeman, behind her.

'There's no one else here. She's on her own.'

'How long have you been on your own, love?'

Questions. Questions . . . I don't want questions I can't answer.

'Who is this, then?'

Teddy!

I reach out to him, she gives me to him.

'How long have you been on your own, love? How long have you been looking after Teddy?'

How does she know his name?

'Are you on your own, love?'

I nod.

'Can you tell me your name?'

Another nod. I know my full name, as Mum calls me by it whenever she's angry with me.

'Jackie Elizabeth.'

'Oh, okay, and your last name?'

'Brown.'

The policewoman sits on the floor next to me.

'Where's your mum, Jackie?'

'She's at work.'

'How long has she been at work, then?'

'Dunno. I lost count, maybe more than ten sleeps.'

'Do you know when she'll be back, love?'

'Most times she comes back before the bread is finished. I'm doing okay; I've got money for the shops and she'll come back before the bread is finished.'

The police man disappears, speaking on his radio.

'Where's he going? I'm doing fine. I eat and sleep and have money.'

'He's just off to see if we can help find your mum. 'Cos that's a lot for you to do on your own; live here by yourself for so long. How old are you – four?'

'Nearly five.'

The police lady has a nice smile. She seems to use it a lot with me.

'Bet you and Teddy could do with something to eat. Will we see if Mrs Simpson has something nice? Maybe after that we can find you somewhere warm to stay and a clean bed, just until we find your mum. Does that sound all right with you? Do you want to give me your hand?'

I nod. Her hand is soft, like my mum's.

'Maybe we should wipe your feet first. Sit there.'

The police are going to help me find my mum.

Outside the flat, with clean feet and a pair of Mum's socks on, Mrs Simpson is standing with a warm blanket which she wraps around me.

'I knew it. I knew it. George, didn't I tell you? I knew it. Who leaves their kid on their own? Never, George, in all our years of bringing up the kids, never once did we leave them on their own . . . Well, not for more than ten minutes, anyway, not once. Who does that kind of thing? I knew it. I did. Didn't I tell ya?'

George smiles at me, agrees, then tells her to, 'Shush.' He stretches out his hand to Teddy. 'Who's this, then?'

'Teddy.'

'Nice to meet you, Teddy. Come on then, you, into the warmth. Would you like some juice? Cuppa's ready. After you, officer, and Teddy, of course.'

George has a big laugh. Their house is nothing like mine. It's just next door, yet is all flowers and warm smells; it's nice, but it's not home.

I want my mummy.

Abby. Aged nine.

When I open the front door, tension greets me. I walk down the hall into the living room where I find my mum and Lee doing his chores. He's on number four. He doesn't look up, he knows not to. Mum's face is like thunder.

What's wrong now?

She's there, curled in the corner of the velvet blue sofa. Her blonde hair is tied back in a ponytail, tight, lifting her face, a Croydon face lift my step-dad calls it. Her jumper flops around the upper half of her body, just about covering the tyre at her middle. Cords, brown, decorated with food spillage on her right thigh, crumbs scattered over her top.

God, you've worn those trousers for three days now.

Not much make-up, she never bothers, doesn't see the point, says her skin don't need it. Plain, my mother is. A shadow hangs around her milk-white face and the frown which is always there seems darker today. Sometimes we hear her laugh with my step-dad, but any laughter stops as soon as my little brother, Lee, and I, the 'little buggers', come into the room.

Today when I look at her, she looks more dark than usual. A hand reaches out to the table next to the sofa. There's an envelope there. Chipped nails and nail varnish reach out to part the top of the envelope; it's already opened. Before pulling the contents out, she changes her mind, stops, fingers halfway inside the envelope, teasing me with the contents. She decides to have a rant instead.

'Do you know what this is?'

My head moves from side to side.

'It's a letter.'

Well, I know that. Don't say, though. Best to keep quiet.

'Nuh.'

'Do you know what it says?'

'Nuh.'

'Don't you nuh me! Yes or no?'

'No, Mum, I don't.'

Keep calm. She's mad as . . .

'A letter. From the school.'

She lets this hang in the air.

Okay. Keep quiet.

I don't take my own advice. I ask, 'About me?'

'Yes about you, you fuckin' thievin' bitch.'

Despite her large size, she and the letter are off the sofa in a single movement. I look down at the floor, crumbs spill from her, all over the bit of carpet Lee has just finished. I see him reach out for the tweezers again and move back to re-clean that piece of carpet. My heart breaks, but he doesn't look away from his task. He knows better than to risk it.

Her red-wine-coloured slippers approach me. She steps over Lee as if he wasn't there. The letter is flapping in front of my nose. A hand reaches out. Pulls my chin up, away from my chest. Fingers either side of my face. I can see my lips purse outward with the pressure.

'Ow!'

'Some thievin' little bastard has been stealing from the school cloakroom. Is it you?'

I try to shake my head, but she's holding my chin so hard I can't move.

'What's that?' she questions.

'No,' I reply.

She releases me, pushing my head to the right. When I bring it back, the letter is still there, being waved in front of my nose, a breeze is created.

'Lying bitch. I know it's you.'

'No, Mum, it isn't, I swear. What does the letter say?'

She pulls it out of the envelope.

'Here – you read it.'

The letter is thrust into my hand. I open the letter, scan it, take it in: 'A series of thefts at the school … Cloakrooms … Perpetrator not yet identified … Increased patrols … Reassure parents … Doing all they can … If any child is affected, let the teachers know …'

They don't know it's me. She doesn't know it's me. I can blag it . . .

'I know it's you.'

Her eyes have narrowed. A finger is pointing.

'It's not, Mum, it's not.'

'Do you know how I know it's you?'

Her voice is strong, sure. Mine less so now, 'No, Mum, you can't. It's not me, Mum.'

'I know 'cos you ain't been hungry enough when you come home from school. You ain't been askin' for food all the fuckin' time. Normally, it's whine, whine, whine . . . food this, food that. You and your brother. Nag, nag, nag. "Give us something to eat, please, Mum, please." There's been none of that recently.' She pauses for effect. Grabs the letter from me, scratches my hand with a ragged nail and continues, 'So this letter comes and I get to thinkin' – where they getting their food from? 'Cos it ain't from me . . . Ain't from me.'

We stare at each other. She's looking at me as I stand in front of her. I can see the anger rising up her face, into her eyes.

Shit.

She grabs my arm, we both spin round as I'm dragged into the kitchen.

Shit.

'Sit.'

I obey and lower myself on to a kitchen stool.

She reaches into a cupboard. A glass. Another cupboard. A container.

'Please, Mum, no, not this again, Mum. I didn't do it, Mum.'

'We shall see, shan't we?'

'Mum, please. Mum?'

She fills the glass with tap water. Salt is in the long, thin, white container, the red top is flipped open to make a small spout.

She pours the salt into a glass, the same glass as the water.

Please not again.

A spoon is taken from the drawer. She stirs it to dissolve. Picks up the salt again.

No, no more.

Pours more salt into the glass.

She turns round to face me. Her hand with the glass is outstretched to me. I know what to do; she tells me anyway.

'Drink.'

I shake my head.

'Drink, you little shit. You stole the food and I need to prove it. Drink.'

I take the glass. She's standing over me.

'Drink.'

I take a deep breath but she's impatient. Pushing the glass up towards my lips.

'Don't keep me waiting. Drink. All of it. Now.'

I do.

First I gag, then choke, then rush to the kitchen sink. The contents of my stomach gets to the sink before me. The salt water comes back, mixed with undigested bits of ham, bread, apple and crisps.

The contents of my stomach, staring up at me as she looks down at me and the sink.

She turns away, going back to her spot on the sofa, a final verbal shot: 'See, I told you you were a fuckin' stealin' bitch. Clean this up. I've got guests coming tomorrow. Then go to your room. Stay there. I don't want to see you until the morning. I'll decide what to do with you later. Fuckin' stupid bitch.'

Robert. Aged six.

She's so beautiful, even without her make-up. I know Dad's coming home, because she's sat me on the floor of her bedroom with Curious George, who is a monkey teddy, and the Lego that I got for Christmas, a tipper truck and a plane. I can't quite make them yet, but she wants me to try.

'Sit there quietly, love, while Mam does her make-up for Daddy coming home.'

I watch her as she selects a dress. She chooses one that's long, with puffy sleeves that will hide the bruise marks on her arm. I don't like that it takes me mam longer to choose the dress than it does for me to make the tipper truck, even though it isn't looking like the one in the picture on the box and I've four bits left over. But it's okay 'cos I've all day to make it right before Dad comes home.

Maybe he'll like my day's playing and give me a cuddle and say, 'Well done, boy', like he did once before. Maybe if I do this properly he'll be less angry and won't hit me mam. Must try and get all the bits on to the truck.

Mam is questioning herself, looking at the dresses again, even though we chose one just now.

'What do you think of this one, Robert?'

'It's very pretty, Mam.'

'Do you think your dad will like it? No, I think he'll like this one better? Or this one?'

She holds up three different dresses, one red, one green, one blue, which is the same one we chose before with the long sleeves. I stare back.

In the blue one you fell down the stairs when he pushed you accidentally on purpose. You went to hospital in the green one and then came home with a patch on your eye. The red one has blood on it from when your head bounced on the wall and you fell down and he said he didn't mean to hurt you, and then helped you clean up afterwards instead of drinking beer.

'Oh, I don't know. He doesn't seem to be liking anything I wear these days.'

'The blue one, Mam.'

That's the one you got hurt least in.

She places the three dresses carefully on the bed, like they're so precious, it's a big decision. We both know the right choice means she'll be safe and the wrong choice means he'll shout at her and tell her he had a bad night and she's not supportive and does things wrong and so she deserves it. But, whatever she wears, it doesn't matter 'cos he'll make sure she deserves it anyway. It used to be that we didn't know if he'd be in a jolly mood or a shouty mood when he came home. Now we know. Always shouty, always angry. It's the level of anger that we can only guess at these days. We know we're in for it when the door opens, we just don't know how much of him we're about to receive until he starts on her. She tries to look nice with make-up before he knocks her about.

Why does she do that? I'll protect her. I will. I will.

She goes back into the wardrobe. It's big for the number of clothes in it, so I go into the wardrobe, too, right inside, sitting on the bottom, looking up at me mam, who is looking at some other dresses, as if one of them will solve all her problems. From down here, I count five other dresses, but I already worked out that three need mending 'cos they're ripped and another green one also has a bit of blood on that she hasn't managed to get out yet. I haven't seen her do any mending today so nothing will have changed.

Why are you checking them again?

'Oh, Robert, what do you think?'

'I like the blue one, Mam; the one that looks like the sky on a lovely day. It has the flowers at the neck and the flower belt. It goes with your sunshine hair and blue eyes. You look like a fairy angel.'

She smiles, but her eyes are sad. I use her legs to climb up and stand in the wardrobe reaching out, giving her legs a hug.

'Don't be sad, Mam; you really will look like an angel in that dress.'

'Thank you, Robert. Now, get back to your Lego as I need to do my make-up and hair.'

I pretend to play with my toy, to build a plane that will take us away but, really, I watch me mam.

Her dressing table is made of wood, a dark wood, shiny and polished like her blonde hair. There are three mirrors, one big one in the middle and two more, one on each side. At the top of the mirror, they are round shaped, a bit like the dome on the place where they exchanged corn in Leeds and where we changed on the bus when we moved from Newcastle to Leeds without Dad. But then he found us and moved us back 'cos he said he'd changed, but he soon showed us that he hadn't.

Can't we get the bus somewhere else today, Mam? Why can't I protect you? Why are you sitting there putting on make-up? Why can't we live somewhere else? Somewhere safe.

The side mirrors are attached to the bigger middle one and they move forward and back, unable to do their own thing without the middle bit.

The mirrors are like me and me mam, both attached to me dad. Unable to live without him letting us.

When she moves the mirror on the right backwards to see her ears, I can see the suitcase on top of the wardrobe.

Why aren't you packing, Mam? Why aren't we running away? Why are you going to all this effort when he's just going to make you cry and make you asleep on the floor. Even after you fall down and stop saying, 'No, please, no,' he carries on. Why bother getting dressed up like this? Pack a bag. I know where he keeps the money. Why are you sitting there trying to look your best, Mam? Can we go, Mam?

Thoughts filling up me head mean I can't do me Lego.

It hurts, it hurts. She won't let us run. He'll come back, blame her, beat her. I can't protect her. Me Lego just looks like a blur. Me head is so full. It feels like it's gonna explode. I don't care. I don't care.

'Robert!'

Her voice snaps me back from wherever I was.

'What did you do that for, you know we don't like that kind of behaviour round here.'

My Lego is broken back into all its little pieces. All over the floor. I must've thrown it, but I don't remember. It takes us precious time trying to find all the pieces. They're under the bed and the wardrobe and the dressing table – everywhere. It's a mess we've to clean up before Dad gets home, otherwise he'll be mad.

I scream back at her, 'He's gonna be mad anyway, so what's the difference?'

'Robert, don't speak about your father like that. Maybe this time it will be different; he's promised to change and we've to try and make it work. No one else wants us. We've nowhere to go. I wouldn't manage without him. I can't do things on my own. You know that. We've to make this work and he says he's changed. Now tidy this up while I finish my make-up. He'll be back soon and everything has to be perfect.'

She turns her back on me, towards the mirror. Picks up her mascara, the brush making her lashes bigger, longer, stronger, as if this is the only thing in the world important to her right now. I watch her. Her words are strong but the hand in front of her eye is shaking. She misses the lash and a big black dollop of mascara sits on the brim of her cheek-bone. She crumbles, drops the mascara on to the table, both hands press into her eyes. Sobbing, me mam is sobbing.

I run and give her a hug. We both feel sad. I hug and hug and she hugs back, until she says, 'Now come on, Robert, it will all be fine. You tidy up while your mam re-does her make-up. Look at me, I look like a panda! Let's start again and get this all fixed up.'

She does a little smile, which is more straight across than up, but we both know the full smile comes when she finishes her make-up and he comes home. It's a smile that comes on to welcome him, in the hope that he's kept his promise this time. It's a smile that stays as fixed as the make-up on her face until the moment that he reminds her with his left fist that whatever dreams she's had about the evening, and future evenings together, they are different from his.

Mam's dreams ended up meaning she stayed in hospital for a long time. I ended up in care. In a place called Chesterfields.

Hope. 1981.

I love my dad so much. He's got no job and we live off the social and what Mum earns, but he manages so well to find us stuff.

All year he collects toys for us for Christmas, his big frame walking through the market, a hand out, coat open, pops something into the inside pocket.

When he gets home, us kids bounce about asking, 'What did you get today, Dad?'

Always a magazine for my mum, or a red Chanel lipstick. He's so resourceful. Sometimes he doesn't tell us what he's brought home. That's when I know it's a toy for Christmas. He hides them so well; it kills me not to know. I never find them, well, hardly ever. When I do, I'm disappointed, so is he. Dad re-hides the toys and then has to get more, to help Santa.

Christmas day all the toys appear in piles, all unwrapped, because, Dad says, Santa doesn't have time. We believe him.

Today I am dancing on my dad's toes, as we do most days. Mum is out working so, for once, it's not to Elvis or Tom Jones on the record player. Dad is playing a new single that he nicked for Mum. It's number one – Michael Jackson, 'One Day in Your Life'. It's my favourite, too.

A new Barbie doll has also joined us today because this afternoon Dad got me a big haul of Barbie things from a skip around the corner.

Barbie is in her best dress for dancing. I found it among the pile of Barbie clothes Dad brought me home. I sorted them out and put all the clothes on the little hangers that he found and then into the white wardrobe. Dad helped me. We set up a whole house for Barbie and her Barbie friends – a bed, a sofa, a wardrobe, a cooker. My dad is so clever to find all this stuff. He was going to hide it, to keep it for Christmas, but he couldn't. He was too excited. As excited as me.

I am so glad he didn't. I am in absolute heaven.

Me, my dad and Barbie in her best dress dance around the room. Me balancing on my dad's toes. Me looking up at him, grinning from ear to ear.

Robert. Aged seven.
Me and me Mam are sitting in the living room of the kids' home, no staff, just me and me mam. Apart from the times Dad put Mam in hospital, she's visited me every week since I've been here, and every week I show her how I can stand a bit better than before. I've been walking normally now for a few months and she's very proud of me. The doctors who help me are very stern and they use the word 'concerned' a lot. 'We are concerned,' I hear them say. I walked like I walk as I've a head trauma. Me mam says it's because I fell down the stairs when I went home for the weekend. She forgot to say I fell down the stairs 'cos me dad threw me down them and then kicked and hit me a bit more with a snooker cue. After that I stopped walking. The

doctors gave my lack of walking a name, 'water on the ear', which makes me lose my balance. But it's okay now as I can walk upright without falling over. I have just been showing me mam.

Normally when she visits, we go out into the garden and I show her where we kids build a den and how well I can walk without holding on or falling over.

Each week I notice she still has bruises in different places. She tries to cover them up, especially the ones on her neck. When she comes, I want to touch them, stroke her skin, make them go away, but I don't 'cos that would make her feel bad and bring attention to something we don't talk about. This time she's come with some news. She wants me to like it, but I don't think I do.

'What do you mean, I'm going back home? No, Mam, no, Mam. He can't have changed, Mam. Mam, he still beats you, Mam. Why, Mam?'

'We love you, son. We want you at home with us. He doesn't beat me, not any more; it's different now. He never really did touch me anyway and he certainly never touched you that much; that was all a stupid misunderstanding. A mistake. Your dad is sorry for everything he did, not that he did much, and I believe him.'

Her voice is getting firmer. I wonder how much longer I can protest. I try once more, 'Mam, no, Mam. I like it here. Please don't make me leave. I don't want to go home.'

'Now, Robert,' she smiles and reaches out to touch my cheek, 'we know things weren't exactly super at home before, but we love you. And your dad, well, he's a job now and, well, I told you already, we love you and we've had chats with the social workers and they agree it's the best thing . . . For you to come home with us. Anyway, you were only meant to be in here a few weeks and you've been here a few months now. So it's time to come home. Robert, are you listening to me? It will all be fine, we shall be a happy family, now your dad has a job.'

It only took two weeks for Dad to lose his job and for things to go back to normal again.

The bath is running hot. I scuttle from my bedroom across the upstairs landing to the bathroom, using both my hands and feet to get about. My bum points straight up in the air and my head straight down. I pause and turn to look at myself in the mirror at the top of the stairs. I look like a crab, though I go forwards, not sideways. Any other way of walking hurts my ears and, right now, there's no point in even trying to walk properly, I just wobble and fall over.

In the bathroom, hot with steam from the running taps, I pull my head up from floor level, to the side of the bath. I rest my head on the side and an elbow beside it, reaching in with my other hand to test the water.

Hot and nearly ready. Must shout to me mam to help me into the bath.

My wet hand pulls itself back on to the floor and I scramble back into the hallway. I edge myself up, hand over hand, along the length of the banister railings into a standing position, holding onto the banister at the top of the stairs.

Careful, take yer time to balance.

Balanced, I call for me mam.

She replies, 'All right, love, coming now.'

I turn round for a moment, forgetting.

Oh no, oh shit.

Whack, everything zooms. I fall sideways. I hear a crash of china. I can hear myself breathing. I'm lying on the floor, my head facing the stairs. A voice from the kitchen calls out, 'What's happened?'

I can't reply. Me mam's head and then her body come into view as she climbs the stairs. Her right hand holding the stair rail, edging upwards, trying to hide the pain of her movements. Her left hand is gently wrapped round her aching ribs. From my floor-level view, a bit more of her is revealed as she climbs, one stair at a time, until we catch eyes and I can see that her already-broken heart crumbles a little bit more.

I can't stand up. I can't stand up.

Her legs dissolve slowly beneath her; she sinks gracefully like air is being drawn out of her until she sits on the top step beside my fallen body. She strokes my head, the tenderness of her action doing nothing to reach through the numbness that hides the feelings I have to bury to carry on with living. I interrupt this moment to get away from the compassion.

'The bath is still running, Mam.'

Using the banister that failed me to haul herself up, she steps over me, towards the bathroom. One foot either side of me, there's a pause as she notices the vase I knocked off the table as I fell and which smashed as I tried to maintain myself in the upright position. In the mirror I can see she looks shocked, fearful, and then her expression changes, she's concerned, reassuring.

'It's all right, Robert. I shall tidy it up while you're in the bath. He's gone now, he won't notice. He's not here to notice. I don't think he's coming back, Robert. I think we might be free.'

Since Dad had an episode of hitting and throwing Mam and me around the house last week, we haven't seen him. Which is good, on one hand, but, on the other, Mam has no money for anything.

Since then, when I try to stand up properly everything goes all wobbly. My head spins and I lose my balance, fall over and whack my head again, though not as hard as Dad whacked it when he had me down on the floor in the corner and boxed my ears. Dad boxed me like Jimmy Young did when he came back after Round 7 to beat George Foreman. Dad boxes me, but our fight isn't as equal as it is in the ring.

It's not so bad, though, when I walk on my hands and feet, bum in air, like a crab. I don't seem to fall over and whack my head again if I do that. I figure I've Dad to do the whacking, so I don't need to do it to myself.

On the day I start walking like this, head down and bum up, me mam tells me to stop playing, it's not funny. I turn my head towards her, from its position near the floor.

'But it feels funny when I stand up, Mam. I keep falling over. If I walk like this, I manage better.'

She stares at me in silence. I know both of us are remembering the snooker cue Dad broke over my back and how he pulled me so hard by the arm, to get me out of the way of me mam, that it came out of the socket for a moment.

'It's the holidays, so I don't have to go to school and I'll get better by the end of the holidays, Mam.'

'All right, then, pet.' She sounds tired, like she can't fight no more, or doesn't want to fight with me.

Now, as she goes to check the bath, she smiles softly and then winces, holding her rib cage with one hand and her opposite shoulder with the other. I stare up at her.

Can hardly see the bruising now, she knows how to use make-up to cover the damage so well.

'How's your ribs, Mam?'

'I'm all right, love. I'm all right. We're going to be fine; seems like he's gone for good this time and we're going to be fine. I'll go to the social tomorrow, tell them he's left us. I'll get some money. It's going to be fine, pet. Stop fretting.'

That night, as we watch the telly, both curled up together on the sofa in our dressing gowns, me and me mam, we hear a key in the door. In an instant, we both freeze and listen. I look up at Mam, she looks down at me. She whispers, 'Shit.'

There's a tear at the edge of her bruised, coloured eye. She stretches out a finger and runs it up her face; it looks like she's trying to push the tear back in, to hide her tears as well as everything else that remains behind closed doors.

We're going to die.

'Robert, quick, go and hide, we can't have him hurting you any more. And, whatever happens, don't you dare try to protect me; he always wins. Better you stay safe. Go. Go now. I'll be fine.'

You won't be, but I know you mean it. I know that voice.

Out in the hall I see him, unshaven and dark with anger. His suit isn't sitting right, it's slumped on him like he, in turn, is against the wall. He looks unlike my normally smartly dressed Dad and, to add to the confusion, he's his own black eye. He looks ugly.

Before I experienced fear or pain on seeing him, tonight there's nothing. I have no feelings. I scuttle past me dad, on all fours, bum in the air, and he slurs at me, 'Where's yer mam? What the fuck are you doing walking like that, boy? Walk fuckin' tall. Be a man.'

Like you, Dad? Be a man like you?

I say nothing. He pauses, as if wanting to impart some other drunken wisdom, changes his mind and kicks out at me instead. He misses. He wobbles, catching himself on the wall with the palm of his hand, a hand that I used to hate, along with the rest of him.

Why don't I feel nothin'?

I take my chance. I pull my head towards the ground like a bull and rush up the stairs on all fours. I hide in the only safe place in the house, under my bed, right at the back against the wall. I stay there for a long time, working out where my feelings might have gone. I cover my ears, blocking out the noise from downstairs.

Please stop. Please stop.

Every so often I listen, hoping it'll be quiet downstairs again. Eventually, it is.

Has he killed her?

Abby. Aged ten.

After Mum poured salt down my throat to make me puke that time, the social worker came and took us away. We went to live with my dad. I told him a bit of what she's like, but Mum persuaded Dad that it was her ex-boyfriend that mistreated me and Lee. We got into trouble for telling lies. Dad believes Mum. So Lee and I now know better than to say anything at all.

Dad says he can't cope with us both, especially as I am starting secondary school soon and he thinks we can't share a room with each other. It's not right, he says. So we've just taken Lee home to Mum without telling the social worker.

Looking out the back window of the car as Dad and I drive off, I look at Lee standing on the pavement outside my mum's house, staring down the close after us, looking as small as his little suitcase.

He stands looking after us and, as we drive away, his shoulders become stooped. We left him on his own outside. Mum didn't come and say hello to me or Dad, she just stood and looked out the window with daggers in her eyes.

I can't bear it. Poor Lee. Dad, Dad, why couldn't you cope with us both? Why do we have to take Lee back to Mum's? Why? Why can't he stay with us? I am not too old to share a room with him. Just because I'm at senior school. Oh, Dad, Dad, he won't even have me to help him steal food. What will he eat? Dad, please, Dad. We'd manage.

Tears are streaming down my face. We've rounded the corner and I can no longer see my little brother left all on his own to deal with Mum.

Last night I threatened to tell Dad about what it was like when we both lived with Mum. Lee talked me out of it; he said he'd be okay, that adults won't believe us anyway.

That it would be better if we kept quiet, said nothing; that she won't be as bad if it was just him at home. As it turns out, Lee was wrong.

Lee. Aged eight.

I breathe out, long and slow, the tension of the day escaping into the air from my mouth. But not from my shoulders, they're still sore from all my chores. Abby has been gone a long time and Mum has got worse.

The only place that feels safe in the house is in here, in the wardrobe. Even though I know Mum is out tonight and I am the only one in the house, it still feels safer here than anywhere else. I blow on my cold fingers and rub them together, then reach out with my left hand to close the wardrobe door. It doesn't shut properly as the cable for my stereo goes from the wall to the wardrobe and I don't have batteries. The gap the cable makes between the wardrobe and the door means that there's a little gap and a small draft comes in to my safety den, but the draft is small enough that if I hug my knees and huddle and put all my clothes over me, and then my bed sheet, I don't really feel it. Even with the draught, it's warmer in here than outside in my room.

With Mum out, I've a few hours to play the stereo that Dad gave me, the one he said I am not to tell Mum about.

As if! It's one secret she isn't going to have the chance to take away. It's mine.

I don't have any new tapes as the security guard at Woolworths has banned me, so I plan to listen to Radio 1. Mum has locked the house up good and proper, and left my dinner out for me.

I'll have that later.

I struggle to get my right hand out from under the pile of clothes keeping me warm in the bottom of the wardrobe to press the button that will bring music to my ears and let my imagination drift to better places, to forget that Dad took Abby to live with him, and that he doesn't want me. To imagine that he'll get another house with an extra room so he can take me, too.

Why can't Abby and I share a room? It's not fair. No one wants me, no one cares.

Pressing the button of the stereo, nothing happens.

What? What's going on? What's wrong with my music? I need my music. Please. Who broke my stereo? Who has made it not work? Did Mum find it and break it? Oh no, please don't let Mum have found it; it's all I have. Please. Please.

My breathing is fast, I can't get a breath, my chest tightens until it feels constricted. Tension, head booming, blood thumping. My vision hazes over. My head rolls. I try to catch my breath.

Have to get out, get out. I can't breathe. If Mum knows, she'll kill me. Beat me. She hates me, they all hate me. Why did they leave me here? I can't breathe. I am caught, stuck, the clothes, they're all round me, I can't get out, I have to get out, I am stuck.

I try and throw the clothes out of the wardrobe but they're stuck in twisted knots around me. The more I try to move, the more entangled I seem to become.

Gotta get out, get out.

I fall forwards, out the door, the stereo slides out with me and a tangled mess of clothes. I land shoulder first on the wooden floorboards. The stereo comes out of the wardrobe at the same time as my bloated tummy. I look up at the ceiling, feet still in the wardrobe, caught up in some clothes.

You're out, control your breathing. Deep, like the teacher told you at school. Slow breaths, focus. Try and control the breathing.

I relax, turn my head on the floorboards, my eyes refocus.

Oh! I didn't switch the plug on at the wall.

Pulling my feet out on to the floor, I reach out and switch the plug on. The chart show is on with Tommy Vance. I wonder what will be Number One this week; he's already playing Number Eleven.

I hope Culture Club still has the top spot, they've had it for a few weeks and it's a good tune; but it might be that song by Billy Joel about a girl from uptown. I wonder what Mum left me for tea.

I rearrange the stereo so it's nearer the socket on the wall and sit on the floor, the wall supporting my back, which still hurts from when Mum took her belt to me last week.

I reach sideways, towards my bedroom door, pick up the dog's bowl and start to eat my tea.

Hope. 1983.

I run home from school, crossing the road to avoid the National Front group handing out their newspaper. With their skinheads and Dr Marten boots, if you are on that side of the road, you feel obliged to take it. So I cross the road, avoiding them is better than refusing them.

I don't want that paper.

When I get in, Dad is holding a box, an empty plastic box, with writing on it. There's a date on the side – 15th February 1971.

'Hope. Disappointed in you I am, really I am. Yer mum

tells me she found this box under your mattress. You stole some money from her box in the wardrobe? That true?'

I nod. No use lying to my dad, he always knows.

'Presentation coins they were. They were yer mum's. What's this stealing from your own? What have we taught ya? Never steal from yer own? Others, yes, but yer own, no. The others are insured, they can afford it, but yer own, no. Haven't I taught you nothin'?'

I hate being told off, especially by my dad.

'Now get the fuck out of my sight, I don't want to see ya. You think about this, Hope. You don't steal from yer own. You better steer clear of yer mum as well for a while, if you want to avoid her tongue. No, don't you go lookin' at me like that. I'm your dad, we may not be perfect, Hope, but at least we're here lookin' out for ya, best we can.'

I run down the street, crying. I hate to disappoint my dad, but he's the one who taught us to survive, to steal.

Other parents teach their kids how to read and write, you teach me to steal. How am I to know the difference?

I sit in the cemetery. I sulk, then my thoughts turn. I think about some of the kids at school whose dads aren't around at all. I sit until it's dark, until I am sure my mum will have gone to work on the bus, gone to work at King's Cross.

As the lights fade in the sky and reappear in houses, I kick the pavement on my way home. I think about what Dad said about being there and looking out for me.

Robert. Aged nine.

After Dad threw us about the last time, Mam finally left him. Well, she went to the social. Didn't want to go to the police. Then she went back to him. They love each other, so he says, so she says. It's a vicious circle. He came back and I watched as he hit her again.

Me mam and me are sitting at the social worker's desk in a cubicle, two grey chairs we sit in, on one side of the desk, and we wait for a social worker with ginger hair and a big body who has been to the house a lot of times. At the house she asked how come I need cushions to sit up and me mam said I fell down the stairs. Me mam lied to the social worker then so today I'm a bit confused as to why she's telling the truth.

Me mam wants rid of me.

The social worker is friendly when she sits down and me mam is on me left, the social worker is across the table. Between me and me mam and the social worker there are files and big stacks of paper. I can't really see over them. Me mam is crying and between sobs she is pleading with the social worker, telling her to write in the file, to take notes and put it on record that she's telling the truth.

Me mam is saying a lot of things I've never heard her say before:

'He beats us, all the time now, every time he comes home. The bastard, just last night, flung Robert down the stairs. I know, I know, I've been telling you everything is okay at home, but my boy, my little boy; his dad did this to him, his dad. You have to help us. I've tried to protect him, but I can't. Robert, he stares into space nowadays, blank, like there's nothing going on in his head. Kills me, it does. Please, I am begging you, please, please. My husband did this to him, you have to protect Robert. I can't do it no more. Please, you have to protect him . . .'

Husband? But you're not married, Mam, that's what you told me, that's why we can't leave, 'cos you ain't a married mum and I am a bastard, and no one will want us. Is the truth that you got married to him and you don't want to tell me, and 'cos you are married, you don't want me no more?

I look at my feet and start kicking the desk in front of me, the metal thuds and me mam doesn't turn round, or stop speaking about how me dad did this. She doesn't draw breath. It's like now it's out there and she's telling the social worker, she can't stop. On and on she goes as I kick the table louder and louder. The social worker's eyes flit from me mam to me, as if that will stop me kicking or me mam talking. On this movement of the social worker's eyes, me mam puts a hand gently on my knee, pushes firm, but not hard. This is her way of telling me to stop, to sit still, to be quiet, while she goes on and on about what a shit me dad is for doing these things. Me mam also wants money, 'cos me dad spent it all on drink and she's got none. That's another reason the social worker needs to look after me and take me away.

Finally the social worker stops taking notes, shakes her hand with the pen in 'cos she's been writing so fast, and suggests me mam goes to the police. We laugh, both me and me mam together. Me mam doesn't answer, so I pipe up:

'Me mam's tried that, didn't work. Me dad's brother's a policeman at the local station and he doesn't believe us 'cos me dad is so clever and even though he gets drunk all the time, when other people are there he's a happy drunk. When it's just me and me mam and him, he isn't so happy and he kicks us and hits.'

The social worker looks a bit sad, but she isn't sure how to help us. There's no space in foster children's homes for now, so Robert, that's me, would need to go to a residential children's home. She thinks there's a space at a children's home that I've been to before, when me mam was in hospital – Chesterfields. Maybe they would take me for a little bit.

Me mam is speaking in a small voice now and is ever so grateful. It can be just until she gets sorted somewhere else. And she says that anything is good and that it doesn't matter where, 'cos the main thing is getting me away from him. That for too long I've been a floppy baby as a result of his violence, and she's worried he's gonna kill me. So if Social Services can give her a break and protect me, then that would be very good.

Why just me? Why not you, too, Mam? He'll kill you, too, Mam.

The social worker says she'll do all she can, but she asks us again about reporting him to the police. Mam has this bit rehearsed, I heard her this morning in front of the mirror.

'I am considering reporting him to the police,' me mam says, 'but I want to think over it some more.'

I know she's lying as her hands are pushed tightly together to stop them shaking. I know she's doubly lying 'cos really she is scared what my policeman uncle will tell me dad, and what me dad would do if he found out is not worth thinking about.

But once she has said it, the social worker seems to believe her. I know and me mam knows she'll never risk going against me dad to the police 'cos, even though he beats her and me black and blue, afterwards he always tells her that this time is the last time, that he's going to work and change and she believes him. Even when he runs out, for days sometimes, when he comes home, she opens the door and welcomes him in, 'cos he's got her believing he's changed, got her thinking she's the piece of shit and worth nothing that he tells her she is. She knows no one else will have her 'cos she's an unmarried tart. Time and again he says it. And if you hear a thing often enough you believe it; if you beat a thing often enough you make it so scared you own it.

Me mam believes me dad. I heard him last night, sitting on the floor next to her, stroking the head he'd just used as a punch bag, saying sweet nothings about him being sorry. Sitting here in the social worker's office, I remember something else he said. I remember he told her that they might just work better as a couple, if, just for a little while, she got rid of me. I feel my eyes go wide. He was slow in his speaking, was careful to tell her she needed to make the decision, that he wouldn't force her to do anything, but if she loved him, as he loved her, then she would do the right thing and give them a chance.

He loves you so much he beats you.

So whatever she tells the social worker, I know and she knows that she won't go to the police. Instead, from here, she'll go back to him. He's waiting in the pub. They will kiss and laugh and have a night of fun, until she says something he doesn't like, until he does it again. I look at my shoes, knowing his control over her – whatever she's saying right now to the social worker, it was his idea.

He don't want me. She don't want me. I don't want me to be hit no more. This way, we all get what we want for a bit. Please, please say yes.

Debbie. Aged ten.

Keep away, keep away.

My hands are over my head. She's raining blows down on to me. Crouched in the corner of the living room, she's towering over me. Every whack stings. The furry front of the slipper caresses my face as her hand passes across, no comfort after the long scratch mark of a kitten heel on my cheek.

Blood, she's drawn blood.

I spin out for a moment, the shock of the multiple wounds being inflicted. I rearrange my fingers to protect my face better.

Crap, lumps already forming.

I push myself back, further into the corner. My stocking-soled feet provide little traction; my hands little protection against her barrage. I am beyond speaking or asking what I've done, or asking her why.

Please, please, stop. I'll be good, I promise, Mum. Mummy. Please stop. Tell me what I've done.

She stands back and leaves the room as suddenly as she rushed at me. I've no idea how long she's done this for, but as I move my hand from my head, it's sticky. Blood covers my fingers. I pat my head again to check the damage, pull my hair gently to separate it from the blood. A clump of hair comes away in my hand. Tears well but don't release. I start to shake.

Is it over?

She comes back in, still looking like the devil has over-taken her, accusing me of being a liar. There is a key in the door.

Oh no, what if it's the babysitter?

A man appears. A man who has a key to this house, but my mum and the lodger, who was the babysitter, have until now managed to keep many secrets from him.

He stands in the frame of the living room door, the front door must still be open as the evening light that shines through it is bathing his face. From my viewpoint in the corner this makes him look like he's in a painting. He moves towards me, out of the light, looking at my mum. He says, 'What have you done to her?'

Mum spits a response, 'Nothing she didn't deserve; nothing she didn't expect. Nothing, really.'

He takes a step towards me; the colour drains from his face as he does so.

'But look at her. How . . .? What . . .? I don't understand. Come on, Debbie, can you stand?'

Another step towards me and my mother puts up her defensive wall and steps in between us. Vicious, all-power-ful home rule.

'Don't you dare. She's fine. It wasn't hard. Leave her alone. Don't you touch her.'

My mum's boyfriend stops in his tracks, doesn't look at me but stares at Mum for a long time, straight in the eye. Finally he says, 'Look at what you've done to her. I am going to call an ambulance to help her. You will let them in. After that, I can't be with you. Debbie, I'll check on you now and again, but I am sorry, I can't stay.'

He turns to leave. From my corner I hear him closing the front door, the light from the hall disappearing as he does so.

Mum's boyfriend reported her, not only to the police but to the social as well. When they came, she turned on the tears. Said it was a one off, that she wasn't coping, she needed a break. Social workers got us a temporary placement so she could get herself together. And then they say we will try again.

Abby. Aged thirteen.

I lie in bed. My brother Lee is on my mind. I met a kid from his school who was wondering why Lee hadn't been there.

Why wasn't he at school? What's happened? What's Mum done to him? I should tell Dad, but he believes her, not us.

'Abby! Get up, Abby. You'll be late for school.'

I can hear my dad shouting from downstairs, but I'm not going to school, 'cos it's shit and no one likes me there.

'Abby. Now, Abby.'

My bedroom door opens. I pull the covers over my head. Dad grabs the corner and with an expert swoop pulls the covers off me and onto the floor, covering the mess of clothes I left there the night before. I lie on my bed, no longer quite as warm, curled in the foetal position, wishing he would piss off and leave me alone. I turn towards the wall, trying to pretend that not having my duvet doesn't matter.

I don't want to go to school.

Dad turns and pulls the curtains open. I open one eye; it's a grey old day, as Granddad used to say. Dad is standing holding both curtains open, arms outstretched at ten to two, hands above his head, staring out the window, motionless.

Oh, Dad, sorry to give you a hard time. I can't help it; I just want to be me.

His hands lower, he turns and starts to pick up my dirty clothes from the floor.

'I don't know, love. Ever since your Granddad died and Lee went back to your mum's, you've become a nightmare. You settled down when you first came here, but, you know, I just couldn't cope with you both. And it's better for Lee to be near his mum and his school.

You're wrong! You don't know what she's like with him, with us kids.

'You used to be such a nice girl, staying in, watching telly, writing your stories, playing with your Sindy dolls and looking after the rabbit. I don't know what to do with you, really. I don't know – skipping school and so on. Since you became a teenager, I dunno, you've been a nightmare. School's important; it's how you get on in life. You must want better things for yourself than this? I want better for you.'

I growl, 'Stop picking up my stuff, Dad, it's embarrassing.'

'I don't know, Abby. Who else picks these things up and looks after you? Look, a damp towel from yesterday on the floor, you planning on using this today? If you hang it up it gives us all an easier life. I don't know, I really don't, you are out of control, and I don't know what to do. I just want the best for you, so help me out here, eh? Breakfast in five minutes, or you will be late. I've got you some Frosties, as you like those. Tell you what, I can get off work a bit early today, and you and I can spend some time together after school. I'll take you swimming and then we can have fish and chips after. How does that sound? Yes, that's a good plan. I'll pick you up after school at the gate.'

I hate my school. Hate it.

I'm waiting outside the school gates like Dad asked me to. I haven't been to school, though. Today I spent my pocket money on a new look – nose ring, getting my head shaved, black eyeliner, a Union Jack T-shirt, Dr Marten boots. And I blew the rest of my money on a bomber jacket. I already have drainpipe jeans, which I picked up off the floor. I've been saving up for this new look for ages, telling myself this is the day I become who I want to be, and fuck the lot of you.

I'll wait at school to get a lift home, but am I going swimming? Am I fuck.

Dad doesn't recognise me when he arrives. I watch him, laughing, before shouting, 'Dad, over here.' And waving.

His face drops and, for a second, I feel disappointed in myself.

Oh, Daddy.

But the moment is gone.

Hard, girl, be hard. That's who you are now.

'Abby! What have you done?'

'It's my new look, Dad. What do you think? Like it?'

I dance and spin around in front of him in my Dr Marten boots, my head is a bit cold 'cos I've no hair to bounce around in, but it feels good.

'Your hair, your hair, what have you done to your hair?

What have you done? You won't get a decent education or a job looking like that. You're a clever girl, why are you throwing it all away, Abby?'

Dad slumps down on the front of the car. He's looking at me in disbelief. I charge over, my face right up close to his face.

'Well, it's the new me, Dad. This is how I want to live my life. My life! Not yours, not school's, not anyone else's. Mine! Mine!'

He stands up, towers over me. He's angry.

'Who cut your hair? Who did this to you? Your beautiful long hair?'

Oh no, Dad, you are so disappointed. I'm sorry to hurt you, Dad, but I just want to be me. You can understand that, can't you, Dad? Dad?

A small voice comes from me now. 'The hairdresser on the high street.'

'Right, come on.'

Dad marches into the hairdresser, with me very close behind him. I expect him to shout at someone, but he calmly asks to see the manager.

He is firm, clear, decisive, obviously angry but not rude.

As we wait for the manager to come out of his office, my dad refuses to look at me or speak to me, not that I try and speak to him.

The manger comes, stands behind the desk for what seems like protection. My dad stands, shakes his hand and asks, 'Why did you do this to her?'

'What, Sir?'

'Shave her hair off?'

'We are a hairdresser's, Sir; it's what she asked and paid for. We're here to cut hair and that's what we do. In this case, cut and shave.'

'But she's thirteen years old.'

'Yes, Sir, and a very determined young lady. I think this look suits her.'

That angers my dad. His voice is slow and steady in that non-shout way but you know he's seriously angry. I now know where the expression 'through gritted teeth' comes from. This is a new side of my dad, not shouting, just calmly stating his case. He's angry on my behalf.

Oh, I like this, he cares, he cares.

The manager doesn't help things, though. 'We did the piercing as well. Nice job they did, too. These need to be looked after, to avoid infection. You can't take them out for two weeks, and make sure they're kept clean with Dettol or another antiseptic.'

My dad almost loses it, but grabs onto his own fist instead.

He's setting me an example, a good one. Go, Dad, you tell them!

He controls his voice.

'What? You are irresponsible. She's thirteen.'

The manger gets a bit haughty now, 'Well, Sir, with all due respect we *are* a hairdresser and a beauty salon that does piercing. It's not unusual in London for people your daughter's age, even younger, to have piercings, and not just in their nose and ears. Belly buttons are getting fashionable now.' He backtracks. 'Not that I want to give your daughter any ideas, oh no. But, really, what can I do? We're a business, a service providing hairdressing, or in this case cutting and shaving, and piercing. We provided a service which she asked for and paid for. Presumably with pocket money that *you* gave her. It's not my fault, or concern, that you don't like what we did. We can't give a refund, as we provided a service. If she comes in again and asks for the same, we would do it again. I'm sorry, Sir, but you are disturbing my other customers and now I need to ask you to leave. Besides, if you can keep control of your daughter, it will grow back.'

Dad turns to me, 'You are banned from coming in here again.' He turns back to the hairdresser, 'Maybe you are right; you are a business, you do provide a service, but it's irresponsible and you are not a responsible business. Come on, Abby. Home.'

But I thought we were going swimming and having fish and chips.

The hairdresser who cut off my long locks opens the door for us. The manager is chatty as we leave.

'This is the eighties, love, it's all about the money. Thatcher is a babe, a star of mine. Responsibility, pppfff, responsibility doesn't come into it.'

As the door closes, we hear laughter in the salon behind us. I'm divided, I love my dad for setting boundaries, for caring enough to fight, but now he's given up. He's been humiliated. I don't understand.

In the car, I ask.

'Dad?'

'What?'

'Why didn't you ask more questions? Why did you let him beat you?'

'Oh, Abby, you've a lot to learn. Don't you know there's more than one way to skin a cat?'

'What?'

'Well, I work at the council, right?'

'Right.'

'So I know that each and every hairdresser who offers piercings will soon need a licence to operate. It's a new act of Parliament that's just about to come in. Thatcher's Britain loves money making but they also love a regulation and a licence to operate, which you have to pay for. Sure, the government wants people to make more money, but they also want a slice of it, too. In that little fucker's case, he's gonna have to get a licence to make money. Only that little cat, he might just find he doesn't get a licence and can't operate one side of his money-making shithole of a business. Hit 'em where it hurts and, in his case, in the pocket. It's who you know, Abby, who you know.'

I feel like a little girl being protected and am slightly scared at the speed at which my dad has picked up on this plan, this revenge.

'Can we go swimming, have fish and chips? Dad?'

He doesn't answer, just drives home with a dark cloud hanging over his head. He sends me to my room. I put on Bob Marley. Despite my new skinhead look, he's my secret pleasure. But today Bob doesn't calm me, so I change it to Skrewdriver, All Skrewed Up, a seventies band one of my skinhead friends told me about. With this music, I dance around my room. I become all grown up and angry again, twisting what Dad did from kindness into embarrassment and misguided feelings.

He was not protecting me, he was sooo embarrassing. He doesn't care, didn't talk to me when we were in the car. Didn't try and understand me. No one understands me. I hate him. I hate him. That's it,

I'm gonna do my own thing, run away. I'm not going back to school, whatever he says. It's my life. I'm not staying in now neither. It's not late, I'm going out. The guys are down the park. I'll go and show them the new me. They understand; they know what it's like.

Slowly, slowly, I prise open my window, move the needle on the record player back to the beginning to give me a bit more time before Dad notices I'm gone.

I look out the window.

Yup, I can get down onto the garage roof below my window and then shimmy down the drainpipe to the ground. Easy.

With one leg out the window and the other still in my bedroom, I look back at the room of my childhood, with its white walls, fairytale lampshade and posters of punk bands, and a slight sadness over this clash of understanding takes me for a moment.

Dad just wants me to be a little girl for ever. But I'm grown up now; I'm a teenager.

I turn and look out towards the street where dusk is touching the night and the streetlights have just come on. I look back to my warm home. The pull of adventure is stronger and I jump onto the garage roof.

In a moment I'm off into the night to find my new friends, the skinheads who are part of a bigger gang, which they call the National Front.

Lee. Aged eleven.

Today, a miracle: the social worker comes and she has got past the front door. She even goes upstairs to the toilet. I can tell Mum isn't happy 'cos the social worker is getting her way, not Mum's way. The social worker is being firm but polite.

'I insist on speaking with Lee on his own, please.'

Don't make Mum unhappy; please don't make her mad.

'He fell down the stairs, I told you. Little boys do that. They fall, tumble. Y'know how it is.'

'Yes, I understand. Did you hear him fall down the stairs?'

'No.'

'Lee, come here, please.'

I don't move until Mum tells me to 'Shift'. She jabs her head towards the social worker. I move, double quick, and stand in front of the social worker, tall like the little soldier I am.

'He's a very large bump on his forehead. It's quite dark. Full of fluid. You are quite pale, Lee, are you feeling okay?' I don't move. The social worker carries on, her voice light. 'We need to take him to hospital, just to check that bump.'

My mum purses her lips and replies, 'If we must.'

'Right, that's settled, then. We shall take my car, shall we?'

Mum and the social worker are in the front of the car, I'm in the back and no one is speaking, but that's okay 'cos the radio is on and I like music. I am not sure what's wrong with Mum but she doesn't seem to like this social worker. I like her 'cos she's a nice face and looks at me, not just at my mum. This social worker has made Mum take me to the hospital. I hope they look at my back as well as my head. I think my back will have a big bump on it, too, 'cos it's a bit sore. The air in the car feels like it did in the house before Dad left Mum. Really heavy.

*   *   *

I'm on a hospital bed. It's nicer than my bed at home, it smells like fresh leaves fallen from a tree. I am a bit bored as they've pulled a big green curtain, like a tent, around me and there are lots of adults who chat on the other side of the curtain before coming in to see me in my green tent. They all look serious and have little frowns on their heads when they come in. Then they examine me and the frowns get bigger. I tell them I don't want to be any bother, as I heard someone say they were bothered about me.

I've been here a very long time now. I don't know where Mum is, but lots of adults have come and gone. They've given me some juice and a biscuit for being so good. They keep asking me when I had my last hot meal. I don't remember so I feel a little stupid.

The social worker is back, she's outside my green tent. She's speaking to someone. I've almost finished my hot lunch of mince and watery potatoes. I manage to use the spoon, but I couldn't get the last bits off, so I lick the plate. I'm bored now, so I try and listen really hard as I think they're talking about me and my mum.

'The family room is perfect, and so clean. But when I went to the loo, I checked the rooms upstairs, and found what I guess to be Lee's room. There's just a mattress and a wardrobe. The wallpaper is torn off, there's no other furniture, there isn't even a carpet. I know I am only recently qualified, but I didn't expect to see things like this. That's why I called you. His room is much colder than the rest of the house. I think the radiator must be broken. Oh, there was a stereo in the wardrobe, with a sheet, which I can only guess is his bedding. Poor little boy, he looks so vacant, like there's nothing there behind his eyes; so pale, resigned to his fate. So thin, too.'

A male voice asks her, 'What should we do?'

'Help him. But let's see what the paediatrician says. They've been doing all sorts of tests.'

I keep making big sighs and am tapping my fingers and toes. The nurse has brought me her personal stereo, but her music taste isn't that good. I don't want to draw, 'cos I don't know how. I don't want to read, 'cos I can't read very well. They'll think I'm thick. Music is okay, even though it's not my choice of music and the nurse seems to like me. Though the last time she went out she didn't shut the curtain properly and so I see her put a happy face on just before she opens the curtain to come in.

Why is she sad?

My mum isn't allowed to come and see me. The nice social worker keeps popping in and asking me things. There have been lots of doctors coming in and out. A doctor with a special name beginning with 'p' asks me what the marks on my leg are. I tell them my mum's cigarettes did that. The doctor takes a little step back, then asks me about the bruises on my back. I tell them my mum's belt did that and my back hurts all the time. Now I am on my way to have an X-ray of my whole body.

Another lady is here to speak to me now. She's asking me what I think of my mum. I say that she's my mum and shrug my shoulders. She asks me how long my mum has treated me like this. I shrug my shoulders. She asks me if there was ever a time when things at home were better. I shrug my shoulders. And then I remember.

'When my dad lived at home. Then it was better. But he left, and me and Abby got shouted at a lot. When Dad took Abby to live with him but not me, Mum got more upset more often and she says all the time now that Dad doesn't want either of us. I think it's my fault he left us and took Abby.'

'Why do you think that, Lee.'

''Cos of Mum. She says that it's my fault he left, she says that all the time.'

After a few phone calls and an even longer time, my dad arrives. He's looking worried. He says he's sorry and that I can come and live with him and Abby for a bit.

He hugs me.

I never want to let go.

Debbie. Aged ten.

I'm sitting on the bench outside in the garden of my foster parents' home. My sister and I are in foster care for a few weeks. According to Social Services, my mum is sorting the house out, trying to get a job. The truth is, she's gone to a beach with the babysitter.

My eyes are shut as I am imagining myself elsewhere, on another bench somewhere, enjoying the sun, far from here and far, far away from my mum.

I smile when I think about the girls at school and the laugh we had today about something I can't remember but it was hilarious at the time. A shadow crosses my face and stays there. Thinking the sun has gone behind a cloud, I open one eye to find myself staring at my foster mother.

She doesn't even say hello, instead, 'Look at me and take that dirty look off your face.'

I open both eyes like she asks me but she doesn't like that either. I don't know what she means by a 'dirty look' so I don't change my expression and I keep my smile, even though my insides have sunk from high up into my boots. I tell her that my chores are done, so I don't know what she's complaining about.

In a flash, her hand is up and down. She catches the back of my head, hard. The contact point stings as I tumble forwards, on to the concrete slab that supports the seat.

My hair is being pulled up, my legs follow, raising me into a half stance. We half run, half stumble through into the house and up the corridor, where my sister is standing in the doorway. We lock eyes, and mine plead with her.

Don't come out, don't get involved.

My sister steps back into the living room and closes the door, leaving my foster mother to drag me by the hair up to my room.

As she locks it, she screams, 'You can stay here until tomorrow. No food for you today.'

Throwing myself on to my bed, I bury my head in the pillow. I feel betrayed, hurt, ashamed.

Why did they move us from Mum if this place is just the same? Chores here, chores there. Hitting, standing, waiting for punishment. All adults are the same. Foster parents, they don't know nothing. Alone. Alone. I feel so alone.

The thoughts stream round in my head. Thoughts of running away. But if I did that then my sister would be left to face this place on her own. Even though my sister is older, she isn't able to cope on her own very well. She likes to be told what to do. She'll do anything that anyone says. She doesn't know how to think, especially when my mum and the babysitter are around.

Thinking about how the foster mother hit me, grabbed my hair, dragged me, I decide to take control.

She doesn't treat her natural kids like that. Why me? Why me? I'll tell my social worker. I'll tell her and she will take me away to somewhere better than this.

It's dark before I eventually drift into a fitful sleep, thankful that the sheets are clean and warm, and that at least here I can sleep knowing there isn't anyone coming into my room in the middle of the night to touch me.

The next morning I'm on my back, looking up, staring at the ceiling. I like to wake up early and not move from this spot for a while. My covers are holding warmth and for the first time in a long time, I feel secure in my own bed, if not in the rest of the house. It's a good feeling that I like to hold on to before I have to go down to do my morning chores. I am one person in this house – a quiet, obedient, sullen type – and at school I become the person I really want to be – a bubbly, funny, popular girl. I am me at school, until I head home again. Well, it's not really home, just a place we've been put 'cos my mum doesn't want us. She can't cope. She needs a rest.

They put us in here so Mum can go on holiday, more like. She says she's exhausted, needs support, to take the focus away from what's really happening. It will all start again the minute we go home.

If only the social workers knew that it wasn't just once, about what really goes on at home. If only they knew, then this wouldn't be temporary. But I can't tell them because Mum and the babysitter would kill me. They threaten to kill us if we utter a word. Me and my sister are not liars but we're very good at keeping secrets. Family secrets. Babysitter secrets. I lie in bed and think that there's no one I trust enough to tell what really goes on at home.

But today I remember it's the first proper day of the school holidays, so we won't be going in. I need to be the quiet person all day and do my chores. I lift the covers, colder air from the room sneaks in to push me out of bed. I get dressed and move towards the door. I try the handle, willing it to have been unlocked already. It has.

Of course it's open, otherwise how would I be able to get the breakfast ready for everyone or feed the animals?

Breakfast done, and after my sister and I have washed up the dishes for three foster kids, two natural kids and one foster mother, I can hear my foster mother on the phone. It's only a few minutes after nine.

Who is she talking to?

The phone is in the living room and there are wooden sliding doors between the living room and the dining room. I make my way, very carefully so as not to make a noise, along the wall of the kitchen, into the dining room and to the gap between the two sliding doors. Me and my sister, when cleaning the house, always make sure we don't shut them properly, that way we can stand on this special spot and find out what's being said about us in the living room.

I can hear my foster mother. She's talking about me.

'. . . Before she tells you, I thought I'd best let you know that Debbie lied to me last night. She's such a fibber that one. She's probably going to tell you I hit her . . . Yes, it's just not true. I've never, never come across such a liar as that one . . . Yes, I knew you would understand. Yes, no there's no need for a visit. All's fine. I just wanted to let you know before Debbie says anything . . . Yes, you know how these kids are, the damaged ones particularly . . . Yes, they all lie.'

I can't hear the other person but I know it's the social worker. I am so angry I can't speak. I'm frozen to the spot, looking through the gap in the door at the smug face of my foster mother having a conversation, then at her even smugger face as she replaces the phone back in its cradle.

The social worker won't take her word, she won't. She won't.

I run back to my room, fling myself on to my bed, my pillow being washed with tears. Sobbing.

How can I escape this? I am told I am a liar, but I am not. It's not true.

Some weeks later, I sit in my best clothes, new clothes, bought for this visit and wait. This morning the social worker is due to come for her scheduled check-up. As I wait, the courage to tell her about my foster mother seeps away into the sofa.

The social worker believes my foster mother instead of me. She didn't ever check my side of the story. She didn't ever ask me what happened. She didn't ever wonder why my foster mother was so keen to call and tell her I am the liar. She didn't ever check.

The social worker arrives on time and we three, me, my foster mother and the social worker, have a cup of tea, in the best china, with cake. The social worker speaks first and then I reply, knowing that if I say anything out of turn my foster mother will hit me before the social worker has even left our driveway.

'So, Debbie, how are you?'

'Fine.'

It's crap here, she hits us, has a separate fridge for the real family, makes us do chores.

'Tell me, have you had a nice summer?'

'Yes.'

'What have you done?'

'Played a bit, learnt to bake; that's my cake you ain't eating.'

Have learnt to be respectful at the end of a horse whip, have learnt how to keep a house nice and cook and clean.

'Very nice, I shall have a piece in a moment just because you baked it. Everything's fine, then?'

She cocks her head slightly to the side in the way concerned adults do, as if that will make me more comfortable. My foster mother just stares straight ahead and, sitting straight-backed at me, her eyes narrow at the end of each sentence spoken by the social worker. I know I have to say the right thing. My foster mother is the person who will decide if I do.

'Yes, it's all fine.'

No! No! No! Can't you see? Are you blind? It's a horrid house. She isn't a good foster mother. I hate it. I hate it. Can't you see how I hate her?

'How's school?'

'I like school.'

That's true.

'That's good. So, everything is fine, then?'

'Yes, it's all fine.'

I look at my shoes and there's a short silence while the social worker writes something down.

She's just going through her checklist. Stop ticking and writing. Can't you see me crying out to you? Can't you see me?

My foster mother breaks the silence by asking the social worker in her best posh voice if the social worker would like some more tea. The social worker nods and I automatically move to pour from the flowery teapot with a knitted teapot warmer.

Just tell her you want to leave. Blurt it out. Tell her. No, I can't. My sister prefers this to home. This is better than home. But this is rubbish. Can't you see?

I am so upset at not being able to tell the truth, at being branded a liar, that I am shaking. As I pour the tea, my hand, as much as I try to keep it still, moves and I spill a little on the table.

Oh, no! I'm for it now. The social worker will see how crap I am at pouring tea and blame me for everything. She'll see that I'm not worth it. She'll believe my foster mother.

The social worker says it's okay, puts her hand out to steady mine and asks my foster mother for a cloth. Then an interesting thing happens; when my foster mother says that I can get it, the social worker just smiles and replies that it would be nice if she, my foster mother, got the cloth as I was pouring the tea and the social worker would like me to cut a piece of the cake I made for her. I can't do everything at once.

As soon as my foster mother grumphs her way out of the living room, my social worker uncovers the note she wrote earlier. It says:

'Is everything okay? I know you might not be able to speak. Nod or shake your head. If not okay I'll be back soon.'

I stare at the note.

She knows. She knows. Don't cry. Don't cry. She saw.

I place the teapot down and press my thumbnail into my middle finger to stop me crying.

The social worker is carrying on a normal conversation about how easy it is for her to get here, while tapping the end of the pen on her note. Waiting for an answer. I stare at her, tears are in my eyes, my thumbnail is pressed into my finger. I shake my head. She writes. 'I thought so. Don't worry. I'll make a plan.'

She reaches out and squeezes my hand. The door opens, her hand is on the cake, accepting it, admiring it, and the social worker is saying how hard I must've worked to learn how to bake so well, so quickly.

As she leaves, the social worker invites me to lunch later on in the week. She says it's to mark the end of the school holidays. She is very light-hearted about it and tells my foster mother she must need a break, too. She puts it in such a way that there's no way the foster mother can say no. As the social worker gets into her car, my foster mother comments at how stupid she is, how she can't see anything in front of her face and it's a good thing, too, from my foster mother's point of view, 'cos she needs the money.

I don't change my expression but inside I am smiling. My foster mother is wrong, so wrong. This social worker is beautiful to me. Even better, in two sleeps' time, my foster mother will learn just how clever the social worker is, too.

*   *   *

A few weeks later, we're in the social worker's car heading back home. My sister is in a horrible mood. Mum, tanned and back from her holiday in Spain, heard how we were being treated at the foster carer's, because the social worker told her that she believed me.

As we haven't told anyone what's going on at home, and as everyone in Social Services just thinks Mum can't cope and needs a rest every now and then, and as Mum has just had a holiday and has the babysitter to help with the rent and around the house, and as Mum says she can cope now, the social worker doesn't know any different, so she believes her and agrees to send us home.

No one asked us. Just assumed.

As my sister and I walk up the path to the house, we see my mum at the door with the babysitter, the lodger, standing behind her. My sister hisses at me, 'You should've kept your trap shut. I hate you. The foster home was shit, but it's better than walkin' into this.'

I look back at the social worker, my shoulders are bent. My face is sad. I half raise a hand to wave cheerio. Standing by her car, she copies my half wave.

If only she knew. If only we could tell her.

I turn, sigh, and walk up the path, through the front door, into the living hell that is called home.

Robert. Aged nine.

'Robert, I know your mam's coming to visit today, but it's only 7.30 a.m. Come and have some breakfast first; she won't be here for a bit.'

I'm standing by the window, looking out. On hearing the housekeeper's voice, I turn to the door of the living room in the kids' home and grin from ear to ear. The housekeeper moves towards me, ruffles my hair.

'Come on, you. How long have you been standing there staring out, then?' I don't answer. She replies for me: 'Since silly o'clock, I bet. Come on, you can help me set the breakfast out. Give you something to do, rather than staring out at nothing happening.'

Throughout breakfast I get told I've ants in my pants and that I need to sit still, eat nicely. I try not to drop any food down my front, otherwise I'll have to go and change my T-shirt, which I chose from the clothes box and, as I don't want to be away from the window for longer than I have to be, I eat nicely but still a bit faster than I am meant to.

As the other kids come into breakfast, instead of saying good morning to everyone, I tell them me mam is coming to take me out today. This gets me into trouble for being insensitive to other kids' needs and situations; but I don't really mind, and I don't go hide under the bed like I normally do when I am in trouble. I am too excited about me mam coming to think about things like that, or to go hide.

I wonder what dress she'll wear and if she will be wearing too much make-up to try and hide that she's been hit by me dad again.

Maybe he won't have hit her; maybe she's left him. Maybe she's coming to tell me she'll take me home now 'cos he's finally left her for that floozy. I don't like it when me mam comes and then she's to leave at the end of the day. It all feels a bit strange. It hurts. But I want to see her so bad it hurts more than the pain that comes after she goes away again.

The best bit is seeing her coming up the drive. I imagine it as I sit by the window waiting. There's a clock in the living room. Tick tock goes the clock. I can read the time and when she isn't here at 10 or 11 o'clock, I ignore it and stare out the window.

The bus is late. The traffic is bad.

Lunchtime comes and I refuse to go in to eat. Still me mam makes me wait. My breath makes steam on the windows and with my finger I draw what I think she'll be wearing today when she comes. In my head I match the colours, blue and greens, soft material floating along with her, and faded jeans, flares, with platform shoes that are the same colour as her blouse and a hat to protect her from the sun. She looks like she could be a pop star.

She'll be here soon. Will just have missed the bus.

After lunch, the other kids from the children's home who are not expecting anyone to visit, go out and play in the sun. One of the smaller boys takes advantage of my sitting at the window and takes out the blue-framed bike, my bike, the one with a box on the back and a tin lid. I spend all day on that bike and the other kids put things in the box so I can set up a swap shop later on like that programme on the telly.

More of my breath goes on to the window – a new palette to draw dreams. I guide my thick thumb across and down, shaping both the trees next to the bus stop that she'll get off at and the bus she's on. Then I turn my hand, to connect a longer fingernail to the window and draw thin lines of the branches and leaves that will shade her from the sun when she gets here.

I should really clean me fingernails; she won't be happy when she comes and sees I haven't cleaned them. In a minute, though. I don't want to miss her coming. She'll be here in a minute.

It's afternoon snack time, the clock confirms it – 3 o'clock. Rather than calling me to join the others, the housekeeper brings me my snack and ruffles my hair again. On the plate is a sandwich, as I skipped lunch, as well as my snack and some milk. I like milk.

She doesn't say anything, just looks down the drive, a bit sad like. So I reassure her.

'The train's late. I'm sure she said today she would take the train. Maybe she's stuck on the train because a signal broke, or something like that. She'll be here; she said she'd bring me a rocket and some new marbles.'

She responds with a pat on my head and an, 'I hope so, poppet. I hope so.'

Why isn't Mam here? What's happened to her? Why doesn't she want to see me? She's late, she's just late. The train, the bus, they must've broken down. She wouldn't forget. I want her here. Why doesn't she come? Mam, I love you. Don't you love me? Have you forgotten me? Mam, are you coming? Mam, why aren't you here? Mam, you ain't coming. Mam, I hate you.

As quickly as these thoughts run through my head, the feelings and emotions follow round my body, ending up as a big brick in my stomach. I wipe the window clean of my art and run, slam the door back with all the force of a nine year old, but it's restricted in its movement by a spring so, as I run up the stairs trying to hold back the tears, the door gently moves back to fit snugly into the door frame, where it belongs.

Under my bed feels safer, more secure, than looking out the front window at a dream that will never come.

Hope. 1984.

Even though me and my brothers have been at Chesterfields a few months and there are lots of kids, I am not used to how quiet it is at night.

It's a very different night from our last night at home, when the people attacked our house. The quiet is filled with their abuse which swims around my head.

'Get them.' 'Get out.' 'Good throw.'

I wonder where Dad is. I hope he's okay. Mum's in prison and he is never too good when she's not at home.

It's so nice here. It's warm, it's cosy. I fall asleep. Warm. Safe. Sometimes in the middle of the night I sit bolt upright in bed and look around me.

What? Where am I? Mum? Dad?

I look around and there's another bed in the room, but it's not my mum and dad's bed, it's my room-mate, sleeping soundly.

We're at Chesterfields, remember. They took us in. We had warm toast and baked beans. A bath! They let me share a room on the first night with my brothers. Feels like yesterday.

I fall back into bed. My head hits the pillow. The softness, the warmth of the covers and the feeling of being safe enveloping me. Even though we've been here for months, I still love this warmth. Then I feel a little odd, it's like a rush of stuff is being swept off my shoulders. I no longer need to worry about how me and my brothers will eat, when we will eat, how to stay warm. Here is our new home and, as I think things over in the warmth of my bed, I am sure, I am sure this will be a place of happy days for me and my brothers, like hundreds of kids before us.

We shall live here forever, won't we? They can't send us home, can they? Mum will be so mad I did this. Oh, Dad, I'm sorry, Dad. I just couldn't take it no more. They will let us stay here, forever, won't they? Are Mum and Dad allowed to visit? I need to ask about that, but there's no way I am getting out of this bed until I have to.

I smile and put my head under the covers.

Love it here.

I met with my social worker yesterday, asked her about fostering. I like her but she just said 'We shall see' in a voice that means I know we won't. She also wants me to see Mum and Dad this weekend. I want to be fostered, to have my very own family, mine, just mine, all mine, and I don't want to see Mum. But it's all arranged.

Who asked me?

Craig and I are turning into our street, Hamilton Road in Hackney. My old school is there at the end of the road and my heart does a little leap. I don't like my new school, they are horrid to me 'cos I'm in care. I'm not allowed to go to my old school any more. I think it's my mum's fault, as she kept turning up at the gate a bit drunk. My tummy isn't so happy at seeing my mum, or my house, and is doing somersaults that make me feel sick.

We park the minibus outside the house. Everyone can see the sign 'Chesterfields Children's Home'. The neighbours will know we're in care.

Mum won't like that we brought the minibus with the sign on it.

I look up; Mum is at the bedroom window looking down on us. She disappears from the window.

This ain't gonna be pretty.

Craig and I walk up the steps to the house. The windows are still broken and boarded up following the vigilante attack on our house, on us. The night that pushed me into making the decision to ask to go into care. The word SLAG, in part painted over, is still just visible.

Mum opens the door, leans against the frame, her stance far from welcoming. Dressed in her trademark leather skirt and red blouse, one of two blouses she owns, she positions herself across the doorway, blocking our way. Her arm is high above her head, her hand supporting the open door. Her long blonde hair is framing her body, which seems to be positioned diagonally across the entrance, and ends in red stiletto shoes. She tells us to 'Fuck Off' before we're even at the top of the stairs. I take a step back. Craig opens his hands in a gesture of reconciliation and steps forwards.

Mistake.

'Get the fuck off my property. Who the fuck do you think you are, coming 'ere without an invite?'

'But, Mrs Daniels, this is an arranged meeting; the social worker should've sent you a letter.'

'I didn't get no letter. You have no right comin' 'ere. Didn't you get my letter, you nonce? You fiddlin' round with the girls in your care? I've written, I have. No nonce is coming in my house, so fuck off and take her with ya.'

'Yes, Mrs Daniels, we've received a number of letters from you about my character; which I assure you are wrong. No, we are not leaving; Hope has come to see you, as arranged.'

'I ain't seein' her with you 'ere. Fucking nonce get lost, get out of 'ere. I don't want to see her neither. Running off to the police, telling them about our business. What goes on at home, stays at home. But, oh no, not according to her. My kids, all taken off me 'cos she went to the police. So fuck off, the both of ya.'

'Mrs Daniels, from what I understand, Hope had no choice—'

'Yes she fuckin' did, could've stayed at home. We were managing okay.'

'Mrs Daniels, rather than discuss this on the street, can we come in and discuss it inside?'

I don't want to go in, I don't want to.

'No, fuck off. I told ya, no fucking nonce is coming into my house. So get lost.'

With that she turns and slams the front door, which bounces back open again as it doesn't have a lock and is always on the latch, so we see my mum stagger down the hall, bouncing against the banister, unable to balance in her shoes.

'Can we go now, please?'

'Yes, Hope, we can.'

Jackie. Aged nine.

I am back at Chesterfields. I've been here for six sleeps now, after Mum went away and the neighbours found me 'home alone' again.

There's a social worker sitting next to Craig on the sofa. Craig tells me her name is Dorothy, but we can call her Dot. She's something to tell me. But first she wants to ask me some things. They must be big 'some things' 'cos I've been given both orange squash and chocolate biscuits with wrappers on, and the lady social worker, Dot, has tea served out of a pot, not just made in the mug like the parents get when they visit.

Us kids know that the orange squash, chocolate biscuits in their wrappers and the tea pot on the table in the front room, together with a social worker and Craig, mean that the adults are about to tell you that you have to pack your things and go. This set-up means the decision has already been made and the adults just pretend to ask us what we want.

When I see the table set out with the teapot and biscuits, I think: *They must've found Mum!*

I know now that when I'm at home, Mrs Simpson keeps an eye out to see if Mum is at home, too, or if she's gone for a rest in Spain or Portugal with her new boyfriend. Mum doesn't cope too well without a break from me, but I never know where she goes. This last time, though, I manage not to let Mrs Simpson know for six sleeps that Mum isn't at home looking after me.

Mrs Simpson says that now they know the history, they keep an eye out for me and call the police when they think I am home alone. Mrs Simpson asked the social worker if she could take me in, just until Mum comes home. The emergency social worker says that is kind, but they prefer kids to be with their relatives, even if the family are struggling.

Mrs Simpson puts on her sad but true face, where she bends her lips from being constantly happy, to flat and sucked in a bit. Then she looks down to the floor and tells the social worker in one long sentence, and with me and my cup of milk right there, too, 'Me and Mr Simpson have spoken about it, but we just don't have the money and couldn't cope with a little one, besides the Mum hasn't asked us, and I don't think she cares for us at all, so how would such a thing go down with Mrs Brown is an entirely different matter.'

I didn't really understand that last bit, but when I ask Hope Daniels, who has lived at Chesterfields for a while without going home for a sleepover at all, she tells me that it means my mum hates the neighbours.

When Mum's home, Hope is right, my mum hates the neighbours 'cos they keep sticking their nose in when she isn't at home, and the Social comes to take me into care. Care is good, though, 'cos every time I come, I get new clothes that fit me. I also get a clean bed. But I have to share a room so it's not the same as being at home with my mum. When she's there and not spread out on the sofa all day with her dressing gown and a lot of chocolate and even more tears, it's so warm and happy. Even when there's no heating, it's warm as we wrap ourselves up in the same duvet and cuddle while she tells me a story she made up about princesses and dragons, or we listen to the radio and dance in our blankets like we've never danced before. It's good to keep warm. Mum even cooks when we have gas. It's like this until she gets a new boyfriend, then she forgets I exist.

But now I am sitting in the front room, waiting to be told they've found my mum and that I am about to go home.

I hope you don't pretend like I have a say. I want to trust you. Can I trust you? She's looking at me funny.

Dot, the social worker, speaks, 'Jackie, your mum is

back. She was in Spain with her new boyfriend, Trevor. They've split up now and she wants you back. She's sorting herself out and I want to know what you want.'

Mum's home! Mum's home! Why are you asking me? You already know I am going home, you've got tea out the teapot and I have a chocolate biscuit. It's so warm and cosy here. I've friends who understand. I don't have to be alone. They look after me. We laugh here. I don't have to think about anything except my school, homework and sometimes setting the table before I can go and play. Has Mum really changed? The social worker says she has, so it must be true.

I stare at the social worker. I look at Craig, he looks very intense with a few lines on his forehead which, when he first arrived, I thought meant he was frowning but now I know they appear when he's thinking.

'I just want to be back with my mum.'

Craig's forehead lifts in a question. I ignore it. The social worker nods, writes this down.

What's she writing?

Craig's face has gone from questioning to looking a little concerned, like he does when one of the kids does something that's a bit silly. Often when a new kid arrives and they do something silly, Craig has this face on. It also appears when someone has been here for a while and is naughty. In both cases, Craig asks that kid to think about what they're doing and how they're behaving. You hear him asking if the kid thinks their behaviour is acceptable, and to go to their room for a bit and think. Then he tells them to come back when they're ready to tell him what they have decided. Sometimes, this is heard quite a lot in a day, especially for new arrivals. But we all get the talk and we all calm down and stop 'being silly'. Then the new kids wake up one day and the blank face they arrived with has gone and it has turned into a face that's more of a happy face than a sad face. I like those days, even though no one speaks about it happening. Not even in the toilets where us girls of all ages meet to chat about stuff and work out what's normal in the world outside. We're beginning to work it out and we think that when we're given points for good stuff, this must mean we're acting how kids from normal families do.

What's best of all is when we do things that Craig, or any of the staff, like and they tell us how brilliant we are, even if we just did something like set the table. We all like being brilliant and getting points. Points mean prizes.

But today the look on Craig's face makes me think that I am doing something wrong and the points I got yesterday for doing my homework without being asked for the first time might be taken away. I look at him.

What? What am I doing wrong? I shouldn't be in care. I should be at home with Mum.

Craig asks me, 'Jackie, I would like you to tell us what it's like when your mum leaves you and you come here . . .'

I don't want to remember. I don't want to know.

I try to think of something else but I can't. A big, thick lump rises in my throat, pushing tears out of my eyes, as he lists the times Mum has left me alone and I have come here to stay; two times of home alone. I start rocking backwards and forwards. I am hugging my knees.

I know there are bad bits, I know. No one wants me. Not here, not there. But I want to be with her. She wants me back this time;

I know she wants me back. I want to be with her. She's changed.
She's changed.

Craig is kneeling on the floor in front of me; his eyes are
level with mine. His hands are on my shoulders, he's
encouraging me to stop rocking, to come back from where
I've been.

'It's okay, Jackie, it's okay.'

I look at him, tears in my eyes. In a small voice I tell him,
'She ain't perfect, but she's my mum. She's changed, the
social worker, Dot, she says so. Mum will have changed
'cos she loves me. I like it here but I want to go home. Craig,
don't be angry with me.'

'I'm not, really I'm not. I just want what's best for you.'

Dot adds to this, shuts her folder, and agrees with me.

'Yes, that's settled, then. Jackie can go home and Mrs
Brown can come in the next day or so to collect her.'

She was a bit too quick there. What aren't you telling me?
Can I trust you?

Craig looks sad. He's kneeling in front of me, looking at
the floor. I try to comfort him; I reach out and pat my little
hand on his big shoulder.

'Craig, it's okay. I want to go home, really I do. Anyway,
the way the table is set, with the teapot and the biscuits in
a wrapper, to us kids, this always means someone is leaving. This time it's me. It's okay. Don't worry, Craig, I'll be
fine. Mummy loves me.'

Craig coughs, wipes his eye, gives the social worker a look
I don't understand, but I'm glad I'm not on the end of it.

As I leave the room to go and tell the others, I pause at
the door; I want to hear what they say about me after I've
left the room.

Craig is complaining about government cuts and how vulnerable kids are being sent home. 'It's not right,' he says.

The social worker agrees, 'It's so hard right now. We're being encouraged to keep kids at home. It's just the way it is these days.'

A big sigh from Craig, 'It doesn't make it right, though.'

'No, it doesn't, but what can we do? The kids are being affected. Thatcher is having her say and her way. But with all the cuts and the fact that there are no jobs out there, we've to tow . . .' Her voice tails off. When she starts to speak again, it sounds professional and strong as if she has forgotten that she showed a softer side. 'Now, Craig, you know we all do the best we can with what we have, but the decision is made. And besides, Jackie, she wants to go home. I'll call you tomorrow to arrange a date for pick-up.'

'Maybe, or maybe she felt she didn't have a choice. Which, to be fair, she didn't. Thatcher had already made it for her. What would you have done if she'd said she wanted to stay here? I wish we could've just been honest and told her straightaway the decision had been made. But, who'd've thought, the kids know they're going home anyway 'cos of that ruddy teapot.' He laughs and continues, 'Well, that's one thing that won't change, whatever Thatcher tries. Didn't I tell you, Dot? They're all clever little blighters! The teapot . . .'

I hear him moving towards the door, still laughing – nothing seems to make Craig sad for long. I run upstairs, confused about Thatcher.

What's the prime minister got to do with the decision about me going home? Oh, Mrs Thatcher must've been there in my

*case review. Mrs Thatcher must know how much my mum loves
me . . . She must be very pleased that I am going home.*

Hope. 1985.

I've been caught. 'Hoarding food', the staff say.

*But it's just . . . I just see it as my emergency rations, like the
people had in the war. I learnt about rations at school.*

Food, food, food, it's all I can think about, is food. I love
food. I hate food. My mind is always thinking about food.

*How to get it, where to eat it, is there going to be enough?
What happens if it runs out? Gotta eat as much as I can while it's
there. Trust no one, like Mum and Dad tell me. 'Don't trust no
one, Hope . . . They're all thieving bastards. Nicked you off us.
Nosey-parker bastards is all they are.' Is this place just one big
lie, like Mum and Dad say?*

I love the larder, it's my favourite place. Full to the rafters with food. I love the milkman, Roy, too. He brings so
many yoghurts that I think I'm dreaming.

Yoghurts, yoghurts, yoghurts. I nick 'em, put 'em under
my bed. Bread, too.

The staff found it all.

*Need to think of somewhere else to hoard my emergency
rations.*

Today, it's a buffet for Easter tea, the last treat before we go
back to school next week.

A buffet tea, what's that?

My key worker, Craig, pulls me aside before the buffet,
to talk to me about food. 'Hope, you don't have to hide
food. You don't have to go hungry again. You don't have to
eat so quickly; your tummy will hurt.'

Trust no one. My mum and dad said so; they're right.

The table in the dining room is covered in trays and trays of food.

You are kidding me.

Food, food, food. Tons of it. My head hurts. Where do I start?

I start stuffing food into my mouth and into my pockets.

Grab as much as you can while it lasts, Hope.

My stomach hurts.

A voice, I don't acknowledge who it is, says, 'Slow down, Hope.'

I can't, I just can't.

I start to cry, I don't like having all this food in front of me. My head hurts, muddled. I can't stop crying.

I want my dad to be here. Why can't my dad be here? Fucking food.

Debbie. Aged thirteen.

'Sit properly, for goodness sake, Debbie. What's wrong with you? Always fidgeting.'

I'm in the car with my gran on my dad's side, his mum, and my baby niece. We're driving down the M1, taking the baby with us to the Brent Cross shopping centre. Gran wants to help the baby buy a present for her mum, my sister, who is fifteen next week.

The baby is ten months old and belongs to my sister and our babysitter, who is now the lodger and my sister's boyfriend. Since my sister had the baby, she and him have lived together in our house.

'Sit properly. Sit on your bum, not on your hip.'

'Gran stop naggin', would ya?'

She slaps me on the side of my leg.

'Sit properly, Debbie.'

I turn my head to stare out the window so she can't see the grimace that I know is coming. I slowly turn my hips to move my bum flat onto the seat. The pain is too much. It travels sharply through my body into my head. I swallow, but it's not enough. Tears held for so long inside me release. They come out, all at once, with a sob that comes from deep within. The baby joins in.

'Debbie. Debbie. What's wrong?'

Gran speeds up, crosses the motorway diagonally, pulling in front of no less than two cars, onto the hard shoulder where she screeches to a halt. Horns screech at us.

Her seat belt is off, she's round the car, opening my door.

'Out. Now,' she commands.

She's pointing into the air at her side, behind the car. I cower.

'I'm not going to hurt you, Debbie. Why would I hurt you? Get out of the car, please.'

Me, my tears and my sore backside are screaming in their pain. She brings her pointing finger down, turns it, extending a hand of help, her voice matching this gesture, soft. 'Come on now, love.'

I grab onto her wrist. Her hand also wraps around my wrist. She pulls me, the stiffness of my bones means I struggle out of the car.

'Turn round. Undo your belt.'

'What?'

'Do it.' Her voice is stern again.

I focus on the cars rushing south on their way into London. I'm so used to complying I do what she asks.

She pulls up my top. She pulls down my trousers. She lets go. She turns and gags. I'm looking out at the M1, behind the car, with my trousers round my knees. I hear her throw up. I just stand there looking out at the cars.

Hello, enjoying the view?

She grabs me, turns me, presses me against the car so it hurts more, but smothers me in cuddles and kisses.

'Oh, my poor child. My poor girl. It's okay, it's okay.'

Tears flowing along with the traffic, which slows to look at two women standing on the side of the M1, the car protecting my dignity as we hold each other as if the world has collapsed, when, in fact, from here on in, now Gran knows, it can be rebuilt.

We're sitting in a coffee shop in the Brent Cross shopping centre. My niece is in the kids' club. My gran and I have managed to find a quiet corner at the side of the shop. We're standing at a high table, the high stools ignored by us both.

'He said I didn't shut the front door when I went out. But I did, Gran, I did.'

'Yes but who did this to you, Debbie? Whatever happened, it doesn't deserve these injuries. You are scarred and bruised from your knees to your back. There are welts. I've never seen the like. Why didn't you tell me? How long has this been going on? Oh, darlin', I'm sorry. Why didn't I see? It's not the first time, is it?'

Her head lowers so she's now looking up at me; I'm looking down into my cup of tea, my head lowered in shame. Her hand reaches out, covering my hand with hers. Kindness I'm no longer used to, have never been used to from anyone other than my gran. Tears are falling like raindrops into my cup of tea. My mother's voice in my head: 'What you moaning about? He only gave you a small slap.'

The police arrive at my gran's house. I hear her telling them that my dad is away working abroad, has been for years. That he and my mum split when we were very little. No, she doesn't see me that often, but still she doesn't know why she didn't notice.

The next doorbell is the social worker. Everyone is very kind to me. I'm asked to go and play with my niece in the dining room while they talk in the front room. They close the sliding doors between the front room and the living room.

I'm able to lie and play on my hip so it doesn't hurt too much. The phone rings. I stand and put my ear to the door that leads into the hall, where the phone is. I can't hear anything but after my gran goes back into the front room, the sliding doors are nowhere near stopping the conversation flowing through, and in snippets I can piece together what they're saying.

It was my sister on the phone. She called my gran's house to see where the baby is, we were due home ages ago. She denies anything happened. She says she's happy. She tells my gran to fuck off and to bring the baby home. The social worker tells my gran that this isn't going to be possible. While Gran lives in a different borough, social workers in our borough are aware of our family. She's discussed things with the social worker who visits us and care proceedings had already started to take us into care, even before today's turn of events.

I hear the social worker explain to my gran that both the baby and Debbie and me, need to go into emergency temporary care while they sort out what's wrong. The baby doesn't have any surface injuries, but they need to check at the hospital anyway.

I don't want to go to hospital. Am I going to be given a choice?

I lean towards the gap between the sliding doors. The social worker is still speaking, my eyes are vacant, apparently, and I'm very pale. The injuries my gran has found are severe and need to be looked at. There appears to be a bump on my head, and my legs, lower back and bottom are black and blue with gashes consistent with a belt buckle.

The social worker is holding my hand, the doctor isn't a nice person. She acts like she wants to get this done and forget me for ever.

'Lie down there, please. Strip off your bottom half. Yes, I know your back hurts, but we have to do this.'

No you don't. It's so painful. Don't make me lie down. Please don't make me be examined, please.

'That's it, lie down. This will just take a second. Have you had a smear test before?

What's a smear test?

'Knees bent, please. That's it.'

The doctor pulls down a light; it's shining into my fanny.

The doctor looks up at the nurse. Something funny on her face.

What? What? Don't make me feel stupid. She looks like she doesn't want to be here. Doesn't want to do this. It's not her this is happening to. It's me. She hasn't even said my name. She doesn't even know my name.

I grab the social worker's hand tighter. I close my eyes. I don't want to see the light and the doctor's head at my fanny. The social worker starts stroking my head, saying it's okay.

What are you putting into me? Ow! That's cold. What are you looking at? What? What are you doing?

My eyes are open now and I'm looking straight at the tiled ceiling. There's nothing up there except grey speckles. I squirm.

Ouch, that feels funny.

'Lie still. I'm just going to put my hand on your lower stomach. You will feel it going in a bit further.'

What? What are you putting inside me? That's cold. That's hard. What is it?

'Good girl.'

My name is Debbie.

'I just need to widen it up a bit. Then we can take the swabs.'

Why are you doing this to me? Why me? Why me?

The social worker catches sight of the tear that has escaped from my eye and is rolling down my face; she looks away from what the doctor is doing to me.

What's that? You're scraping my insides? Why are you scraping me?

Then suddenly, I contract back into myself. The cold thing is gone. The light is pushed away and the doctor is looking stern.

'I shall be back in a moment.'

She turns to leave. I hear her in the corridor with another person who I can't see. 'There's a lot of internal bruising as well as external. A lot of damage. I think she has an STD . . . Taken swabs for tests.'

Are they talking about me? What's an STD?

A question is asked by someone I can't see or hear.

'Yes, I am glad the police are already here.'

What? Why?

The person I couldn't see or hear speaking to the doctor is the social worker who sometimes comes to my house and when she comes, the whole family, including the lodger, have to pretend we're out by hiding upstairs. Sometimes Mum lets her in but we're not allowed to say anything except everything is okay.

The social worker and I spend a long time in a room at the hospital with another doctor lady and she's nicer than the other one. She's softer. She explains that I'm very brave and that they now have evidence of what has been going on at home, thanks to the other doctor.

My arse. She hurt me.

The new doctor asks me to show them with some dolls what the babysitter does at home to me. I tell them he also does it to my sister and it started when I was seven, my mum knows he does it so it must be okay. I'm thirteen but I don't mind playing with the dolls as they're pretty. I tell her about the babysitter giving us presents but it doesn't feel like a present, it just feels sore. I tell her about Mum saying it was okay what happens at home. I tell her that when the babysitter became the lodger, he got my sister a bigger present in the form of a baby. Even though he carried on giving me presents, I've not got a baby.

She asks me if there's anything at home I don't like. I'm quiet for a bit, then as I play with the dolls, I tell her how Mum hits me when she's angry and how sometimes when we do something bad it makes her tell us to strip off, open the window and stand for hours in the cold for our own good, but I don't like that either, as my legs get sore. I really don't like it when the babysitter, who has moved in, comes to stare at us when we are standing naked, as he looks at us funny. He also comes and tickles me in the middle of the night when he should be sleeping with my sister.

Mum says standing like that is the only way to check if me or my sister have done something bad. At the end, the babysitter tickles us and says he's going to make us feel better, but it doesn't, it makes me feel bad.

The social worker explains how the babysitter shouldn't be sleeping with my sister, or tickling me. Tickling like he does is not tickling, it's against the law. The doctor lady asks in a roundabout kind of a way about what I think is right and wrong.

I don't understand. Too much. Too much.

For my own safety I'm going to go and live somewhere else for a long while until they sort things out. They will tell my mum where I am, but are not sure when she'll be able to visit.

'But, I don't understand. Why do I have to live somewhere else?'

The social worker looks sad and explains again, 'Because what happens at home isn't normal, Debbie.'

'Why not? It's what happens in our house. To me and my sister it is.'

The social worker asks me, 'Can you tell me if it happens in anyone else's house?'

'I don't know.'

'Were you ever told to keep what happens in your house a secret from anyone outside the house?'

I nod. Her voice is so gentle. I want her to take me home with her.

'The reason you were asked to keep it a secret is that this behaviour isn't normal, Debbie. You should feel happy at home. You should have food and the right kind of love. You should not be getting "presents" of this sort from anyone.'

We're in the room a long time. I play with the dolls and sit quietly. I don't want to speak to anyone any more, because now I'm not normal.

It's doing my head in. What does she mean I'm not normal? What happens in our house has always happened. What does she mean it doesn't happen in other people's houses? What doesn't happen? Which bit?

The social worker asks me to come with her; we're going to a place of safety for me.

'I don't want to go into fostering again.'

'We've got you a place in a children's home. It's nice.'

She tells me not to worry because from today I'm going to learn what's normal.

Am I going to like it? Being normal.

Hope. 1985.

'How come everyone else gets fostered except me?'

It's a question I ask everyone. Social workers, children's home staff, the girls at the bathroom meet-ups. They change the subject every time I raise it. One of the older girls is giving a lesson to the younger girls about their periods; I see Jackie listening, tomorrow she's off to a new foster mum in Wales.

'You can't use Tampax. It ruins your virginity. And you can get toxic shock. Just use pads. Come on, it's dinner time.'

The dining room is bustling, our favourite time of day.

'Hope, be careful. That's two forks you've dropped now.'

We tuck into roast beef with all the trimmings.

I love it.

I look up, Jackie is opposite me. I put a Yorkshire pudding in my pocket for my security food box. As I do, I knock my glass of water over. Betty, one of the residential social workers, is standing next to me.

'Oh, Hope, so clumsy. Due on, are you?' I want to die of embarrassment, all the male staff heard.

The next morning, I need some supplies. There are none left in the bathroom. All the girls seem to come on at the same time here.

'Please can you go and get some for me?' I plead to Jackie.

'No, it's your turn. I am too young to be needing them, and anyway I'm leaving today, so I don't have time. You gotta do it.'

Don't remind me you are leaving, being fostered, and I'm not.

'But only Craig is on shift; there are no women to ask. Please?'

The girls are laughing, telling me I have to ask for myself. I trundle down the stairs in my pyjamas and find

Craig. Bright red, I ask for what I need – towels. He says I know where they are, they're in the cupboard. If I need a clean towel, I don't need to ask.

'Um, not that kinda towel.'

'Ahhh,' he says, unphased.

Packets are handed to me. He doesn't seem bothered.

When I come out of the larder, where everything we need is kept, Jackie's new foster mum is standing in the hall.

Why didn't you pick me?

Inside I'm cringing with embarrassment and jealousy for Jackie and her foster mum.

The girls giggling at the top of the stairs say I look like a bright-pink salmon when I come back with bundles of sanitary pads to restock the bathroom.

It's not fair, it's not fair. Why can't I be the one who is getting fostered?

I hide in the bathroom, my thoughts interrupted by a voice calling through the bathroom door.

'Hope, come and say goodbye to Jackie.'

I am so jealous of her that, to my shame, I pretend not to hear.

Jackie. Aged ten.

Mum is coming to collect me from my foster parents in Wales today. It's only been a few weeks since I left Chesterfields and already I'm going home. Except I'm a little worried 'cos it's not home. It's a whole new city, somewhere else that doesn't sound like home at all.

The social worker tells me Mum's sorted herself out and is ready to look after me again. Everyone seems happy.

The last time Mum came to visit me, only last week, she did look good. Or at least better than before. She said that she'd got a job working in Aberdeen so we won't be broke all the time. This is the same place my foster carer comes from, even though she now lives in Wales. Mum said it was almost sorted and when it was she'd come and collect me, and that we'd both be moving to Scotland.

I didn't really know where Aberdeen was, and I don't know if Mum knows. I know better now as my foster mum showed me on the atlas that they got for a wedding present.

It's a long way away. A city she says. Mum says it is big enough for us, somewhere we can get lost, and no one will know us and we can start again. I don't even know if she's got a job, but I know she told the social workers she did, and that's good enough for them to let her come and collect me from the foster carer's house.

Mum's coming to collect me at 2 p.m. and we're getting the bus. I don't mind moving again because I'm going to be with her. She isn't leaving me this time and, even though it's nice with the foster carer, I haven't made any friends and her own two kids are much older than me and are going off to university soon, so they don't bother with me.

The foster carer has been very kind and I now have some super new clothes, but I still miss my mum. Today, while I wait for her to come, I'm wearing a pair of denim dungarees, which are not too big and they're not too small. They are just the right size. This is the first time I've had clothes that fit me properly. I now have so many things that they also gave me my very own case to carry them in, not a plastic bag. The case even has wheels. I can't wait to show Mum.

I'm so excited about living with her again that I've been ready since just after breakfast and I've been standing at the window since lunchtime. At lunchtime we made some extra sandwiches for me and my mum on the journey, as we shall be travelling overnight. I even have some home-made shortbread to share with Mum.

Right now, though, I feel like I need to go to the toilet every five minutes, but I don't want to move as I really, really want to see Mum coming up the path more than I want to go to the toilet. So right now I'm crossing my legs and holding it in.

What if she doesn't come?

It makes me sad to be away from my mum. The family I'm staying with are very nice. They've a big house with a big garden in the West End of Cardiff, so it's posh. They live in Wales, but they're all Scottish and talk funny, especially when they're all together as a family, so I don't understand them all the time. Sometimes I just say 'Uh huh' to make them think I know what they're saying. They've a Volvo and we go on nice outings to the countryside. Rural Wales reminds Mrs Cameron of going 'up Deeside', a place near where she was born. We drive up into the hills with home-made bread sandwiches and home baking and at lunchtime we stop to have a picnic somewhere surrounded by hills and sometimes a lake, and Mr Cameron tells me that in Scotland a lake is called a loch and, as I am going there, I try and pronounce it but end up calling it 'lock' instead, and we all laugh. If it's raining, we still go but we eat sitting in the car. Mrs and Mr Cameron both like to do this, to get out of the house.

Mrs Cameron likes to bake and the family all like her baking.

She wants me to call her by her first name, Lynda, but I like to call her Mrs Cameron, as I'm only here for a short time and it seems to be that young people in Wales call old people by their last names and I want to fit in.

But now I'm waiting for my mum and we're leaving. Next to the front door is my case, full of new clothes, so it was worth coming here to get those. But even though people are very kind in this house, I'm lonely. I'm on my own a lot. I go to school but people in my class don't like me and they make fun of my English accent. Somehow they found out that I'm in care and a group of them follow me around saying that I don't have a proper Mum or Dad and I must be really stupid not to be able to keep them.

I don't have a Dad at all and never have, as my mum is a single mum, but I don't tell the kids in my class that; I just turn round and try to surprise one of them by throwing a punch. Then they all fight back, the whole group all at once are against me, pulling my hair, kicking me, trying to knock me down. But I'm stronger than I look and only once have they got me to the ground. Other kids stand round shouting, 'Fight, fight, fight!' until the teachers come running and shout 'Oi!', pulling us by our shoulders to split us up. We all get detention on a Saturday and we have to do this together 'cos the teachers think this will be a way of getting us to like each other and be friends. But it doesn't work like that; they still hate me for not living with my mum and I'm still lonely and not living with my mum.

The garden gate wedged between the high front hedge opens. My heart leaps like the salmon Mrs Cameron made me watch on TV. She shouted, 'Jackie, come quick, watch this. This is where you will be living. This is near Aberdeen. This is the place called Deeside, where I was born.' Fish, salmon, are on the telly; they are swimming, jumping, up the River Dee, near where the Queen goes for her summer holiday at Balmoral Castle. I hope we live in Aberdeen for a long time. The countryside looks very nice. Mr Cameron says the salmon do this, jump up river, to get home, to lay their eggs.

I start to shout, 'Here she is!' but stop myself when I realise it's the postie with a parcel and not my mum. My joy falls back as quickly as it rose, like the salmon who don't do a big enough jump up river and get washed back against the flow to try again.

She's late. She's five minutes late.

I go to answer the door to the postie. Behind him stands my mum. As I moved from the front window to the front door, I must've missed her coming through the gate. I don't care I missed that moment.

She's here, she's here!

I ignore the postie and shout back into the house to my foster mum, 'Mrs Cameron, the postie has brought my mum! She's here, she's here! What is it you say when you are happy?'

Mrs Cameron comes through from the kitchen, apron on and rubbing flour from her hands. She gives me a smile that lights up her whole body.

'The salmon are jumping, dear, the salmon are jumping!'

*   *   *

Mum and I have moved to Aberdeen, Scotland. She says that, with the oil industry starting here and ships in the harbour, that's where the money is and we can get away and start again. She doesn't have a job, though she told my social worker she did. But it doesn't matter, as we're together again. A friend of hers lives here and does very well. We came on the bus with a suitcase each. I have the one the foster carer gave me, and Mum has her red one. It's a long way from Lincoln, where I was born. The people speak funny here. In the day I go to school and my teachers are nice, but it takes me a little while to understand what they're saying.

I stay in the loft. Well, at night-time anyway, when Mum and her girlfriends have visitors downstairs.

When the doorbell rings for the first time in a night, I'm 'shoo-shooed' by one of my mum's friends up the step ladder and into my room in the loft. Once they know I'm safe and I've closed the loft hatch, I can hear feet, one set light and one set heavy. They follow me up the stairs, but they don't come up to the loft. The feet turn right at the top and go into the bedroom. The door closes behind them, stopping the sound of moving feet, and replacing it with other sounds. The room they go into is below my bed.

When they're inside, I can hear them, low voices first, then sometimes, but not often, a giggle. Then thud, thud, thud, which goes on until it ends with a man's groan. I know it's the headboard that thuds against the wall because before I knew what was making the sound, I went to investigate the room in the day-time, when no one was here. It's an okay room at night, there's soft lighting and drapes hang from the corners of the ceiling, I guess that's to hide the paper coming off the walls. But in the morning it smells musty and funny, and in the daylight you can see the colour in the drapes is beginning to fade. Every day, when she wakes up, one of Mum's friends opens the window in there and lights incense to make it smell better, then she comes out of the room and shuts the door. This always annoys the other ladies who stay here, including Mum, as it makes the room cold. But I agree that it takes the fusty smells away and, even though the others complain, they say to her she can do what she wants. She agrees and puts 'Tainted Love' by Soft Cell on the record player. They all love this song. They sing along every day, over and over, even though it was in the charts when I was two years old. They seem to like the words 'cos they sing from beginning to end. I wrote the words out from the back of the record cover in my notebook, so I can try and learn them and join in.

I practice the words and the actions all the time. So that I remember when to use my arms, I have put ** next to the words 'Tainted Love' where my mum and her friends add a 'boom, boom' with full arm outstretched, hand punching the air motion, and then a * when they're pointing a finger in the air as if telling me off. Then *** next to a line that means I give myself a cuddle – all while singing at the same time. I copy Mum and her friends and I practice on my own, so I do the same actions at the same times as them. If I don't practice, I find I get a little behind trying to remember the words and the actions together.

Early in the evenings, the five of us girls, as my mum calls us, sit together in the living room. They are all made up and look so pretty. One of them puts this record on and we all start to sing along from our chairs, arms above our heads. When it's finished, we've a moment of being quiet when I know not to speak. Someone will put the song back on another time and they start all over again. I only join in the first couple of times, after that I just watch as I get a bit bored. They do it again and again, until the doorbell rings and the chorus is broken by my mum saying, 'That's us, girls. Someone calling for another bout of tainted love.'

They all laugh. I don't understand, but I laugh with them before I'm 'shoo-shooed' upstairs.

On the day I work out what makes the noise in the room below my loft at night, Mum comes home and asks, 'What have you done all day, love?'

I reply, 'Played with my dolls in the kitchen.' But that's a lie and I think my cheeks are a little 'liar, liar pants on fire' pink because she just looks at me and says, 'Really?'

I nod and leave the kitchen, go upstairs and past the room where I did my earlier investigations.

Next to the headboard there's a dent in the plaster. I wobbled the bed back and forth, and I was pleased with myself as it made the same noise I hear when I'm in the attic – thud, thud, thud.

Now I know what that is.

But as I move the bed, I realise that without a man and one of Mum's friends, there will be no groan at the end.

So, what makes the men groan?

Sometimes when I'm in my attic, I lift the hatch and place a book between the boards and the trapdoor. This gives me enough space to look through the hatch towards the stairs and see which girl and which man go into the room. Even if I couldn't see them coming up the stairs, they pass right under my loft hatch, and I've seen them so often from up here, I know all the girls from the top of their heads. There's a blonde whose hair is always down, and a second blonde whose hair is always up in a pony tail; there's a redhead who has wiry, frizzy hair, my mum, and the dark-haired girl whose hair is always in a bun when she goes into the room.

When they go into the room, their hair is all nice and smells of Charlie perfume and Silverkin hairspray. When they leave the bedroom, the girls' hair has changed. The one with the bun, her hair changes the most. It's up when she goes into the bedroom, but it's down and all over the place when she comes out. But however messy their hair is when they come out, it's fixed before the doorbell rings again and they come back up with another man.

When my mum comes up the stairs, I don't look. I hide under the pillow and think of living in the countryside with my grandpa, who has forgotten that he doesn't speak to us and instead shows me how to cook eggs and weed the garden.

I stay there, under the pillow, for a long time, until I fall asleep or I'm sure she's back downstairs again. It's warm and safe in the loft, and they always have a snack ready for me so I don't have to go back downstairs. If I need the loo, I've to wait until the bedroom door closes then sneak downstairs, quiet as a mouse. Sometimes I have to cross my legs and wait a while because no one is upstairs and they might come up while I am in the loo. I don't want to be seen.

If I think really hard, I don't cry. But most of the time I cry. When my mum or my mum's friends hear me, they come up to the loft and give me a cuddle. When it's not my mum I cry harder, 'I want my mum. Let me go and see my mum.'

'You can't just now, she's working.'

'Where is my mum? I want her.'

'Now, Jackie, you always want her for no reason, and then when you get her you don't need her. Now go to sleep, or she'll be pissed with ya.'

My bed is warm and the smell of Charlie perfume and Silverkrin takes a while to leave the attic after they've gone. I feel a little bit sick with the amount they put on. It keeps me awake.

Some of the men I've never seen before, some come to visit at the same time every week. The men are all different shapes and sizes, but they've one thing in common – they all make the girls giggle at the same point on the stairs. Every time it's the same stair. Right now, I'm doing an experiment to prove myself right, or wrong, and then I can tell the girls what I find out. I'm writing it down in the same notebook that I have the 'Tainted Love' by Soft Cell words in. According to my notebook and the notes I've made over the last week, I'm right.

All my mums' friends laugh and stop on the same step every single time. I don't see what my mum does, 'cos when she comes up, I don't look and my head is under the pillow. But my records show that each of the girls puts their foot on the third stair, starts laughing or giggling, then she stops, turns round, looks at the man below her on the stairs, smiles, and then turns back, and loses the smile straight away. The man doesn't see her smile switch off, 'cos she's got it back on by the time she gets to the top of the stairs. Sometimes I see that between the third step and the top step, the man's hand is on her bottom.

Yuk.

Or it goes up her skirt.

Even more yuk.

Or sometimes he isn't touching her at all, but just has a weird look on his face.

Yuk to him touching and double yuk to that look. If we moved to the countryside, they wouldn't find us, these horrible men. It wouldn't be like it is here. It would be sunny and perfect.

Debbie. Aged thirteen.

We drive up a gravel path to a big building; there's a minibus at the front door.

I get out of the car with just what I'm wearing; the rest of my stuff is at home. It's a big house. On the drive here, I didn't speak, instead what Gran said is going over and over in my head. How she reacted; what the people in the hospital said about what's normal; and how they said that I'm a victim. The words swim in my head.

Not normal. Abuse. Victim. Brave. I don't feel brave. Feel dirty.

The front door of this place is under an arch and it swings open. A girl rushes past, she looks a bit younger than me, she's laughing and smiling. Another one, too, a few years younger than the first. Both are wearing fashionable clothes, they look like Duran Duran fans in Mum's magazines.

I'd kill for them clothes.

The older one stops, stares at me, smiles, then speaks, 'Hi. You new? We're off shopping. What's your name?'

'Debbie.'

'Nice to meet ya, Debbie. See ya later.'

'Um, what's your name?'

'I'm called Hope. Pretty bitch, ain't ya?'

Her grin is huge. She turns and runs after her friend. As I watch both girls rush down the drive, for the first time in a long time something stirs. It feels strange. I realise a bit of Hope's smile is left behind and just a hint of it has appeared on my face. This feels different; it feels better than what I feel at home.

Is this normal?

My smile grows and, as I watch Hope disappear, I realise what's happening.

I am free.

I am sitting on my bed. I share the room with two girls, Hope and another one who is pretty sulky. The room smells of paint. It's so pretty in this room and each bed has covers with pink flowers.

Hope is lying face up staring at her posters and a wall of birthday cards she's collected, with her personal stereo headphones on.

My suitcase is on top of my wardrobe, now empty of the things my mother bought me to make me shut up and be a good girl and say nothing when I threatened to tell the social worker that the babysitter was living there with my sister and he was renting out his other flat and claiming benefits.

Some of my stuff has gone missing. I am sharing a room with a thief.

How do I deal with this?

I go over and stand over Hope. Her eyes are open but she doesn't move. I lean over her, reach down to prod her arm. In a flash she's got hold of my arm and has removed the headphones.

'What do you want?'

'Ummm, I just wondered, ummm, some of my stuff . . .' I take a deep breath, 'has gone missing . . .'

'So? I don't have anything to do with it; you don't steal from your own.'

'I just wondered if you had seen anyone in our room or if, um, you knew anything about it.'

She has posters of pop stars on her cream-coloured walls. The pop stars seem to surround me, to be on her side and she senses this, too, as it gives her the strength to fight back.

'What? What do I know? Are you accusing me of stealing?'

'No, I, uh, I, uh, just wondered.'

She's sitting up now, headphones pulled off and thrown on the bed where she'd just moments before been listening to the music. Now she's angry, spitting as she speaks.

I wish I had never asked.

'You wondered if I was a thief, is that it? A thief? You know me, and so you should know I don't know nothing about your stupid stuff.'

With strength I didn't know I had, I haul Hope from the bed by her right arm. She remains in her sitting position as she's flung across the room and lands on the floor by my bed. I throw her in a way that the babysitter did to me and my sister many a time. It's a sweeping movement of grab and throw. It's surprising and effective. She screams as her back hits the frame of my bed, but I don't care. I am convinced that I am right.

My stuff. She nicked my stuff.

I look under her bed, there is a cardboard box there. I haul it out and lift off the lid. It is full of food. Saying nothing, I shove it back under the bed. I lift her mattress in another smooth motion, throwing it to the side so it, unintentionally, lands wedged between the bedroom door and the bed so no one can get in. I take advantage of this, and hiss, 'It's just you and me, then.'

Her eyes widen in fear.

'I know nothin'.'

I turn back to her bed and look for the spoils which must be hidden under the mattress, but there's nothing except a metal box, which doesn't belonging to me, sitting in the space between the base of the bed and the mattress. I open the box, in case some of my stuff is in there, and the colour drains from her face as I do so. At first glance it looks like a first aid kit. Then I look closer. There's a knife in there; I look towards her and say gently, 'Lift up your sleeves.'

She doesn't do it, but I know how to be forceful. I just need to copy the babysitter when he's angry and he manages to get me and my sister to do what he wants. In the same tone of voice I say, 'Do it.'

She pushes one sleeve up, then the other. Nothing.

'Your legs?' I ask, my voice softer.

She nods. 'And my tummy.'

I don't need to see the scars. I know it, I've seen it. She pulls up her top anyway, just a bit. I show no surprise.

The air in the room between me and Hope is heavy. She looks embarrassed, is waiting to be told off because her tummy has scars from left to right, and right to left, of old wounds turned white, newer ones, still scabbed, and others, fresh, I guess from today, which have not even started to heal. I stare in silence at her. She stares at the floor, then up at me. The way she's patterned her body by taking this knife to herself to release the pain is standing between us.

I close the lid of the box and sit myself down on the floor, at first leaning against my bed. But this seems too far away from Hope, so I spin myself round, still holding the box, and push myself backwards with my feet, until she and I are side by side on the floor leaning against the frame of her bed.

I hand the box back to her, she accepts it with one hand, pulls her knees up into her chest, then balances the box on her knees, seemingly protecting the contents with both hands – one hand curled round the side, the other on top, checking the lid is back in place.

She speaks first in her London accent.

'You won't tell anyone, will ya?'

'Look, we're roommates, so long as you don't steal my stuff or do that when I'm in the room, then we're cool.'

'Um, I didn't steal your stuff. Maybe she did.'

Hope nods her head towards our roommate's bed. We both stand up at the same time and lift the other girl's mattress. There they are, my things. We stand and stare at the items. I pick them up, one by one, and move them over to my bed: a Sindy doll, a walkman, my Wham! tapes, some chocolate, now a bit melted and leaving a brown stain on the bottom of the bed.

Hope watches me as I go back and forwards. I say to her, 'You know, we're good, ummm, we're sorted . . .'

'What about my, um, box.'

'Your business and, as far as I am concerned, your secret. Whatever we need to get us through the day? Come on; let's get your bed sorted out.'

We smile at each other.

Should I tell her? Should I show her my upper legs and say I get it, 'cos me too, me too . . .?

Jackie. Aged ten.

I wake. It's a bit cold. Half asleep, I reach for my covers but they're not there. With my eyes still closed, I pat my hands around the mattress. I touch bare skin, my skin.

What? Where is my nightie?

I lie still, listening.

There's someone breathing. Someone else is here. Smells of whisky.

I screw my eyes tight shut.

Go away. Go away.

He speaks, 'You awake now, then? Yer mum sent me up to see you're doing okay. Up here on your own, are ya? Sleep up here, do ya? While the girls entertain?'

He's not from Aberdeen. More like the south of England. I open one eye. He smiles. It's not a nice smile. I don't know this man; this isn't one of the men who come every week.

I don't believe you. Mum would never send anyone up here. That's why I'm here. To be safe.

His face is covered in stubble, his hair is greased over to one side with a big parting, but there's a bit sticking up on the top. He's wearing a brown suit with shoes that match, a belt and a different-coloured brown shirt, which is lighter and looks like puke.

I don't like you.

Little eyes and he smells like he's musty. A picture of a house where the windows are never opened flashes through my head. I see him sitting there with dirty thoughts and a green armchair.

Mummy, Mummy, Mummy. Oh no, Mummy, there's a man. He's peering over me, Mummy. I'm naked, Mummy. How did that happen? Mummy? Mummy?

I open my mouth to scream. Nothing. My voice is only working inside my head. Only silence comes from my open mouth. My eyes lock with the man as he stands on the left of the mattress, which means there's nothing between me and the hatch. Nothing stopping me, except him grabbing me.

If I'm quick. Can't speak. Try and move. The hatch . . . Light coming up from the hatch. It's open.

My gaze moves down from his face to where his hands are. I don't want to look there, so quickly I move my eyes back to stare at his face. I push myself away from him standing at the side of my bed. Again, I go to scream, to shout, 'There's a man staring at me when I'm asleep.' But nothing comes out. I slowly push myself to the other side of my mattress, away from him; an inch or two nearer the hatch. He's got the same look the men have when they're coming up the stairs with Mum's friends.

Where is my nightie? Why am I naked? What do you want?

His hands move to undo his zip, then they move to his belt.

'Come on, then; I've paid good money to be up here with you.'

I feel my eyes getting bigger.

Mum's friends were complaining of a lack of money, of slow business. Of how the men wanted younger girls these days. Oh no. No! No! No!

'We can play some. Come on. There's a good girl. You look so good. Come on, over here. Or do you want me to come over there, is that it?'

Shit.

He's undoing the button on his trousers.

Shit. Mum, or her friends, sent him here. But I don't want to.

The thud, thud, thud from the room below starts up. He looks round behind him and, as he does so, his face changes, like he's wondering what it is.

Now!

I leap off the mattress. Towards the hatch. I feel his surprise, his arm in the air behind me, a swoop.

'How the—? Fuck!'

He's switched to anger. I'm halfway down the ladder, butt-naked. He reaches down the hatch, touches my skin. It feels like a sting.

Run. Run. Run.

At the bottom of the ladder, I steal a look back. The man must've tripped in the loft as he tried to grab me. He scratched my arm but there was a thud after that.

His bottom half is lying across the hatch, his trousers round his ankles and big, dirty, grey pants still where they should be. One of the girls comes out the living room. She's pissed off.

'Get back up there, Jackie, for fuck's sake.'

Why? Why do I have to go back? Help me, please . . .

She tries to grab me but I'm fast, darting past her and then she is distracted by a new man who is coming in the front door, who doesn't seem to notice a naked me.

Run. Run. Just run.

Out the door, the cold air of the street hits me. I look left and right. I cover my naked bits and go left.

Run. Run.

The street is cold, dark. My bare feet stub on the uneven pavement. I move to the middle of the road. My chest hurts from breathing in the cold air and not being very good at running.

Keep going. Keep going.

I stop for a second, look up. There's a light ahead.

The pub. The pub.

I burst in, just as I hear the bell and 'Time ladies an' gentlem—'

Then everything seems to stop at once. It's so quiet, no one is speaking. People are looking at me. I stand in the middle of the double doors, holding them open with my hands, the Scottish night air coming in with me. My breathing is heavy, the cold air sharp in my lungs, but I'm determined to speak and I hear a small voice escape me, 'Help.'

'Oh my good God. Someone cover her up. Yer jacket, man, gi'e me yer jacket. Wha' did she say? Johnny, call the police. Now, man.'

The police station is calm, but the copper says I have to go back to the house to try and find the man in the brown suit.

I don't want to. Why can't I stay here?

I'm wearing a blanket and some clothes that are too big for me. The landlady gave them to me in exchange for the man's jacket while we were waiting for the police. I tell the police lady in one breath what happened at the pub, 'cos I don't want to tell her what happened at home.

'These clothes, they belong to her, the landlady's daughter who used to be at my school, the daughter not the landlady, 'cos she's too old, but the daughter left and now goes to the big school, but the landlady knows my name as she's seen me around. When we were waiting for you she gave me some hot milk with chocolate and called me a poor wee mite. But I know that's an insect that bites and lives in your bed, so I told her in an angry voice that I am not. She, that's the landlady, replied by saying in a very kind voice – which surprised me – that, "It's okay, dear" and, "There, there." She said I must've had an awful fright and to put these on. She said they would be a little bit big and they are, but, no matter, better than nothing, which is what I was wearing when I came into the pub.'

'Why were you wearing nothing when you came into the pub, Jackie? Can ye tell me?'

I shake my head. I know the police lady is only trying to be nice, but I don't want to tell her that I sleep in the loft when Mum and her friends have other friends, men friends, round and then, when the men have gone, they go to sleep, get up and sit around and smoke pot and do other stuff that lets them forget what they've to do in Maggie's Britain to make a bit of money. Entrepreneurs is what my mum says she and the girls are.

To start off with, the streets that we're driving through aren't ones I know, then the police car turns into a street I do know 'cos it is the road my school is on. It's near the one where we live. To distract myself from having to go back and see the man at the house, I concentrate on how Mum wants me to get my accent to be more like Maggie Thatcher's. If I manage to do this, Mum says I can be anything I want. I've asked my English drama teacher if she thinks it's possible to change my accent to be posher. She says my English speaking is already good, just needs a bit of refining. I like that word, 'refining'. Although, I don't think it's the same meaning as the oil men have. Sometimes when the men come to visit Mum and the girls and they want a drink before going up, I listen in. The talk is boring most of the time, especially when it's about the oil refinery and all the money it's making us in the north-east of Scotland.

As we drive up from the police station towards my house, past posh houses made of granite blocks that sparkle when the sun shines and are grey when it doesn't, I feel a bit bad. I've told the police lady what it's like sleeping in the loft, how the men come and go, about how I can hear the thudding. Her response is to tell me in a soft accent that I've done very well and not to worry, and that I shall be safe.

So why are we back here, then? The loft is no longer safe.

'Which house is it, Jackie?'

'That one, the one with the shoe in the window.'

Why are you taking me back? You said I would be safe. It's not safe there any more. I wanna see my mum.

'Of course, that would be the one.'

The social worker sitting next to me looks up at the house. The policeman and police lady look at each other. They share, in that look, something I don't understand.

What don't I know? Tell me. Tell me.

The police lady turns to the social worker. 'Mrs Edwards, we're goin' into the broth— sorry, the house. Will ye please stay here wi' Jackie? Please don't get out of the car until we come back. You will be perfectly safe.'

What? Are you leaving me? Why? Why?

My view from the police car lets me see the people running back and forth inside. It's all happening behind thin curtains – people standing up and waving arms, shouting, 'Tainted Love' playing, again. I can see the police and my mum's friends but it doesn't look like there are any men shapes in there, except the policeman in his hat. From out here it kinda looks like the beginning of the *Professionals* on TV, silhouettes Mum calls them. I can't see Mum's shape in any of the windows either.

Where is my mum? I want my mum. Maybe she'll come out the door and find me here in the police car. She's gonna be pissed with me for running off to the cops.

Our house is different to the ones near the police station. Our house is covered in a grey paste that's bumpy and called harling. When I asked about it, I was told it makes the house waterproof. On the houses in our street the harling doesn't go all the way to the door and you can see the bricks framing the door. They, too, look grey and, not for the first time, I wonder if they ran out of paste when they were building.

Why is everything in Aberdeen grey?

I stare at the front door, which is open; the light from inside means I can play my game of counting the bricks around the door.

One, two, three, four, five, six, seven, eight, nine, ten, eleven, twelve, thirteen, fourteen, fifteen – where's Mum? – sixteen, seventeen, eighteen, nineteen, twenty, twenty-one – why haven't they found her?

I carry on counting. There are twenty-seven bricks up the left-hand side of the door and eight across. It could be nine, but half a brick on each side of the top of the door goes bigger than the door, and I learnt at school that two halves make a whole, but I haven't counted that as a whole.

There are twenty-seven bricks on the other side of the door, too, but as I don't know how to add up twenty-seven and twenty-seven and eight all in one go, I have to count each brick individually, from the bottom of one side of the door, over the top and down again, 'cos I can count to high numbers.

With one plus one plus a lot more one plus ones, there are sixty-two bricks that go round the door, not counting the two halves that stick out and make a whole, that would make sixty-three. When I've finished counting, I start again and get the same sixty-two bricks. Halfway through the fourth time of counting, the police lady and the policeman come out. The police lady tells me my mum can't be found and there's no man in a brown suit there.

You don't believe me. You don't believe me.

'No mum?' The social worker repeats. The policeman shakes his head.

I know the social worker has been speaking to me all the time in her thick Scottish accent while I was counting the bricks but I don't know what she said 'cos I was counting bricks and I didn't want to listen, not until they found my mum.

Mum will know what to do.

'How is she?' The police lady asks, nodding towards me.

What? I'm here! Ask me! No one bloody cares if I'm here or not.

I cross my arms and sink into the back of the seat like I do when I don't want anyone to see me, but really I just want them to see me and give me a hug and tell me I'm safe now.

'In shock, I think; she refuses to speak to me.'

Are they gonna make me go back in there?

'What happens now?'

'Well, she can't go back in there, at least not tonight. We need to do some further examination, see if she's been harmed or not. We shall need to take her to ARI.'

Um, hello, I'm here. What do you mean? ARI? That's the big hospital – Aberdeen Royal Infirmary. No. No. I don't want further examination. Oh no. I don't want anyone to look at me. He didn't touch me; I told the police lady that. Tell her I don't need anyone looking at me. I got away. I don't want to go to ARI. I don't want to go back in there either, 'cos Mum's gone and gone, again.

'Well, it's late now, but my colleague will be able to let me ken if we've got an emergency foster placement. If we have one we shall take her there; if no, we shall need to have a rethink, I suppose. Maybe her old kids' home will take her back. I dinna think there are any other relatives that care, the poor wee mite.'

I thump the social worker on her arm, hard.

'I am not. I am not. I am not.'

After what happened in Scotland, a judge decided, enough is enough. He thinks Mum will never change and has put me in care. FOR EVER. Well, until I am eighteen, which is a long time away from now, as I am eleven on my next birthday. The social worker, who helps me pack my case, told me a court order has been issued and I am now a ward of court, belonging to no one and with no one wanting me. She was very kind and chattered away, which was fine at first, but she carried on all the way from my house to Chesterfields again. It's a long way.

On the drive, I just wanted her to shut up. If she'd asked me whether or not I wanted to talk, I would've said I would like to be quiet. I managed to ignore her chatting about what a good place I was going to, how they put on a Christmas show, go on holiday and how they know what special attention we need. How the kids do well there. How even the worst kids turn themselves around.

What? Did she say, 'the worst kids'? So we're the bad ones? Why do we need special attention? Why me? Why didn't the judge see my mum loves me, she just needs a break from me every now and then, that's all? Maybe it's because I am a bad girl that she keeps needing to go away. 'The worst kids' the social worker says. I must be one of them.

Debbie. Aged thirteen.

I'm straightening my new school tie in the mirror next to the front door of Chesterfields. It's not quite ready when Craig calls me from the doorway.

'Come on, Debbie, your new school is waiting, the minibus is waiting. Everyone else is on the bus, which is a minor miracle in itself, so I don't want to give them any chance to get off before they're meant to.'

I love learning. Ever since my first teacher read me a book, I've been reading. No one had read me a story before

I started school. No one had told me about the magic of reading. I take a look in the mirror and at my tie.

I'll fix it on the bus. Happy. Happy. Happy. I remember sitting on my teacher's knee as she read me my first book when I was five years old. All the way through, she told me the words, one by one. Magic. After that I taught myself, secretly, at home with books from the school library. I stole a torch from Woolworths so I could read under the covers in my room and Mum wouldn't know. I worked it all out, one letter here, another there, letters that make words, words that make a book. My mystery world that took me away from home. Love books. Love books. Love numbers, too, but books more.

'Debbie, come on, please.'

I don't need to be told a third time; I turn and run out to the bus that will take me to my new school.

I have a tie because my social worker identified that I am 'gifted' and has got me into a school with a high academic record to stretch my abilities. I stop at the front door, get on my tiptoes and throw my arms around Craig to give him a hug.

'Thank you,' I say. I look back at him as I run towards the bus, where Hope and the other kids are all waiting. As he turns to shut the door, I see Craig smile and then follow us out to the bus to take us on the school run.

As we drive off, I ignore the rest of the kids jumping around, playing sillies, and stare out the window.

My new life. So much better than home. Safe, secure and there's no doubt that I'll get to go to school every day. Mum can't stop me now. Love it.

A hand gently pulls at my hair, a happy voice asks, 'What ya thinking?'

It's Hope. Her blonde head and cheeky grin plonk themselves down beside me.

'Oh, just how much I like learning, maths and reading and stuff.'

She stares at me, understanding, she loves them, too.

'Word of advice,' she says; 'don't go tellin' no one at yer new school that, or that yer in care. Okay?'

Why? What does she know? She's almost a whole year younger than me.

'Okay,' I reply.

'Good on ya. You'll be fine, then!'

She spins herself out of the seat and re-engages with obviously more interesting people on the bus.

Why can't I be more like her?

The English class is reading *Anne Frank*, but I've read it before, twice. I stick up my hand.

'Yes, Debbie?'

'Please, Miss. I can't read this, Miss.'

'Really, why not? It should be within your reading ability. Have you been missing school? Is that why you can't read?'

The class sniggers, someone whispers that they saw me getting off the care bus and that's why I can't read. The teacher pulls them up on whispering and she asks them to stand and 'Repeat what is so interesting to the rest of the class'.

The person behind me stands, blushes, looks down while he says, 'She's from the kids' home, Miss. Maybe she missed school and that's why she can't read.'

I try to speak, 'But, Miss, that's not the reason—'

The teacher talks over me. 'Right, Debbie, if that's the case, then we need to send you to the Head for an assessment. Come with me, please.'

'But, Miss?'

'No more talking. Come on, Debbie, we shall get you into the right class.'

The Head wants me to do an exam to test my ability. None of them listen to me. None of them give me the chance to explain that the reason I couldn't read *Anne Frank* is that I've read it twice already. That I'll get bored. They should give me something more challenging to read.

They all assume I am thick just 'cos I'm in care. Play along, do their stupid exam, show them what marks you can get and then they will eat their words. Better do the exam than go back in class now when the fact I am in care is fresh in their minds. Maybe when I go back and they see how clever I can be, they'll forget where I live.

The key turns in the lock; for a moment I am back at home with Mum locking me in. Panic.

Keep calm. Stay in the present. I am not at home. I am in the stationary cupboard.

It's dusty, with a single yellow bulb. I look up and around me; I am surrounded by books, blue jotters and textbooks. I run my finger over the spine of a row of books. I love the way they feel, the way they smell. The shelf label says the books are for a class two years above me.

I can't wait to learn what's in these.

The exams on Maths, English and Geography are all piss easy. I'm finished in no time and reward myself by looking at books for the class two years above me, finding only disappointment.

Trouble is, I know this stuff, too.

When the Head reopens the cupboard door, I am sitting looking at one of the text books. I smile when he opens the door, and say, cheekily, 'You took your time; I finished ages ago. Should make it harder next time.'

A few days later I am called to the Head's office again. This time his secretary seems to be frowning more than smiling at me; last time she was friendly and welcoming.

What have I done?

I sit and the teachers pass me, looking at me as if they know I am a child from care. They make me fidget in my seat. In my head I scream at them.

WHAT?

The door to the Head's office opens. It is a long, dark room, with wood panelling reminding those who enter that he's in charge, that it's a school with a long history, with a good academic record, even if it is run by the government. This room tells me that this is a school of learning and I get a shiver of excitement at being in such a place, of knowing how well I have done in the entrance exam.

The Head looks stern. He stays on his side of the table, which is never a good sign at school. He looks me straight in the eye.

He's summing me up. Sit up straight. Good impression.

He lets the silence hang in the air between us. The anticipation of my doing so well waiting to break. His voice doesn't match the 'well done' words that I am expecting, though.

'Debbie, have you something to tell me?'

What's he getting at?

I'm confused. 'Um, no, Sir. I don't know what you mean, Sir.'

'Well, your entrance exam troubles me.'

What? Why?

He pauses for effect; this lets me build up a picture of being in trouble, but for what, I'm not sure. I don't respond or ask why, though my head is jumping around keen to do just that.

He breaks the silence.

'You see, Debbie, it seems you got one hundred per cent in each of the three exams. Now, no matter what your social worker thinks, someone from your background with, I assume, sporadic education . . . Well, how can this be?'

Someone from my background? My background? Are you assuming I'm thick? That the social worker knows nothing? What do you know about me? What do you see? You decided already. I am obviously not worth as much as other people, as much as those without my background . . .

My voice is small. I am careful to pronounce all my words properly.

'Well, Sir, I have always gone to school. I love school.'

'That may well be, Debbie, but, again, with your background, even you must admit the results are a little, shall we say, surprising?'

He's leaning slightly forward now, both forearms creating two sides of a triangle on his desk, his body providing the third side. His elbows are balancing on the edge of his vast, leather-topped, dark-wood desk, his hands hover slightly above it, clasped together as if in prayer.

I want a desk like this one day.

I rub my forehead and speak again, 'I don't understand.'

'No, neither do I.'

Damn, done it again. I mean, I don't understand why you think I couldn't get one hundred percent, not, I don't understand how I got one hundred percent.

'No, what I mean is, I like—'

He cuts me off mid-sentence and, while speaking, he moves from the back of the desk to the front.

Really in trouble now, girl. A head moving from behind their desk to the front of their desk means you are in big trouble, and he wants to prove it. But why am I in trouble? I did nothing wrong. I got one hundred percent.

Before he finishes his sentence, before he sits on the edge of the desk next to me and looks down on me, a light bulb comes on in my head.

He thinks I cheated.

'All right, Debbie, you can tell me.'

'Tell you what. How could I have cheated? You put me in a cupboard. Locked the door.'

'Yes, but that cupboard is full of text books, you were even reading one when I opened the door.'

'That was after I finished the exam,' I plead, but he ignores my desperation. He raises his clasped hands to bounce his thumbs off the top of his mouth before speaking through his hands. 'But who says you weren't reading them during the exam?'

'Me,' I say.

He releases the first two fingers from the clasp, puts the thumbs between them and points at me, the rest of his hand still clasped and hovering in front of his mouth.

'But, who, except you, knows what really happened in that room? Eh, can you tell me that?'

You've made up your mind already.

He carries on, 'No one gets one hundred per cent in all three papers in our exams. No one. I've checked with the administrative staff and the other teachers, they all confirm it.

That's why they were all looking at me funny.

He releases his hands from their grasp to point his left hand and one finger at the ceiling, I stare at his plush, leather-topped desk, listening to the lies he believes.

'But what really doesn't surprise me, or anyone I spoke to in the staff, is that someone from your background cheats. So we shall have to work on that with you . . . Well, have you anything to say for yourself?'

What's the point? You've already decided I'm thick. What's my background got to do with anything? What's my background got to do with how intelligent I am? You just ain't listening to me. Just look at the bad bits of my record, did you? See what you wanted to see? If you bothered to look at the other records, you would know I haven't missed a day of school, except for the one time when Mum hit me with the kitten heel of her slipper and I bled from my head. You will see that my social worker thinks I am 'highly intelligent'. Not once from my own doing have I missed a day of school. I love school, it's my sanctuary. It's not my fault you gave me an easy exam. It's not. It's not.

I cross my arms, sink into my seat, become the teenager he's expecting.

'Sit up, Deborah.'

'Debbie.'

His hands are now still, splayed out on his thighs as he sits, balanced on the edge of his desk to the side of me, looking down at me.

Bad news is coming, his hands are stock still.

'As I was saying, no one in this school has ever got one hundred per cent in their exam so, sadly, you have let yourself down. The cupboard is full of text books and we can only assume you finished your exams by cross refer-encing these books – very resourceful of you but, in my book, this is still cheating. We've no choice, therefore; we will put you in the lowest stream, with special education and take it from there.'

What? I don't suppose you mean the lowest stream of the year above me? No, of course you don't. Listen, Mister, you are gonna see the worst side of me in this school. My behaviour is gonna be baaad.

The minute I leave the Head's office, I decide to set myself up in business, selling homework to the richer kids. Less than a month later, I can buy so much – proper clothes from Topshop, records, a record player. I laugh – because I was labelled a kid in care, a cheat and thick, no one suspects it's me who is raising the academic standards of the school all by myself. By the end of the first term, the social worker meets me to discuss my upcoming case conference. She notices my new wealth. I trust her and, as I am pleased with what I've achieved, I tell her.

The social worker goes to my case conference and objects to the way I've been treated by the school. She insists that I am given the chance to sit the Maths test again. I do and I get one hundred per cent this time as well. Even though a teacher sits in the room with me as I do calculus and Pythagoras and work out their sums; it makes no difference. They reward my efforts with detention. Because of my background, they decide I somehow got hold of the exam paper, so I knew the answers before sitting down.

Detention teaches me that people in authority don't like to be proven wrong. The social worker tells me to stick with it, tells me that it's all a misunderstanding, that there's more than one way to skin a cat.

In detention, as I write my lines about cheating, I think up words that describe me better. Every time I write: 'I am a cheat, I promise not to cheat and to work hard.'

In my head, I replace the words with: 'I am resilient, I promise to be resourceful and to work hard.'

Again and again, as I write my lines out, I vow never again to let my background hold me back. The skills I have are the skills that will give me an edge, so I can achieve anything. Until, of course, my head gets in the way with: *It's all very well saying that, but do you believe it?*

In response to self-doubt, I write my lines out faster, harder, all the while thinking of the replacement words in my head. I write one set of negative words and think of the strength I get from the positive ones. So focused am I on the new words that the old ones write themselves quickly and I am finished within minutes. For the rest of detention I stare out of the window, dreaming, thinking of the skills I have, and a new voice soon appears: *Yes, of course I believe it.*

PART THREE

SECURE

Hope. 1999.
I'm shattered after my day at the CAB, but still I go back to my files and look at my life.

Mr D – was himself in care from age three to sixteen. Unhappy childhood. No experience of being parented.

As I slowly read these files and my notes again and again, I receive confirmation that the things I thought were secret were already known. I research and research the files and, despite only finding pain in the truth revealed when all I was looking for was solace, I carry on.

My parents were offered help to stop drinking, support in how to care for us, but they were addicts and they chose to live with addiction. Like a disease, what power addiction must have? They chose addiction over us.

I take notes to help me remember and, when I look at them again in the cold light of day, this only serves to remind me that my parents were offered help, when I assumed they had not been.

Shit! They refused help for their addictions. Why did neither of my parents care enough to fight their addiction and learn to care for us?

Reading the files again reinforces this.

My parents cared more about their addiction than they did about us.

It's here in black and white, Mr and Mrs D unable to cope or support the development of their children. They turn up drunk to Social Services meetings, to court, telling the authorities what they think of them for taking their children. For keeping them.

But they didn't take us. I walked into Stokie nick and insisted that me and my brothers weren't going home any more. Home was attacked. Home was not safe. I needed to protect us.

Sitting back on my knees, the realisation of what I've just read runs through my body. Tear-filled eyes overflow and my pain finds another deeper level to burrow inside of me.

Wine flows into me, trying to fill the confused, empty void that, no matter what I seem to do, soon finds itself isolated and alone again.

Yuck, it's warm. Do I care? No, I don't. Finish this, then bed.

Maybe if I sort the papers by location it will help me find the answers I'm looking for.

I pull all the piles together and start again. The beige carpet, with small red and black triangles scattered equally across it, is once again revealed, but not for long.

I spread out my family's history. It is overwhelming, but still I go on.

Somewhere in here is the answer. Was I a disgusting child? Did the staff hate me? How do I keep my kids with me? I must keep my kids with me.

Tonight I read the locations in my head as I place one piece of paper on top of another, to make new piles showing the places my family lived:

Hamilton Road, Hackney, Calakow House Secure Unit. What? This isn't a file about me. Oh my God! This is about Mum.

I read quickly taking it in. Mum – Calakow House Secure Unit as a teenager. It's there in black and white. The papers fall from my hands on to the floor. I bend; I'm still holding the one that tells me the harsh truth. I reach out clenched hands on the files. I mess them all up, so there's no order at all, but I don't let go of the one causing such pain. I hold onto it.

No! No! No!

Tears fall onto the paper. I collapse forwards from the sofa onto the floor, on top of the papers, my body covers them. My fists hit the floor. I'm still clenching the offending paper.

That can't be right. Mum couldn't have been in the same secure unit as me.

I turn my head, still lying on the floor. I open my hand, uncrumple and read the offending piece of paper again. The words have not changed. Mum was in Calakow House, just like me. At a similar age, too.

The same place. The same age. What? No. No. History can't be repeating itself. It is. It is. That dirty old man said I would turn out like my mum. Is history repeating itself? No. I gotta believe I can break the cycle. Generations in care, doesn't mean my kids will be, too.

The social workers, the key workers, they all thought I might have gone on the game. At thirteen? Don't be fuckin stupid. I hated men then. I didn't want to be my mum. I only ran away 'cos no one wanted me; no one wanted to foster me. Why didn't anyone ask me? The only people that want me are the protestors in Trafalgar Square.

I'm back there in my mind. I feel it all again, just like it's happening now.

Trafalgar Square, shaking cans, collecting money.

Night after night, the protesters give me an education. They tell me about world affairs, apartheid, Nelson Mandela, the ANC, segregation. I help them put posters on sticks so they can hold the signs up. Words calling for freedom, calling for sanctions. People from everywhere. I'm just one of them, helping out at the non-stop picket. They've been here since April 1986 and now it's 1988. They just hit 600 days. I write the number of days on posters, then go and shake a tin to collect money. They look out for me – feed me in return for raising money from people on a night out and tourists from all over the world, except not many from South Africa.

I'm part of something.

When I get bored, I go down the road and find some other friends. The homeless people who hang out there. We chat. Drink cider.

Ha ha, love it. Woo hoo, black cab. From Trafalgar Square to home. Travel in style. Great day out. Got loads of money for Mr Mandela. 'Freeeeee Nelson Mandelaaaaa,' we sang. Sat and drank cider in Leicester Square. Wander, wander round the city. Love London.

We arrive back at Chesterfields, I point at the door, mumble to the driver, 'They will have to pay. Got no money, mister.'

He sighs.

The engine of the black cab is ticking over. I fall out of it. *Ooops.*

I stand and go in a zigzag line to bang on the door until Betty opens it. Even though she's got money in her hand, I slur, 'I've no money to pay the man.'

My head is thrown backwards as I walk up the steps past Betty. My mouth catching flies as she pays for my taxi.

'Hope, go to bed. We shall speak in the morning.'

The next morning, me and my sore head have been unable to avoid Betty. I sit in the front room, shutting the curtains, creating my own little den. I have a lot to think about and she's sent me away, out of her sight to do just that. All I know is no one cares. My social worker is coming later. I have to talk to her, too.

Years later, my files show me different – people did care. The staff cared deeply about my welfare. So did my social worker. They were all concerned that I thought it was okay to wander the streets of London at night. The files show that they were worried at what they saw as the re-enactment of my mother's behaviour – black cabs, getting drunk and disappearing.

Black cabs were just a safe way of getting home. They should have just asked me.

Sheets of paper about whether or not I was following her into the same profession.

Why didn't you ask me what I was doing? I was shaking tins, collecting money for the people of South Africa. Sitting with the homeless people. Drinking. But not selling myself. A need to run away, yes, but only from my own head. From my mum turning up at the home, drunk, screaming. I ran away to be part of something normal. But I was not following my mum into her profession. Men disgusted me.

The files tell me concern was mounting, a decision needed to be made. At thirteen, they didn't talk to me, find out what I was doing. At thirteen they sent me away to a secure unit, for my own safety.

It was there that I met Abby. It changed my life.

Hope. 1988.

We're looking out of the window of the secure unit; I've been here a few weeks. My social worker says it's for my own safety.

We chat to pass the time of day, as Fiona, a girl who has been here for over six months, calls it. I'm bored.

A car pulls up; often this is a sign of a new arrival. Fiona shouts to me, 'Come quick, Hope; let's go and have a look.'

It's a day of excitement when someone new arrives at Calakow House Secure Unit, especially if it's their first time in care.

This one walks sure, steady, hard.

She's not a newbie, she knows the score, what to do. She looks like she's in the National Front. That won't go down well with the girls in here . . . Hang on, I've seen her before.

I stand up.

'Do you know her?' Fiona asks.

'Yeah, yeah I do. She's older than me, like everyone here. But, yeah, I've met her before. Always remember a face, me. Now, what's her name? Begins with A . . . Abby, that's it!'

'Abby!' I shout.

She turns round but she doesn't see who's called her. I remember it feeling like a long walk from the car to the first set of locked doors of the secure unit. The nerves, the slightly sick feeling as you realise that this is it.

The adult with Abby guides her towards the main door. The metal gate opens and as Abby steps through, I shout after her, 'Abby, see you in a bit, yeah?'

I don't know if she hears me 'cos, without turning round, she's through the open door, which only stays open long enough for her to step through. Then it closes behind her with a bang of metal on metal and a sound that, no matter how hard you are, sends a shiver of fear through you. It is a reminder that you're locked up.

From here I can hear the heavy metal bolts closing, welcoming her to the new world of Calakow House Secure Unit. Someone walks over my grave.

Abby. Aged sixteen.

The sound of the heavy metal door and a bolt being pulled across sends a shiver through me.

I'm sure I heard someone call my name. But who's here? I hope it's not that girl I was nasty to as I was being sent home the last time, the black one. I didn't expect to be back in Secure, at least not so soon. She can't be here; it's a different place. If I had known I'd be back, I wouldn't have said all that shit to the black cow when I left. I was just tryin' to be hard, play the game. What if it was her? If she's here, then I'm in real trouble.

'Abby, over here, please. We need to take your details.'

I go over to the desk, trying to walk in a manner that matches my clothes, shaved head and earrings.

Fuck. What is this place? Shit, shit, shit. Why was I so stupid as to run away again? Dad wasn't doing such a bad job . . . Why do I want to run away all the time?

While at the desk, I turn to my right and see two women of different sizes standing face to face, talking. As the tall, skinny one talks, the short, fat one turns to look over at me. They are very serious. Another woman is standing behind the desk in front of me asking questions – we both know the answers are already in my file.

What are those two whispering about?

'What the fuck are those two talking about?'

'Mind your language, lady. Respect at this desk and while you are in our care, please. Don't worry, that's just the warden, so I'm sure they aren't talking about you.'

'Yes, they fuckin' are.'

'Abby, what did I say about language and respect, please?'

'Sorry. But they're talking, about me, I mean.'

The skinny one steps forward, I guess she's the warden as the other lady looks like a security guard, even though she's not in a uniform. Keys, never seen such a huge bunch of keys.

'Abby, for your own safety in here we're going to have to give you a change of clothes. You can't be dressed like that in here.'

You see, I fuckin' knew it.

I posture and bounce in front of the desk in my Dr Martens. I tell her, 'Well, you can fuck off. This is me, this is who I am, and I'm proud to be different.'

'We understand that but, for your own safety, we cannot let you go into the secure unit looking like the

National Front. We would also advise you to think seriously about your language and the way you approach things in here, and indeed longer term. We don't discriminate or segregate here, everyone is in this together, and everyone in here, no matter what their colour is, is in our care.'

Her eyes narrow, like she's marking my card, or testing me, I'm not sure which.

I never mentioned anything about who's white or black and who's not. Is she trying to wind me up?

'Nuh, I ain't doing it. You ain't taking my clothes. Besides, Bob Marley, he's one of my favourites. Look, look in my bag. I've a tape of his music. I ain't racist. Just 'cos I dress like this and you think I am, I'm fuckin' not.'

She persists, 'No, but your file says you are a member of the National Front. Look up what they stand for. In here, being a member of the National Front will place you at risk. For your own safety, I can't allow it.'

What? What does it stand for? It's just the name of me gang, name of the gang me mates are in. What, what don't I know? Nah, they've been nothing but nice to me, ever since they first started chatting to me. They look after me, they do.

She doesn't stop. 'Think about this, Abby. You are about to enter a unit where a lot of the girls don't agree with your look and what it stands for, never mind any views you may or may not hold. The way you look is asking for trouble, both on the outside and in here. Look, let's do a deal. Make life easier for yourself. Just while you are in here, wear ordinary clothes and keep your thoughts to yourself about people of a different creed or colour. Deal? Good. That's agreed, then.'

She could've at least waited for me to answer. What she's saying makes sense, but this is me, this is my look, this is who I am. I want to stay like this. I don't give a crap what other people think. I don't wanna give it up. But maybe . . .

She clicks her fingers. The big lady comes forward and, behind her, a doctor.

Search me more like. You won't find anything, I don't have anything on me. Don't do any of that stuff, drugs. I told ya, it's just a look, to protect myself. It's just a look, the way I dress, and I like it, looking so tough.

After the doctor has done her examination, weighed me, measured me, taken notes, looked at me, made me feel uncomfortable, looked in my hair for lice, taken more notes, and asked me to remove my earrings, my nose piercing, under the guise of checking for infection, she's done. She doesn't give me my earrings or nose ring back, but instead hands them to the woman who looks strict and who, in turn, puts them in an envelope.

I'm in my underwear.

I feel naked, exposed. I don't like this; it feels like they're stripping me of my identity. I want to keep the earrings, at least. What are you doing to me? This isn't right, I feel so small.

I'm standing in the middle of the room, stripped of my identity. The doctor doesn't look up from her notes but waves her pen at me and speaks, 'Right, you can get dressed now.'

My clothes have gone. Where I left them, there's a pair of jeans and a plain top.

What the fuck?

I pull myself up; I don't feel so confident as I did in my clothes.

'My clothes, where are they?'

The big lady is back behind the desk, she speaks for the first time, her voice is softer than I would imagine from the look of her.

'As the warden mentioned, Abby, it would be dangerous for you to have your own clothes in here. It's our job to make sure you and the other girls remain safe. So we've provided you with some new clothes for today, and we shall get you some others for tomorrow and the next day. You will get your clothes and jewellery back when you leave here.'

'But it's my identity; you can't strip me of my identity!'

'When we believe your safety, or the safety of the others, is threatened, then, yes, we can.'

Her voice is firm. The staff, the adults here, they know how to pick a fight.

'But you are violating my rights. It's my identity, it's me, it's what I stand for.'

She lets me mouth off, saying nothing in return, lets me go on and on until I see myself in the mirror, a teenage skinhead, naked in her Marks & Spencer pants and bra, in a room where the adults have all the power.

In a smaller voice, I ask, 'What will happen to me if I don't?'

'There will be no privileges. There are battles that you should pick and I would suggest this isn't one of them. The warden always wins. Besides, Hope Daniels has been jumping up and down with excitement to see you. She says you helped her, so you can't be all bad. You wouldn't want to disappoint her now, would you?'

Hope, Hope Daniels – that must've been who called out. Oh, I did wonder what had happened to her. But she's young to be in here. How's she coping? And, besides, that's what the guys at the National Front say, too – pick your battles, know your fights. Is this one I want to fight? It's so unfair what they are doing to me, stripping me of who I am. I still have my skinhead, I can keep that. Show them who I am. My, my . . . Hope Daniels has found herself here. Be nice to see her.

As I'm thinking, I see my hand automatically reaching out, pulling the top over my head, the jeans up my legs, putting socks on, plastic shoes, and covering up part of what I was before I walked though the metal series of doors into the secure unit. Surprisingly, the clothes fit.

Hope. 1988.

Abby and I are roommates. We're both here for a short time to be assessed. The other girls are here because they've got themselves locked up. It's late in the night and I'm tossing and turning in the heat.

Today, a girl kicked off; it was horrible. That girl – the wardens stopped her, they rushed in the room, they did, caught her, pushed her down, she was struggling, bent forwards, arms back, they threw her in her cell. She banged on that small window in the door for hours and hours.

I don't want that to happen to me, the wardens grabbing me, bending me backwards. Better keep myself to myself. I don't want that happening to me. I just want to do the assessments.

My train of thought is interrupted by Abby, 'Hope, you awake?'

'Yeah, can't sleep.'

'Me neither; that was horrible today, wasn't it? I can't help thinking how she is. I was gonna ask ya, is there a way out of here?'

'Nah, I've tried. I tried to get out by the food lift once, but I got stuck there for a few hours until Fiona heard me and pulled me out. What did you do to get in here anyway?'

'I just didn't go to school, hated it. They say I'm "out of parental control". Don't care about anything and I don't give a shit, but I ain't sure how I've ended up here.'

'What happened at school that made you hate it?'

'Dunno. I missed a few lessons as I wanted to hang out with me mates and all of a sudden, without asking me and even though I hadn't done nothing wrong except not be there, they put me in the dunces' fuckin' class. I ain't thick, you know I ain't. Stupidest thing they ever did, as I wasn't gonna go back to school after they did that to me.

'It was shit at home with me mum, really shit, so I went to live with me dad. He couldn't cope with both me and my brother, so Lee, that's my brother, went back to live with Mum. She hasn't let me see Lee since then . . .'

There's quiet in the room for a bit before she carries on.

'One time, when I was in a kids' home they put me in 'cos me dad couldn't cope, they took away my clothes after school. They did that to all the girls, so we just wandered round in our pyjamas and did our hobbies. One of the girls showed me how to knit and I found out that I love it.'

'You, a skinhead who loves knitting?' We laugh.

'But this one weekend, I had an urge to go see me mates, run away, you know? Me mates were having a big party in Kingston and I wanted to see them . . . It had been ages. I was saving money for some wool, so I started walking all the way to London. I got to Kingston in the end. The party was wild, scared me a bit, if I'm honest, as me mates had got into drugs while I was away. I was up for a drink but I'm not into drugs. But this guy, Robert, came in, saying there was an old guy outside with a photo of me, asking everyone and anyone if they'd seen me. The old guy was going round town apparently, in and out the shops, asking everyone, shovin' a photo in their face. I went out to the road and there he was, Dad, looking all worried and asking everyone if they'd seen me.'

'Fuck, he cared? So what did you do to end up in here?'

'I didn't see it like that. But, yeah, I suppose he did. Not sure he still does. My mates, they told me not to bother, that I was better off with them, that Robert liked me and that I'd miss the party if I went home with me dad. I liked it, though, him searchin' for me. But I knew if I went home with Dad, all he would want to do was talk and talk, and analyse where I was going. So boring, there was nothing fun about it, and I wanted fun. So I stayed at the party. Robert and I got on well. Turns out he'd seen Lee at the football. Told me he was in and out of foster care, runs away a lot. It was fun at the party, though, y' know?'

'Kind of. My mum and dad weren't like that, though.'

'The police found me when they raided the party. There were so many drugs there, they took me back to Southend, then took me here. I just wanted to be out with me mates and I want to get back to them now. If there's a way out of here, I'll find it. I just didn't want to go to school and now here I am banged up with other girls who are much worse than me, who have done really bad things. Shit, there's

even a girl who murdered her brother in here. You didn't
do anything like that, did you? Nah, I know you didn't.
Shit. We gotta get out of here, Hope.'

'There isn't a way, I've tried. The windows only open a
tiny bit so you can't get past them. When the fire alarm
goes off, they keep you in the lobby . . . If there was a way,
I'd have found it. Anyway, I'm tired now. Night, Abby.'

'Yeah, night, Hope.'

*Her dad cared but just couldn't cope with her behaviour. Was
that why my dad couldn't cope. 'Cos of me? Is that why he
drank? 'Cos of me?*

Abby. Aged sixteen.

The next morning, we're all getting breakfast and something makes me turn round to look at the door. There's a
girl standing on this side of the door, she's about my age,
she's a black girl I recognise. The same black girl who told
me that if she ever saw me again she'd be my worst
nightmare.

Shit.

She's staring at me with such hatred and she starts to
walk towards me.

Try and ignore her.

The last time I saw this girl was when I left Midrange
Lodge, the secure unit I was at before this one. She was
washing the stairs. I leant down to whisper in her ear and
called her a 'black bitch'. As soon as I'd done it, I felt
ashamed, wanted to say I was sorry. My abuse of her was
false bravado; I didn't think I would be back inside so
soon. I don't know what happened; I just wanted to be
hard. But I think I made a mistake. I wanted to say sorry,

right there and then, say that I didn't mean it, but I couldn't, as I was back to being a skinhead, being hard and part of the National Front. I needed me mates to survive, to fit in, to be like everyone else. As I left the corridor, she called her warning after me. I didn't listen. I'm back inside now and there she is, and even though it's not been long, she's bigger than I remember. She walks past me, leans down and whispers, 'Later, bitch.'

Fuck, that mistake is coming back to haunt me now.

I'm on the stairs. I want to shout out, but the look on the face of the black girl makes me freeze. I'm not able to go up or down, because at both the top and bottom of the stairs there is a pack of girls waiting for me. Fear keeps me where I am. She's staring at me with such hatred.

In an instant she's next to me, like a cheetah selecting its prey. She pushes me downwards. I fall, headfirst down the steps. I am at the bottom of the stairs. Other girls pounce, all converge on me like a pack of hyenas. Their collective weight is on me. I feel my leg being held at the ankle, twisted, being twisted further, the girls suddenly get off but someone still has hold of my leg. Through their feet I can see there's no one to help me. The weight is reapplied quickly, with a number of the girls jumping on my leg. There's a crack, a shooting pain inside me. Then nothing. The girls are off me as quick as they jumped on top of me.

Now the atmosphere changes from anger and revenge to all the girls acting the innocent, all standing round me, calling for an adult. The girl I abused in the last secure unit, who has now got what she wants, smiles. She's standing over me. She hisses down to me, 'Don't you dare say nothin' or we'll kill ya next time, fucking National Front bitch.'

One of the other girls, who moments before was in my face, on top of me with all the rest, is now shouting for help. A woman who comes into the unit to teach us English appears. She calls for one of the staff to come and help.

'Miss, Miss, help, Miss, she fell, fell down the stairs, Miss. I think she's hurt her leg, Miss. She must've fallen, accidental-like. Or fell deliberately, wanted to hurt herself. She did this to herself, Miss, you know like self-harm.'

I don't self harm . . . Not like you. Arghh, my leg hurts.

In a moment, a warden is here, looking down at my twisted leg, asking how I feel, calling for an ambulance, telling me it will be okay, that even though me leg is obviously broken, it will be okay. She gets me as comfy as I can be, has shouted to someone to call for an ambulance. None of the girls move until the teacher is more commanding. Then she turns back to look at me and her voice changes immediately to be soft, caring again, a voice that's now asking how it happened. I respond with a lie that will be good for me.

'I dunno, Miss, I just fell. I must've tripped on the stairs.'

The black girl who I had abused turns and walks out, carrying her success and newly found power over me out of the room.

The warden is asking me if I feel sick, faint, and I nod in response. A blanket and some water are brought but I don't want either. The blanket is placed under my head; someone says I look a bit pale. She instructs people not to move me, or my twisted leg.

'She must've fallen and twisted it under her to have it out of shape like that. Did anyone see what actually happened? How far did she fall?'

From my position on the ground, I don't see anyone move or hear anyone admit to witnessing my 'fall'.

Hope is standing over me now. She, too, has turned ashen white. Her eyes travel from my face to my legs and back again.

'Is it that bad?' I ask.

She nods. The warden goes off to find out where the ambulance is, telling Hope to stay with me. As soon as she's out of earshot, Hope asks, 'What did you do to them?'

Slipping in and out of consciousness, the face of the girls who did this turn into Robert, then Lee. I see Lee.

Lee, where's Lee?

Lee. Aged fourteen.

Me and my mate have a video and some sweets. We've saved up some of our allowance and bunked off school. It took me a while to work out which day to do this and, in the end, it became a decision we made this morning.

I know today is okay to bunk off as the foster carer has gone to see her mum and won't be back until 6 p.m., which is the same time her husband comes home every night after work at the bank.

Their son, who is a bit older than me, has football after school. We don't get on too well as he supports Newcastle and I support Leeds United.

Me and my mate have settled in, our feet are up on the table, and we're warm. We've a film, we've sweets and Coca-Cola.

Heaven.

This place is pretty cool and the social worker is coming to visit on Monday. I am going to say 'thank you' to her for getting me into this place and tell her how much weight I've put on. The foster carer says I am still a little thin, but together we're working on bulking me up to where I should be. She says I have to watch I don't eat too much sugar all at once, as it makes me a little high still 'cos my body isn't ready yet.

But today, me and my mate want to feel a little high as it's both our anniversaries of being in care and being safe. We met on the day the social worker took me to hospital and I never went home. He is still in a kids' home but I'm in foster care as the social worker says it's better for me, one-on-one attention. The case conference agreed with her, so I packed up all my things and, as I didn't have a say, I just moved.

I didn't get my stereo back from Mum's. When I moved here, the foster carer bought me another one, a better one, and some new tapes. I can have this as long as I don't play my music too loud.

The social worker told me Mum must've found the stereo that Dad gave me, hidden in the wardrobe where I told the social worker it was with my cassettes. Mum must've found it on the day I went to hospital, 'cos when the social worker went to get some of my things, including the stereo, she found all the tape from my cassettes pulled out, decorating the floor, along with smashed-up bits of stereo. The social worker also found a hammer, lodged in a hole in the wardrobe door. Mum must've been very upset I'd been taken away, again.

*   *   *

It's getting dark outside when the key is in the lock; I like to listen to the key in this house opening the door, as I know it's followed by a hug and good cheer, not chores and a beating.

Me and my mate are laughing. We've eaten so many sweets, we're high and laughing at the film, the sugar rush and the buzz of being alive.

The voice that says good evening isn't happy. It's the dad, who I am never sure if he likes me or not.

'What are you two doing here?'

'Watching a film.' We both laugh.

'What's going on?'

We both laugh.

'Did you go to school?'

We both laugh.

'My God, have you been sniffing glue in my house? You are so high. You, out.'

He points at my mate, who surges, stands, clasps my hand, mutters it was a good one and skulks away, knowing he's better off out of here. He passes my foster mum in the corridor. She comes in with shopping bags and a smile that disappears on hearing her husband speak.

'Looks like your precious boy has bunked off school and has been sniffing glue.'

There's no point, there's no point. He's arguing with me about something he doesn't know about. Glue my arse. Sugar rush.

She looks gutted.

I am innocent. I'm sorry to hurt you.

He puts his arm around her and her shopping, telling me, 'Go to your room. We shall deal with you when you are off your high.'

You won't get the chance, mate. Big match tomorrow. I was going to watch it on the telly but now you accuse me of something I didn't do . . . I'm off.

Hope. 1989.

Abby and I have both been moved to Beaufort, a community home with education for girls. It's what both our assessments recommended. It's huge. Like really huge. The driveway is a long road, with a forest either side. It reminds me of a haunted house.

While I wanted them to send me to be fostered, it's actually okay 'cos Debbie was here when we arrived, and one of the other girls is in touch with Jackie, and she says she's coming here, too. Glen, the care worker at Beaufort, is laughing with me and Abby, 'You two are inseparable. It's great, but take care when you go into town tomorrow, and please don't get up to too much mischief.'

In unison, we reply, 'We won't.'

'Good, 'cos we've had enough police round here for a while.'

Always wanting to please, to receive praise, I tell Glen what we're getting up to.

'We're going Christmas shopping tomorrow.'

'Oh, you are, are you?'

'Abby is buying her boyfriend, Robert, a present.'

'Hope, shut up, don't tell him anything,' says Abby.

Glen, still looking bemused, asks us to stay where we are in the kitchen for a moment, as he has a couple of questions for Abby about her Christmas present request list. Abby and I look at each other, wondering what she's done now.

Glen returns.

'I didn't ask for anything expensive,' she says.

'I know that; I am just a bit confused.'

'Really?'

'Yes, now, perch yourselves up on those stools, you two. That's it. Abby, look at this list. You have asked for a Bob Marley CD, a free Nelson Mandela poster and a book about the Dalai Lama.'

Abby crosses her arms, 'So? What's wrong with that?'

'Nothing at all. I'm delighted. But I just wanted to ask you if you are aware how much these requests differ from your mode of fashion.'

'Do not.'

'Do so,' I say.

'How?' asks Abby. I decide to shut up, to let them have the conversation.

He really cares.

'Well, the way you dress suggests that you support the National Front.'

'But that group of people are my friends.'

'Or perhaps they just made you feel like you belonged at a time in your life when you felt a bit confused. Maybe they didn't really explain what they stood for. Maybe they gave you something that you needed. You know, all these discussions that we've been having in recent months about racism and the like? That's what the National Front really stand for – they're racists. The world is a better place without racism. The National Front are not good people.'

'I know that, but not the ones I know.'

'Abby, don't be so naive. Think about it. You're a lovely girl and when you came here, you were sent here for your own safety. You had just been attacked and were hobbling on crutches after some black girls had jumped on you. When Hope got here, shortly after you, she told me the reason your leg got broken, because you said you were an anarchist and were mean to a black girl.'

I hang my head, he wasn't meant to tell her I'd told him. He carries on with his speech.

'But yet you listen to Bob Marley and, here, on your Christmas list, it confirms that . . . All I am saying is, have a think about who you really are. I refuse to believe you're a bad person, an anarchist with a skinhead, part of the National Front, with ridiculous tattoo dots on the one hand, but also someone who listens to Bob Marley, doesn't like apartheid and wants to learn about Buddhism. Really? Who is the real you, Abby? Now, lecture over, off you go, you two, and promise me tomorrow you will stay safe?'

Abby is quiet, thoughtful, so I reply, 'We will. We promise.'

Abby. Aged seventeen.
It's doin' my head in. I want to squeeze my head to get all the thoughts out. The staff here say my head feels full like this 'cos my actions and my way of living don't match with my real thoughts.

They say I should be working stuff out for myself now and not listening to those who hate other people just 'cos of the colour of their skin. But they are my friends and when I ran from Dad's because I had no one else, they took me in, they were there, they told me about the world and how Britain was all wrong 'cos of the immigrants coming in and taking our jobs.

The staff here say it's not true and that skin is not a reason to hate people. But they are my friends. But, then again, they say I shouldn't be friends with black people. But why not? Is there something wrong with me that means I can't have the friends I choose? That I want?

I hit my head with my hand. I don't know what to do.

I rub my temples with the ends of my fingers.

Music. Music will help. I got a Bob Marley album for Christmas. He always makes me feel better.

I put the music on, lie down on my bed with my eyes shut and let my mind relax, let the music take me somewhere else, a place where the thoughts disappear and my head isn't doing me in.

Hope. 1989.

What to write. Hope, what you gonna write?

There's a letter sitting on my bed, it's from a guy called Steve. I've been writing to him now for about six months and he's written me back. I write a letter, post it and then a week later the postman comes for me, for me!

I love getting these letters, and the excitement from the other girls has to wait, 'cos I like to read the letter by myself in private first. I'll tell my friend Debbie first, as Abby went home to her dad for the weekend, otherwise I'd tell them together. As I run up the stairs to my room, the girls chant: 'Hope's got a boyfriend. Hope's got a boyfriend.'

I try not to go bright red, but I do, and I run a bit faster to lie on my bed and read over and over again about his life in the real world, running around playing football. We found each other through the penpal pages of *Jackie* magazine. I love the sound of his life. He's a family that seem lovely. He's the same age as me but our lives are very different. He doesn't know I am in care. He's in a world I don't understand, has a life that seems normal, where they go camping and he does stuff with his mum and dad and his sister. He seems to like his family; they do stuff together.

He wouldn't like me, he'd hate me if he knew. I'm not normal. I can't tell him I'm in care, I can't.

He's asking about Beaufort in this letter, he's asking how my house got its name. He thinks this is my house and I am going to keep it that way.

He's asking a lot of questions about my life, about me, about my family. My pen is in my hand, ready over the writing paper Glen gave me, poised, ready to write. My mind is a blank; I don't know what to say . . . I find my hand rubbing the tattoo of his initials, which is really a blue blob you can't read, trying to rub them away.

What can I write? There isn't really much more I can write to him about – the good stuff in my life has been told to him. I'm not going to tell him I'm in care, so what else can I say?

Kids in care are all outsiders in the real world. The rest of the world is too confusing; it's alien to me. My world is alien to him. I ain't going to risk trying to explain it to him. To anyone.

I take a deep breath in and a long one out. The top of my pen is chewed away and the blue ink is coming out of the top. I chuck the pen in the bin and my draft letter to him follows in little ripped-up pieces that I decide mean nothing. His letter is carefully folded, put back in the envelope and placed under a box, under my bed. A wave of sadness overtakes me from my tummy up to my head. But before it takes over, the bedroom door opens and Debbie sticks her head in.

'Secret rendezvous in the bathroom in five mins? Jackie's arrived; she wants a tattoo. She wants her badge of honour. Hope, you comin'?'

I nod. She laughs and carries on speaking, 'You'd better go in and wash up now, Hope, 'cos you got blue all over your face and it don't look like lipstick . . . People will think you have a new tattoo on yer mouth . . . Pen leak while you were thinkin' 'bout what to write to yer boyfriend?'

'He's not my boyfriend; I just finished it. I ain't writin' to him again.'

He was getting too close.

She stares at me for a moment, her mouth goes into a straight line of understanding before she probes in a gentle voice, 'Askin' questions, was he?'

We grin at each other and I reply, 'Yeah, just like you.'

'You'll need a new tattoo to cover those initials. I'll get the kit. See you in five.'

The bathroom is full of girls in the know – me, Debbie and four others. Anyone can call a secret rendezvous and this one is being run by Debbie. She's the perfect organiser. But to get into the meeting, you have to be invited. We've meetings here on all sorts, like finding out about what's going on around the children's home, or to ask the older girls to tell us about things that other kids would maybe learn from their brothers and sisters or their mums and dads. We always meet in the bathroom, and, quite often, someone is having a bath while the meeting is going on. We've spent a long time working out just how much the curtain can be pulled round, so the person in the bath can see but not be seen, except for her head. Today, Jackie is in the bath and our meeting is about getting those that want one a new tattoo.

Since her mum went to jail for what she did to her and her sister, Debbie has, what the children's home staff call 'flourished'. Glen says she's a strength that she should use in life to make something of herself. She's a year older than me and sometimes she's pretty sad 'cos the police didn't get the babysitter for everything he did. He had a good lawyer and Debbie's sister stuck up for him, so he only spent a little time in jail. Now the babysitter lives with her sister and their baby. Her sister doesn't have the same strength 'cos she won't say a word against him and says that Debbie is lying about the babysitter.

I'm watching her now, in our big bathroom, waiting for the secret meeting she's called to start and the tattoo session to begin.

'What do you want, Jackie?'

'I want the dots.'

This statement is greeted with lots of different voices and versions of, 'Oh, yes.' 'Oh, I like that.' 'That will look brill.' 'Go, girl.'

I feel a bit sick.

Does Jackie know what those dots mean?

'How many?'

'Ummm, can I have four on this hand?'

Jackie, no, no – that means all pigs are bastards. No.

'Sure,' says Debbie. I'm not sure if this is a statement or a question.

The excitement in the room is building, high-pitched squeals of agreement and comments about bravery echo off the white tile walls and we all chat about how much we love a new tattoo.

Debbie announces, 'But, girls, girls, as Jackie is still in the bath, Hope needs a new tattoo. We need to get the attention away from those initials and give her something pretty.'

Murmurs, nodding and clapping as teenage girls are jumping up and down in excitement, and Jackie in the bath emits a high-pitched, 'Yes!' The girls crowd round me, pull out my wrist, examining the initials put there six months ago, already merging into one and disappearing, along with my courage to tell him who I really am, to tell him I am in care. One of the girls strokes what's left of his initials, she nods, looks me in the eye and asks, 'What do you want instead, Hope?'

'A flower,' I say and move towards the table where Debbie has set out the pot of Indian ink and a needle.

When she's done, it stings a bit and is bigger than the initials so will be more difficult to hide from Glen. But it's quite pretty; a little flower. Jackie changes her mind about the dots and gets a flower, too. The girls are comparing our home-made tattoos when we realise it's time for lunch.

As soon as I get into the dining room, I slip some of the bread that's on the table at the side of the room into my pocket, to keep for later. I see Jackie doing the same. We smile at each other.

You never know. Biscuits, too, must get one – biscuits last longer than bread. Unless I eat it and don't save it, 'cos I need an extra treat before bed.

I've a selection of goodies in my special food box under my bed. It's a habit that I've not been able to break and knowing the food is there gives a little comfort in the dark of night, when my head takes over and thoughts such as these stop me sleeping:

What happens if they stop looking after me? How will I survive? You can never be too careful. You never know when the food will run out, or stop. Gotta make sure you have a plan. Gotta make sure you have some food for the days there's none, or you need some comfort. Gotta make sure you hide some food.

If things go wrong, at least I know that there's a bit of extra food under the bed to turn to. As my hand reaches out to get some chicken, my new tattoo is revealed, just as Glen walks into the room.

'Hope! What . . .?'

He seems to change his mind about what he was going to say but, either way, I know he's about to give me trouble about something. I turn, put my best cheeky smile on, and my innocent eyes meet his.

He looks mad. What? What have I done?

His hand reaches out to grab mine. I pull it away, stuff it in my pocket. He grabs my wrist, pulls my arm towards him. I protest, telling him he's hurting me when he isn't really. I try to release my wrist from his grip and back away, but he's got a proper hold of me now. He turns my arm over, his eyes fixated on my wrist, until he raises his eyes to mine. I try and avoid his gaze.

'Hope, look at me.'

I don't.

'Hope, look at me, please.'

I do. We stare each other out and I can see he's disappointed, trying to find some words.

'Hope, you will regret this. What's it meant to be?'

'A flower.'

'Really? A flower? It looks like a blue blob to me. You will regret this, mark my words. It's done now but, really, I am so disappointed in you. I don't understand why you girls think these tattoos look so good, or you want a tattoo so much. I know you all have them. I know you all do them to yourselves. But do you sterilise the needle? Do you even think about what this does to you? Why do you follow each other?'

We are all transfixed, watching Glen in full flow, his one-man rant, as we call it. Showing his disappointment, looking round the room at us all, as we hang our heads in shame. He carries on: 'If someone asked, would you jump off a cliff like sheep? Would you? Some of you would. But, you girls, each and every one of you are your own person, and you, Hope, you especially, I thought you had more sense than this. I am disappointed in you. This blue blob is disappointment, that's what it is, Hope, not a flower, or anything else. Now get on with your lunch, all of you. You will regret this, Hope. So stupid.'

Glen leaves the room; we kids finish collecting our lunch and sit quietly. No one dares to say a thing to break the silence. As lunch goes on, the air in the room feels heavy. Normally, lunchtime is a happy, chatty time, with girls of all ages coming together to find out what happened in the morning. But today the only sounds are the knives and forks and, for those who are still learning about cutlery, the spoons, that seem to want to clatter around as our plates are cleared of food.

As I take each mouthful, I see the tattoo on my wrist.

It's there; it will be there for ever. It's a flower; it's not a blue blob. It's beautiful.

My head is right over my plate, my chin in my neck, head down like a bull ready to charge, but I feel broken. I'm thinking about what Glen said. He's disappointed in me.

Why? Why me? Why me more than them? We all did it, why pick on me? Glen must think I'm thick and stupid.

A tear drops into my chicken and gravy.

Gutted.

It's Saturday night in winter so the heating is on and it's hot inside Beaufort.

Despite the heat, all day we've been looking forward to an evening of snuggling up with our blankies on the sofa together.

Looking around the front room, there are girls of all ages – some are playing pool in the other room. As soon as we're called by the sound of 'It's starting', me and my friends Jackie and Debbie all rush to our places and snuggle up with our blankies to watch a new series called *Goodnight Sweetheart*.

Calls of 'Settle down' from one of the night staff, who is watching this episode with us, echo around the room, until we tell her, halfway through the credits, laughing, that she's making more noise than us with her 'Settle downs' and the way she eats her popcorn. Also laughing, she replies, 'Careful, girls, otherwise hot chocolate might not appear tonight.'

Immediately we all simmer down and watch the telly, transfixed.

When the programme is over, we move to the kitchen where the smell of hot milk tells us that the hot chocolate is nearly ready and, to me, it feels almost like Christmas. All the girls in the home are excited as this week we did the first door on the advent calendar and decorated the Christmas tree. We all made our own advent calendars and were given a chocolate button to put behind each door. Mine is standing beside my bed, so each morning I don't forget to open it and have a chocolate treat before breakfast.

We collect our hot chocolates and return to our sofas to discuss the Christmas show we're putting on.

Is this what normal families do?

Looking round me, I see teenage girls snuggled into the sofas, into each other, warm and safe, chatting, laughing, wanting to be heard, tired but not wanting to go to bed, feeling so safe and secure that, even as teenagers, we wander round the home with blankies and baby's dummies in our mouths. It's comforting, even though I was worried about the need to do this at first; the staff constantly reassure me, saying it's OK. It's a phase, they say; all the girls do it, have done it for years. It marks the point when the staff know that things are working, as we start to feel comfortable enough to accept love. They also tell me that when I'm ready I'll grow out of it. All the girls here eventually do. Right now, though, I'm happy, warm, safe. I sit with hot chocolate and a biscuit, my baby's dummy worn as a ring so I can drink the hot chocolate, and my blankie at my chin. A new feeling of security and warmth that, until now, I've never felt. I look at the dummy. One part of my brain speaks to me: *Maybe it's time to get rid of the dummy.* And is immediately answered by: *Not yet, not quite yet.*

Abby. Aged seventeen.
The last weekend I had with my dad didn't go too well. Dad has a new girlfriend and isn't interested in me any more. I didn't get to see Lee and I didn't get any lunch so Glen and I are sitting in the kitchen eating a burger and chips that he cooked for me and him, 'cos I'm a bit mixed-up and confused and he didn't get lunch today either.

'Abby, do you want some salt?'

I shake my head. I shiver as the memory of Mum pouring salt into a glass for me to drink comes back to me.

Glen's face falls, 'I'm sorry, Abby, for a moment I forgot.' He carries on with a brighter voice, 'So, did you watch Mr Mandela being released from prison?'

I nod.

'What do you think about it?'

I shrug.

'Come on, Abby, you're not a typical teenager, by any means. Think for yourself. What did you think of Mr Mandela being released from prison?'

I stare at my food and for a while I say nothing, just eat looking at my plate. Glen doesn't like silence and he has to fill it with something.

'Mr Mandela is a freedom fighter for South Africa. He will end apartheid. Won't that be good? Abby?'

He lets my name hang in the air. I want to fill the gap of silence now, but I don't know what to say. My head is a muddle about what I believe. I am really pleased Mandela is free and gonna get what he wants and South Africa will be less like a war zone; but it's confusing 'cos my friends in the National Front think differently. They were there when I needed them. No one else was. I don't want to let them down.

Glen stands up from the table, puts the kettle on, offers me a cup of tea by showing me a mug and the teabags, but still he doesn't speak. I want him to speak, otherwise I will have to.

'Glen?'

'Yes, Abby.'

'You know when . . . Well, you know how, um, well, how you have one set of friends and then they no longer seem like friends 'cos even though they've been really good people and they looked out for you and all that . . .'

Glen's fingers do a little dance on the work surface, then he turns to face me.

'Yes, I see, I think. What are you trying to ask me, Abby?'

'Well, in South Africa people didn't like each other, the white people and the black people.'

'As I've said before to you, there is no reason for that to be. People are people, whatever their colour.'

Shhhh, let me speak.

'Yes, I get that; it's just that there's a really nice girl at school and, well, now I'm a bit older it seems silly not to have my own friends, like ones I've made myself, rather than just have the friends that my old friends say I can have.'

'Why wouldn't you be friends with her?'

'Well, she's um, she's . . .'

'Black?'

I look down. I nod.

Why did I say that? It's so stupid. She's a great girl; we both like the same music. We both do running. Oh, I wish I could take my question back.

'Abby, how many times do we have to say to you—' Glen stops himself mid-sentence, takes a deep breath and starts a new one. 'Abby, I'm delighted you have a new friend. Does she like the same things as you?'

I nod.

'What do you think about her?'

I shrug. Then, looking down at first, I speak: 'She's really, really nice, funny, can run; she's really clever, too. But I don't know.' Midway through the sentence my eyes start to rise up from looking at the table to stare straight at Glen. I want reassurance when I say, ''Cos my friends in the NF say I shouldn't hang out with people like her.'

He looks back at me, straight in the eye, 'Oh, Abby, be true to yourself. Be true to you and the rest will follow. Let me know what you decide, though, 'cos right now you're on what people call a crossroads in life.'

As he leaves the room he ruffles my hair, smiles and laughs, muttering, 'Nelson Mandela released and a new friend for Abby – both of those sound good to me.'

Hope. 1990.

On the Saturday after Mandela is released, Abby and I rush to get into London, to Oxford Street, to buy birthday cards and an outfit for the party we're going to have for one of the girls in the home. I note Abby hasn't got her nose ring or swastika earrings in today, but I say nothing.

Topshop awaits and we spend hours in the changing rooms with Abby's new friend from school, selecting clothes that we spend our allowance on. Abby's clothes are different from her normal selection of black and dark green. I say nothing except that she looks nice.

The Dr Marten boots are matched with new jeans and a pretty top. She comments that she can't let go of it all at once. But she says that she might grow her hair.

Abby and I decide to head back on the bus, treating ourselves to a McDonald's on the way. We're high on the new clothes and the presents we've bought.

Glen is just leaving to go home as we arrive back at Beaufort. He greets our girly high as he always does, with a big grin and a question about our day. Abby runs with her shopping bags towards him, waves them in the air. Looking very pleased with herself, she dances round him and shouts, 'Glen, I've decided. I am not an anarchist, I am an activist!'

Jackie. Aged fifteen.
It's Friday, and my mum has got permission to have me home; she's beginning to sort herself out. It's just for the weekend, but it's a start.

I am going to see my mum.

My suitcase has been packed and repacked since Wednesday. I've not known what to take, so I empty it and start again. Now I have three outfits for daytime and two for evening. I know there are only two days at the weekend, but I might change my mind about what to wear. As Mum is off the drink and the game, we might actually go for a walk, or maybe to the cinema. Hope and Debbie agree, it's difficult to know what to bring, but they tell me to pack most of the stuff I own and that fits in the case, and then I'll be covered.

My mum has been calling every night this week, except last night, to tell me how excited she is, too.

Why didn't she call last night? Still, I know she's going to be here at 9 a.m. to collect me.

She's also going to meet my boyfriend, Barry, this weekend, too, so I've got to wear the right thing to meet him. He likes to see me in certain clothes that are not too showy, just in case other men like me, so I need to make sure I've those in the case, too. He's twenty and we're waiting until I am of age. He's so gorgeous and he looks after me. His dad taught him to drive and bought him a car so he can drive to college. The car is registered in the name of his dad's business, to keep the insurance down.

Barry is a good driver and, even though he told his Mum and Dad he's passed his test, he hasn't. They believed him and didn't check his papers. We only go for short drives in the car in case the police do a spot check and pick him up. When he's passed his test properly and when I am sixteen, we shall go for longer drives. But that's the future, this is the now, and I only have one sleep to go before I see my mum for the first time outside the children's home, or without a social worker, in years.

I am trying to get to sleep, but am too excited about seeing my mum and my mum meeting Barry. We met when I was at the kids' home in North London, he lived next door. He comes to visit me at Beaufort. I have a photo of him and me together, it's from a photo booth; you get four in a strip. I have two and he's two, so we're always together. One of mine is in my purse and one is on the side of my wardrobe, stuck on with Blu-Tack so I can look at him when my head is on my pillow. The photo was taken last weekend – me and Barry, together for ever. I like that he's happy to wait for me until I am sixteen. Not long now, under a year, but it seems like an age. He's planning something special for my birthday. I reach out to touch his face. In the photo I am wearing the new jacket he bought me that he likes to see me in.

Crap, better remember to pack that jacket. Though I don't see why I should wear what he tells me. Well, better to; I don't want to cause a fuss. He loves me and knows what's best for me. Wearing the jacket and the jeans he likes me to wear, he says, shows him I love him.

Saturday morning is bright with a slight breeze. I wake with thoughts of how Mum has been saving for weeks to show me she's doing okay and that she has treats for me, that we're going to have a weekend shopping, and do all that mother–daughter stuff we should've been doing for years. I imagine it's going to be perfect.

I take my case down to the front door and wait. Miss Smith, the new Principal, comes down the stairs from her flat. We all hate her; she even brings her own plate and cutlery to eat in the dining room, like we are from a different planet. She calls out to me from halfway down the stairs.

'Jackie – where do you think you are going?'

No. No. No. Not today, no, please, not today.

I turn round, she's already right there, inches from my face, spitting as she speaks the 'p'.

'Who told you you had privileges of going home this weekend? Hmmm?'

'I do, Miss, I do.'

'I think not. I hear you didn't do your ironing, or tidy your room this week, so you know that means privileges are cancelled.'

I try not to grimace as spit hits my face again. I try to stay strong.

'But, Miss, this is a special weekend with my mum. It's ages, years, since I have spent time with her on my own.'

Don't mention Barry, it will only make things worse.

'Not a chance, young lady. You know the rules.'

'But, Miss, Mum will be here any minute.'

'Actually, she won't. I called her yesterday morning and told her that things were postponed. Maybe next weekend, if you behave better.'

What? What? You are going to take this weekend away from me, for what? What have I done?

'But, Miss, I did tidy my room, I did do my ironing.'

'No more buts, there's a good girl. This doesn't match the report I got – you did a bit, but not to standard. So, on you go, back upstairs, unpack your things. Your weekend is here. You can help out with some chores and this evening we shall have a film. There's two of you not going home this weekend. You and Hope Daniels. But, you know that she never goes home.'

'But . . . my mum . . . she . . .'

'Yes, she knows. She won't be coming.'

You could've told me yesterday. Why now? Why here? Why wait until I'm ready to leave? Unfair. Unfair.

*   *   *

It's Sunday and it's been a crap weekend. My eyes are sore from crying. Barry has been on the phone all weekend telling me I'm stupid for letting this happen. Every time the phone rings, I know it's him. He says there must be a way out of here and that if I'm a good girl I'll find a way to come and see him.

Why doesn't he come and collect me?

Miss Smith gets me stripping the beds of all the kids who did get to go home, just to remind me that I didn't get to go. This is, she says, punishment for not doing my own ironing properly last week. As if not getting home to see Barry and my mum wasn't enough. Hope is out with Glen and her little brothers, so she isn't here either.

Who told? Who grassed me up?

The washing basket is piled high with sheets of different colours and patterns – pink, blue, yellow, flowers and stars. Sheets that all need different washes. My bed is last to be stripped, tissues that caught my tears last night are strewn all over the floor, between the pillows, under and on top of the sheets – a reminder that I haven't got control of my own life, that any hope or joy and dreams I had about this weekend have been stripped from me, just as I strip beds instead of choosing new make-up and clothes, laughing with my mum.

Mum. Mum.

Before I strip my bed, I pick up a couple of tissues from the floor.

It would be easier to bring the bin over here.

The wastepaper bin is by my suitcase, as I reach to pick up the bin, seeing them together, my hand moves to the right and picks up the suitcase instead.

It's small enough, it will fit.

Quickly, though I am not sure why I feel the need to be quick as I am the only one here right now, I pack some of my stuff into the suitcase, lift out some sheets, drop them onto the floor, then shove the bag in the middle of the washing basket and replace the dirty bed sheets on top of my case to hide it.

That's it, that's how to do it. Run away!

I finish stripping my bed and put it on top of the rest of the washing, with my suitcase inside. In the corridor between the service lift and the kitchen, I meet Miss Smith coming in from her Sunday afternoon walk.

Don't go red. Don't show guilt.

She hardly looks at me as she passes, just says, 'Jackie.' Nods her head and moves on. Not even a hello. I reply equally stiff, like I am in the 1950s, with a nod of my head. I stick my tongue out at her as soon as she passes. No one sees me, but it makes me feel a bit better.

Cold cow. Why did they replace our lovely staff with you? No wonder you couldn't get yourself a husband. No one knows what the rules are any more; you change them just to be cruel. No one can stop me seeing Barry and he'll take me to see my mum. Wait and see what happens after I run away. I'm leaving, with or without your permission.

That night, when everyone is back from their weekend away, I sulk. I eat well and say nothing to no one. My hand reaches out and takes extra food from the sideboard buffet. I put it in my pocket, only stuff that can be eaten easily, like bread and some boiled eggs.

Before everyone got back, I also took a piece of food

from each of the kids who have a secret stash of food in their room. They can't say anything 'cos they ain't meant to have food in their room as there's enough in the larder. But it doesn't work like that for some kids. They learnt before coming into care that if the next meal doesn't appear, there should be a contingency. It doesn't matter how much food there is available downstairs, the fear of starving again is too strong. When stripping the beds, I found that more than half of them have a little box of food hidden under the bed. I only nick a little bit from each, so I hope they won't notice.

Once everyone is asleep, I make my move. The window of the laundry room creaks as it provides my first taste of freedom. I wedge it open with a clothes basket. Lifting my bag onto the window sill is a struggle.

Heavy.

After the third go, focusing on my goal, and some heavy breathing, I get it up onto the ledge and push it through the window, balancing it so I can turn the bag round. I want it to fall on the ground with the wheels up so they don't break.

If I have to walk a long way, I don't want to have to carry the bag.

I follow it out the window, pick up the bag and run through the woods, over a field, down to the road which will take me to the M25, and then to Enfield, where Barry lives. I walk and walk along the hard shoulder, towards Barry and my mum. As I reach the M25, first light is beginning to appear. I look to the sky, which is bringing a morning that will be heavy with grey clouds.

Shit, I forgot my brolly.

Cars are zooming past me as I trundle on, my suitcase trailing behind me. I walk for miles, for hours, anticlockwise in the wet, lorries spraying me with muddy water that I try and jump out of the way of, unsuccessfully, my language going downhill as I walk. Along the M25 I walk, squeezing through the sections with roadworks and no hard shoulder, running with horns blasting.

Junction after junction on the M25 passes and I realise I don't know how far round Enfield is from the kids' home in Essex. I see a sign telling me there's over 20 miles to go.

It's so cold. It's wet. But Barry is at the other end of this.

My mum lives in Hertfordshire now, Potters Bar, I think, so as I walk I convince myself that it will all be worth it. Barry will offer to drive me to see her, even if he doesn't have his licence yet and doesn't want to drive long distances.

Suddenly a car is pulling up in front of me. It parks at a diagonal, blocking my way.

Hope. 1990.

Debbie and I are pacing in the bathroom. One of the old children's home girls, who married an older bloke she met getting off the train, has called us to ask us to a party with a bunch of men she knows. She says parties with adults are fun. It means running away; it means being out all night. I'm nervous about the party but I do want to run away 'cos I hate it here now, especially since Abby turned eighteen and left care for good and the new Principal has started picking on me. For no reason, the Principal moved me upstairs away from everyone I like. I want to run, but I don't really want to go with these men. The men freak me out. They've managed to find a way to bypass the main switchboard. Whenever the phone on the landing rings, my skin crawls.

Debbie says it'll be fun, and it's okay 'cos one of the other girls is married to one of the guys. Still I protest.

'But they're well old. At least thirty.'

'It'll be great; it's just a party. And we'll get some drink and stuff. They're coming to collect us in their car. It'll be wicked! Come on, it's nice to get some attention. Don't make me go on my own.'

The flat the girl and the two men live in, with her brother and another older girl, is small. The party is just me, Debbie, and the two blokes who have been calling us at the home, tellin' us we're special so we begin to believe it. One of them is married to the girl who left care and who introduced us. She isn't around.

My hands are sweating but I don't know why, and I try to dry them on the side of my jeans, but they start sweating again as soon as I've done so. Debbie is getting attention from one of the old blokes; he's sitting next to her on the sofa. I sit on an armchair, far away from them all. There's music, there's smoking and so much drink it goes to my head. I feel a bit hazy a bit too quickly. I don't know why. They want to play a game of strip poker. I don't want to. I tell them this.

'Come on, it'll be fun,' says Debbie.

There's a click at the door. Through the drink I'm not sure what it is, but I shiver at the noise. The guys don't take their eyes off us. I get told not to be boring and to relax. An older man's hand reaches out, rubs my shoulder.

Get yer hands off me.

We play. As we lose hand after hand of strip poker, I look to Debbie. She's uncomfortable now, too.

As the guys are laughing, preparing us another drink from the sideboard, everything we do seems to be met with praise. I see Debbie likes it a lot, but I'm not sure. I like the presents they give us and the words that come out of their mouths are kind and nice. They think we are beautiful. Still, I was expecting a bigger party than this, and they are old.

I lean over and whisper, 'Can we go?'

She shakes her head, 'I think they locked the door.'

What? Oh, no. Scared.

At the same time, an outside door slams shut. The handle of the door to our room moves, but the door doesn't open.

It's locked. Debbie's right.

There's banging on the wall, on the door. A girl screaming, words directed at one of the men in the room.

'Open this fuckin' door. What ya all doing in there?'

Screaming, banging, the men turn on us, tell us to keep playing poker. I try but my hand is shaking.

What's happening? Why is she so mad?

The husband of the girl on the other side of the door replies, 'Nothin' darlin', we're just having a little drink, a bit of fun.'

She screams, calls to someone else. The door is being beaten with something heavy. There's thumping, the girl is shouting, 'Break the door down.' A man is telling her that he's trying. Debbie and I are crying, asking the men to open the door. They tell us it's okay, she's just a bit jealous for no reason. They stare at us, like the men who stare at my mum. A look in their eyes that I don't like. Don't trust.

I want to go home. Back to the home.

She says her brother has a baseball bat. He's using it on the door.

There are sirens. There are other footsteps. A cry of 'Police!' A girl's voice through sobs saying that her husband has got two young girls in there with him.

One of the men tells us to get dressed in a harsh voice. The other one is listening through the door. When we're clothed, they open the door to find four police, the man's young wife and her brother. One of the policemen is holding a metal baseball bat, a bag is wrapped round it.

Evidence?

The men who locked us in speak; their voices switch back to being soft, kind, smooth like honey. The same voices they use on the phone when they try to persuade us to meet them. The police believe them, too.

We get a lift home in the police car, the police accepting the whole situation as being a misunderstanding.

No one thinks to ask us what went on, how these older men got access to us. No one thinks to ask why we would want to be in a flat with old men. Ask how one of those men married a girl half his age. All from care. Yet that night, the wife sends accusations our way about trying to steal her husband.

Jackie. Aged fifteen.

The van is slowing down beside me, it's not the police. Shit, is it the children's home? Oh no, have they caught me? I don't want to go back.

The window rolls down and a hand reaches out, saying, 'Come on.' For the first time what I am attempting to do hits me. The danger I have placed myself in washes over me, soaks into my bones with the pounding rain.

What have I done? Who is this person? What if they are a murderer? What am I doing? Who are you? I don't know the van. There's a logo – what does it say? Something to do with deliveries.

I freeze, standing in the rain, clutching my suitcase with the wheels, surprisingly, still intact. I stare through the drizzle, my hair wet and pressed against my skin. The driver jumps out, she's dressed in a blue jacket with yellow high-visibility stripes. She signals for me to come over. I can't go back against the traffic, so I do.

If she tries anything, I'll whack her with my case. Get ready.

'I saw you earlier this morning. I'm a delivery person for meals on wheels. About an hour ago, I saw you again. Walking the M25? What are you doing? After my last delivery, I decided to come and find you on my way home, see if I can give you a lift somewhere, get you out of the rain. What are you doing? Where are you going?'

In a small voice I reply, 'Trying to get to Enfield.'

'Okay, that's good, it's on my way. Shove your case in the back, I'll give you a lift as far as I can, to the A10. You can get a bus the rest of the way from there. Come on, now, I'm meals on wheels, I'm not going to kill you!'

She laughs. Suddenly I feel the need to be warm and dry. I want to be driven, not walking.

Although somehow I know I am safe, the thought still passes through my head: *If she tries to kill me, so what? She's old, I can fight her off.*

*   *   *

The radio is playing and the heater is on full blast. Despite this, I am able to speak by raising my voice as I dry my hair and warm up in the car. I keep apologising for causing the car windows to steam up with condensation, making it difficult for Sandra to drive, but she wipes the window with a laugh and I know I am not about to be murdered.

I tell her I am running away from a children's home to a boyfriend who doesn't have a driving licence but will take me to see my mum all the same. How the children's home has a new manager who gets a kick out of stopping us going home for the weekend. It was my turn this weekend and so I'm running away instead, 'cos she can't stop me. For over twenty miles I tell her about my life, about how my mum was a prostitute, about how I had to run away down the road naked in Aberdeen, how Barry tells me what to wear sometimes and, even though this annoys me, I love him, I really do.

I don't take breath and Sandra just watches the wet road, negotiates the traffic, and nods now and again. It's like she's letting me get all the frustration out; then, when I've run out of words, she tells me how hard it must be, but I shouldn't put myself in so much danger, and should value myself more, especially in regards to Barry, in fact any man. As she finishes this sentence, we arrive at the junction of the A10 and the M25. She's off the exit, pulling over at a bus stop where a bus that's going to Enfield will be here soon. As I get my bag out the back, she gets herself out the front, hands me a Crunchie, some money for the bus and a telephone number.

'Now, that's my number. You must call me; let me know how you are. You will, won't you?'

I nod, knowing I won't, and knowing I'll feel bad about it later, and long into the future; something else to beat myself up about.

Barry's brother's flat, where Barry lives, has all the lights on. It's a Monday night but the loud music makes it sound like there's a party. I ring the bell, no one hears. I am still soaked to the skin, despite Sandra's car heater.

I ring the bell again and keep my finger on it.

A window opens above my head, a head and an unclothed top half of a man's body holding a can of something that looks like beer comes out the window, followed by, 'No, we ain't turning the music down, it's a free— Jackie?'

It's Barry. When he realises it's me, he looks panicked. He disappears inside the window, then reappears, suddenly calm.

'Hold on, Jackie, I'm coming down. Hang on, I'll open the door. Push when it buzzes. Stay there, I'll help you with your case.'

I do and I stand waiting in the corridor, wondering why the panic, and why at 8 o'clock at night my boyfriend isn't wearing a T-shirt. He's down the stairs in a few minutes, dressed again. He hugs me, calls me Baby, says it's great to see me, and kisses me. He tastes of booze and cigarettes.

'When did you start smoking?'

'Never mind that, great to see you. What are you doing here? Great to see you, really.'

'I've run away, they wouldn't let me see you or my mum, so I ran away. I'm cold and wet and it's horrid. I need a bath.'

'Okay, okay, come on up, slowly, now, you're cold.'

He keeps looking up the stairs, beyond where we're walking.

What's going on?

We walk slowly. He takes my bag, stops to ask me a question. A girl, about my age but a little older, sixteen maybe, passes us on the stairs. She looks at him. He doesn't look back but he tenses. She's past us and looks back again. They think I don't see, but I do.

Entering the flat, his brother isn't there 'cos he's out at the dogs. I am relieved as it means it'll just be us. He picks up an ashtray and I see the menthol cigarette with red lipstick on the filter that matches the girl on the stairs.

What's going on?

Barry is super attentive, tidying the ashtray, running me a bath. There's bath bubbles from his brother's ex somewhere . . . He finds them. Gives me a hot cup of tea, sweet with sugar. I feel in a daze. The walk, walking to him, the girl. Who is she?

I lie in the bath with his promises of everything being tidy when I get out. I hear him running around putting things in cupboards, opening windows to get rid of the smoke as he knows I don't like it.

Running, running, why are you running around after me? You don't do that.

As I lie in the bath, defrosting, feeling the chill of my bones disappearing, I hear him rabbiting on.

'I've some great plans for your sixteenth birthday, you know, when we're going to be together properly, for the first time. Tonight you can stay here and, not to worry, I will sleep on the sofa, so you know I mean it. We've known each other too long to let this go now.'

He carries on, his voice higher. 'But maybe we can have a little cuddle before we fall asleep. That would be nice, wouldn't it? Maybe we can share a little together time, after your nice bath.'

'What do you mean about letting this go?' I call from the bath.

He replies in an even higher voice, 'No, you misheard me. I mean that, even though you're here and staying overnight, we've waited this long, we should wait until you're sixteen, like we agreed. Just a little cuddle, maybe? But you can have my room, and I shall sleep on the sofa.'

I smile. He does make it all seem better.

Wrapped in a towel and feeling warm and safe, I ask him who the girl on the stairs was. Why was he naked when he leant out the window? Who had smoked the cigarette and left lipstick on the end? Had he started cross-dressing? I try to laugh, to make light of it. Before I can ask my next question, he thumps me. I fly across the bedroom onto the bed. He's across at me in a moment. Pinning me down with his legs. He lifts his hand into a fist again. I stare at him, thinking: *Go on, I dare you.*

Within seconds, he comes back to being the Barry I know, melts into me, hugging me. He's lying on top of me, kissing me, saying sorry and that it won't happen again. In moments we're kissing each other, he's tender, we're touching each other and he's telling me how beautiful I am. He stops. He looks into my eyes, telling me we should wait until I'm sixteen. He pulls the towel back over me and just holds me until I say that I believe him when he says hitting me was a mistake, a one-off.

I believe you, I do. I shouldn't have asked you so many questions.

Hope. 1990.

The phone rings; its sharp noise brings a shiver to my spine.

Tell them I'm not 'ere. Tell them, please.

'Hope, it's for you.'

No. No. No.

It's that smooth voice again, telling me he wants to see me. 'You're so special. I saved ya from being beaten by me brother-in-law. You can trust me. Don't worry, I'll protect ya. I'm the one that saved ya.'

He carries on, telling me that it will be a laugh. That he and his mate will come and meet me in the woods at the back of the house and that I should bring my lovely young friend.

'Don't worry about staying out, no one will miss ya. But I'll miss ya, if you're not here. You owe me 'cos I saved ya from a beatin'.'

Why do I feel like I have to go? Why can't I say no? I want to say no. What's going on? I'm so confused.

He'll find somewhere for the four of us to stay, he says. He knows I need to get out, to have some fun. He understands that I feel cooped up in here, that I feel a bit suffocated with all the pressure. Would I like to get away? Yes? Then he can help me with this, because he understands. He'll bring some drink and I should bring Debbie. The voice is smooth, but whiney. Am I there? Am I listening?

'Yes, I am listening.'

*   *   *

'Careful, Debbie, open the window some more. That's it.'

We jump. We run to the woods, the moonlight shining our way. Two men in the woods, waiting. The men are breathing a bit funny, but I can't quite put my finger on what's different. Each man reaches out, takes a hand. One older man, each holding the hand of a teenage girl. They seem excited. Pleased. Mine goes to kiss me on the cheek. I recoil back. He looks at me with a different look; in the moonlight it's harder than the voice on the phone.

I feel sick, trapped by you. You are ugly. Ow! Don't grab me like that, you're hurting me. Do I have to go with you? I feel I have to go with you, but I don't know why.

They take us to a house in Camden. It's dark, derelict. There's nothing here. It smells of piss. Two new mattresses are in one room and an old, beat-up sofa is in another. There's a lot of drink.

Suits me.

We accept a can each. We dance to some music on the radio. I feel woozy. I can't focus.

Why can't I focus?

When I open my eyes, I am on one of the mattresses; the man is standing next to me. I pat myself; I am fully clothed. I can't focus, though. Why can't I focus?

'Don't worry,' a voice says. 'I want you to be awake.'

He's stroking my hair.

Get off, get off. What have you given me?

'Where's Debbie?'

'She's in the next room. My mate got sick with all the drink. He had to go home.'

'So it's just you and me?'

'You've been sleeping. Come on now, come over here.'

My eyes widen. Suddenly I am sober.

I don't know what you are doing, but I don't want to be here with you.

I smile at him.

'Can I go to the toilet first, please? I need a wee.'

His face changes, expressionless. His voice is flat.

'Sure, I can wait a bit longer.'

I go out into the corridor, into the room where Debbie is and shake her awake. I tell her I don't want this. We run. She wants to go back to the children's home. I want to stay out a bit longer. Clear my head, go for a walk. She gets on the bus. I go in search of some more drink. I find a squat. I join the party. Things are fading in and out. Daytime, nighttime. Dark, then sunlight again.

Debbie. Aged sixteen.

I'm pacing up and down the bathroom.

Hope hasn't come back since we were in Camden together. No one knows where she is.

Come back. Come back. You've been away for days.

But it's not just Hope and me escaping from those two. Now I'm involved in something else. Girls are being taken away in fancy cars to meet older men. This has been going on for months and months apparently.

Why didn't we know? Why didn't we see what was happening to the other girls?

I went last night with them. A party. At first it was fancy, a posh house, lots of booze. Then there was an introduction. A man tickled me. Asked me if I like being tickled.

Asked me if I wanted a present from him. I ran to the bathroom. Sick. Covered the nice marble bathroom in sick.

The babysitter used to tickle me. The babysitter gave me presents.

The girls disappeared for a while with men, all older. No one our age. No one wants to be with me 'cos I smell of sick. Next time, they say. She's good. She's young. She's pretty.

I'm here. Don't speak about me like I ain't.

It ends quickly. As soon as the men come out of the rooms the other girls were in, the party stops. Some money is exchanged.

They're using them.

The men give us a lift home, they say next time I'll need to join in. They stop the car, give each of the girls some spending money.

Not me.

The guys say the girls did well. The girls smile, grateful for praise.

They drop us off, ring the bell at Beaufort. They make sure we get inside. They say to Glen that they found us getting drunk in London, thought they should bring us back.

What the fuck do you care? You men don't care about us. You just want to fuck a young girl. I don't like it. I don't like what I've been told I have to do. How do I get away? I feel sick, trapped. I want to cry.

I don't know what to do. I'm pacing the bathroom floor. The staff will be furious with me and blame me for getting myself into this.

I am letting everyone down.

They'll think I am a slag. I feel like a slag. It's not just these party guys, there are the two Hope and I went off with.

How do I get out of this? Tell Glen. You have to tell Glen.

Within forty-eight hours, four other girls and I are in a minibus, each with our own social worker. We get interviewed by the police. Say nothing. Our things are packed for us. We're moved. I am moved to the north of England. I don't know where the others are placed.

I tell Glen to say goodbye to Hope for me.

Hope. 1990.
I'm walking next to Camden Lock. I don't care what happens, but I need some glue. Love a bit of glue to get out of it. I gotta rob some. I turn a corner, straight into something black. A copper. He's got hold of my arm. I'm still out of it.

'Piss off, copper.'

He takes me back to the station. Apparently I'm on a missing person's list. I've been gone for four days. I raise my eyebrows. No shit.

When I get back to Beaufort, five girls have been moved on. Including Debbie. My heart breaks. Again.

They hate me, they hate me, they hate me. I hate me. They sent my friends away. They've taken my new family from me. They hate me. Why did they move me upstairs? Why are they stopping me from seeing the people downstairs? Why can't I see my key worker, Glen? I hate them.

It's been six months since the new Principal at Beaufort decided to move me away from everyone I know and had come to love over the last few years. She moved me upstairs, stopping all contact with those who knew me. The boxes in my room haven't been unpacked.

What've I done to make her do this?

There's a bottle of vodka on the floor, another one in my hand.

I don't give a shit. I hate myself. Life isn't worth living.

I try and focus on the boxes, which just remind me how much the Principal hates me. I think about the struggle I've had to get moved back to the people who care for me, just downstairs. I failed. I have to stay up here.

They want rid of me. They hate me. Well, I'll show them. If they don't want me, I don't want them.

Raising myself up from sitting on the bed, with my only friend, vodka, I stumble over to the biggest box in the corner of my room, the one that holds most of my stuff. It's next to the chest of drawers they put in here and I've never used. Before I reach the other side of the room, I lean forward, bending my torso, my arm outstretched, holding the bottle neck in front of me, attempting to place it on top of the surface. I wobble and miss. I almost drop the bottle, fall sideways and knock against the wall. I reach out again with my free hand to steady myself on the corner of the drawers, with my other hand I manage to place the vodka bottle on the empty chest of drawers. My bum is pushing outwards like a toddler on unsteady legs. I haul myself up and side-step towards my box. I'm quite pleased with myself, but not enough to stop my thoughts.

No one loves you. You are on your own. It's all shit. They moved you here because you are shit and don't deserve to be loved.

Rummaging, pulling things out, dropping them on the floor. Then I find them. Paracetamol. They take pain away.

Perfect. This is the way to do it, to take all the troubles away. The bottle of pills is what needs to happen. This is it, then. They hate me, I hate me. No point in going on. No one listens to me. No one wants to hear me.

I shuffle back grasping the bottle of pills to where the vodka bottle is calling me. I empty all the tablets out onto the surface of the dressing table. Take the lid off the vodka. I'm standing tall now. I pick up a handful of Paracetamol, throw them in my mouth, wash down with vodka. Another handful, more vodka. The third handful and a big swig of vodka sees the last of the pills away. I gag but push the pills back down. Another swig makes me a bit more woozy than drunk.

That's it, that's right. Wash it down now. The pain will soon go. Lie down on the bed. Lie down. Sleep now, sleep.

My head is pounding, I feel drowsy. It's still dark. My room is hot and I feel my nose curling up, reacting to a fusty smell that's surrounding me.

Something stinks.

I'm lying in bed, face up, my head on the pillow. One hand is above my head, it seems too heavy to lift so I slide it down, in a sweeping motion, over the pillow, towards the covers. My hand hits something cold, wet, sticky.

Yuck, what's that? Why do I feel so hot? Shit, I took some pills. Why did I take pills?

I reach back and out with my hand, searching for a lamp, but with my unpacked boxes, I only find empty space. It takes me a moment to put two and two together.

Lamp in a box . . . Have to get up . . . Light switch . . . Have to get up . . . Open window . . . Body heavy . . . Body sore . . . Head thumpin' . . .

I swing my legs round on to the floor, hauling myself up with my arms. I put my hand down onto the covers to steady myself, again, and a hand lands in the cold and sticky stuff.

Ah, shit.

My feet hit the floor with a thud; they feel heavy, too. I'm covered in sweat. I've an urge to push myself up, to stand, to move towards the door. I need to move, to take control of myself. I swing my feet round, place them on the floor. I spin, still woozy. Feet are on the ground now, there's something else cold under and between my feet. It feels like liquid, but thicker. It's so dark in the room, so hot I'm sweating. I want the light. I move myself forward, but my body doesn't respond, I lose balance, fall forwards, face first, my hand reaches out to grab the bed, to try and slow myself down. I fall along the side of the bed, there's a thud on the floor, which I know is me hitting the carpet and the bed at the same time.

Lie here for a bit. Get up and try again in a sec.

The back of my head is touching the side of the bed; my face is in the cold stuff on the floor. Dazed, I just want to curl up again and go to sleep.

Sleep. Sleep.

My bedroom door opens. From my position on the floor I see feet in slippers, with light behind. A voice which seems distant, muffled; I can't tell who it is but I think they're telling me it's 3 a.m. in the morning and what am I doing waking everyone up. Then my bedroom light is switched on and there's a moment's silence. The feet leave and there seems to be a lot of knocking and shouting in the corridors, vague voices drift to me.

'Hope's not well ... There's a bottle of pills and vodka . . .'

A different voice, older.

'What has Hope taken? An overdose? What? Are you saying she's taken something? Where is she?'

My head is lolling around. I'm trying to focus on what's going on. There's a bright light in the room, up high.

Switch it off, switch it off, wanna sleep.

More feet come, different pairs. I add to the pile of vomit on the floor and cover a pair of slippers with feet in, giving them a new pattern. I slump back. I wanna sleep. I close my eyes, then nothing.

Someone is stroking my forehead. I've been vaguely aware of them for the last few hours as I drift in and out of sleep, unable to respond as a cold cloth is brought to my forehead, kind words reaching beyond my hazed state.

My room smells fresh and clean like the spring laundry. My memory jumps back to me and Jackie in the laundry, spinning with sheets and towels. For a moment I think it's her sitting by my bed but I force myself to focus and see it's one of the other girls from upstairs who I don't know that well, Sally. She's staring at me, looking a little confused. When she sees my eyes are open, she smiles, asks how I am. A voice that's so gentle, I know she's gonna grow up and work in childcare. That's her wish, she told me.

The door opens and Laura, one of the staff, comes in. She places some orange squash on the table. Looks over at me and Sally. A soft, Scottish accent speaks, 'Ah, the patient is awake, then.'

I smile, Sally nods.

'You gave us quite a fright, Hope. This one, she's been sitting by your bed since we discovered you. Mopping your brow, giving you water and juice. Hasn't left your side. In fact, she refuses to leave you. You will need to be checked out by the doctor again but when he came this morning, he said that luckily it seems you threw all the pills and vodka up before they could do you any damage. What were you thinking? All those pills and no damage except a room full of sick that Sally here has cleared up for you, neglecting her own sleep and studies. Lucky for you that she's here, and lucky for us.'

Laura smiles and carries on with what we girls call a 'Laura monologue'. It's one of the big words we learnt at school.

'You have a lot to be thankful for, Hope Daniels. A lot. Well, now you are awake, you will also have a meeting with the Principal. I've been told to let her know when you are up to it, so how about I set that meeting up for tomorrow? You should be up and about by then. I'll give you another day in bed. Then, Hope Daniels, we shall all just have to get on with it. Life is hard but you have a lot to be thankful for, so no more of this nonsense. Just live with it and enjoy what you can. And when you are all better, let's have a think about unpacking these boxes and making this room more of a home for you. What do you think?'

Sally and I look at each other. We trade a smile; Laura is like the mum neither of us had but every child should and, in that moment, I make her part of my extended family, too.

But, if we'd known what was coming over the next few months, I would've stayed sick in bed. As it turns out, any thoughts of unpacking my boxes were not to be.

'Hope, you are out of control.'

The Principal's office hasn't changed since the last time I was in here when she told me they were moving me upstairs. She said it would be better for me.

Got that wrong, didn't ya?

The other thing that's the same as last time is the people – The Principal, my social worker and me.

This isn't gonna be good.

The Principal, my least favourite person in the world, speaks at me, not to me: 'Hope, as I said, you are seriously out of control. We can't do any more for you than we have done.'

Believe that, do ya? You know nothing of what you have done. NOTHING. Ruined everything, you did. Took away my family. Moved me upstairs, separated me from everyone. Took everyone away. Banned me from coming downstairs, even for a visit. Why do you think I changed? You, you changed me. You.

I can't believe what she's telling me.

'Hope, this placement is no longer suitable for you.'

This isn't a placement, this is my home. All was okay before you came.

'I've already discussed it with social work . . .'

Without me? Whose life is it, anyway? What's that? You're chucking me out? Bitch.

'I, we, have, um, agreed to, um . . .'

Why are you stuttering? Go on, tell me. As if you can do anything worse to me than chucking me out . . .

'I, I mean, we,' she looks at my social worker, who obviously doesn't want to be here, has just been told this, just like me, 'are giving you twenty-eight days' notice to find yourself somewhere else to live. Hope, I know you have always wanted to be fostered, so maybe now is the time. Social Services will help you. Twenty-eight days, so don't use all that time to pack.' She pauses for effect. 'Ah, no, you don't need to pack, do you? It's all still in boxes, isn't it? Good, good. Off you go, then.'

A hand is waving me out of the room. I stare at her in silence. I am so drained from the experience of trying to end my life, so taken over by pills and drugs, my mouth freezes.

I can't say anything.

I stand, I turn to leave.

I hate you.

I'm standing at the bottom of the drive of a new house. It's late in the evening. In the last four months, I've run away from three sets of foster parents, this is the fourth in as many months.

These placements have only lasted days, the most a few weeks; in between I've been staying at a hostel in Hackney.

I don't want to go back to the hostel. I've felt so lost away from Beaufort, from children's homes. Foster care isn't what I expected, I don't wanna call 'em homes, 'cos they ain't. They are placements. But I gotta make this one work.

My foster mother takes some of the black bin bags that everyone in care uses to carry their things when they move house, and asks, 'What's this, then?'

'My dirty washing from previous foster placements.'

I hang my head.

'Not a bother, we shall get these washed for you, then. No, no, dear, I'll do it.'

Ohhh, you seem nice. Happy you're doing that for me. Good start. I might like it here, after all.

'Come on, I shall make you a cuppa, then I shall pop a few washes on, get this stuff clean.'

We walk through the house, meeting her kids and other foster kids on the way. They are friendly, playing a board game. Lee, Abby's little brother, is here, too. We laugh, say it's a small world. I walk through the house to the kitchen at the back. Every room is warm. The heating is on. She tells them all, now they've seen me, it's ten minutes to bedtime. She smiles at the social worker, who realises the time and leaves.

She seems nice but, yuck, her house is very, very dirty.

The dust in the kitchen has turned to fur. She puts on the kettle, makes herself busy as she moves my washing from the bags into the machine. I look around, think about where I am.

I've waited so long for this, so what if it's a bit dirty? It's only a bit of dirt. If this is the worst thing I gotta worry about, then I'm cool. The last few months I've felt totally lost. I have to make this work, otherwise I'm going to a hostel back in Hackney and I don't want that – no way.

I've my own room here. I curl up, warm in my bed on my first night. My tummy is full. I am so excited I can't get to sleep

At last. At last. Love it. It's so cosy here. The family seem lovely. It's gonna be good.

My foster mum pops her head round the door.

'Everything all right, Hope? Got everything you need? Get to sleep now, you have to go back to college tomorrow.'

'Yes, all's really good. Thanks. Night.'

'Night-night, dear.'

Sitting outside college waiting to go into class, my head is full of money. My head is running overtime.

Gotta get a car. Need to get myself a new job.

My thoughts are interrupted by my psychology teacher.

'Hope, why haven't you been at college? You need to be here, you know. I'm very disappointed you haven't been here much. Are you back for good? Or are you going to take the mickey again?'

'Do ya know what? I'm on me fourth set of foster parents in four months, Sir. Give me a break, will ya?'

His face looks shocked. Sad. 'I'm really sorry, Hope. I had no idea. Tell you what, if you're up for it, we can give you some extra time after college, to help you with your work. How does that sound?'

I get tears in my eyes at his response and nod.

'Thanks, Sir, that would be great.'

Jackie. Aged fifteen.

I am leaning against the phone in the corridor at Beaufort, the phone against my ear. Tears are rolling down my face. Barry's voice is in my ear. 'I'll kill myself if you don't come back to me. I need you. Jackie, are you there? I am sorry. I love you. Are you there?'

'Yes.'

'Come back to me, yeah?'

'Yes, okay then.'

The light in these bathroom mirrors makes me look old. I push a big lump of air out of my lungs, knowing what I have to do, despite every part of me wanting to fight it. I just don't have the energy to do anything, let alone think for myself.

I hide in the bathroom until after lights out. I go back to my room, hoping Sally, who I now share with, is asleep.

I know my shoulders are bent, but I try to hide the tears; my sniffing which gives away my fear over the future. I feel like I need to cut myself off from these emotions, hide the feelings so there are none, so I am numb.

Find a way to survive. Who else would want me?

A voice comes from the darkness, 'Jackie, you okay?'

'Yeah.'

'Jackie, tell the staff, tell Glen. They will know what to do.'

'There's nothing wrong.'

'But—'

I cut her off, sharply, a bit too loudly. 'Shut up, I told you there's nothing wrong. Barry loves me.'

I hear her mumble, 'Love isn't hitting, even I know that.'

'Shut up, I told you.'

A few days later, Barry's parents come and collect me from the safety of the children's home. They reassure social services that they will look after me. They tell Social Services that I will live with them. They lie. They've found us a flat; Barry and I will live together. He's forgotten his promise about waiting until I was sixteen.

Barry and his mum and dad and me, we speak with Social Services. No one speaks with me on my own. It's agreed – I can stay with Barry and his family, as long as I call Social Services once a week. I want to tell them that his mum and dad don't live with us. That we live on our own. That his parents got us a flat. That I am a prisoner. That Barry is nothing like I thought he was. But I am too scared to speak.

I go for milk. I'm in the street. I bump into a girl from my old children's home. I speak to her. Barry comes round the corner, sees me. I don't get the milk, but I do get a black eye. I am not allowed to tell anyone my name, or speak to anyone ever again without Barry being there.

The special sixteenth birthday present that Barry has been telling me about for years is nothing like I expect. What I get is an argument and a knife in the stomach. I am in hospital on my birthday, my boyfriend and his parents are here with me, and the hospital staff don't believe any of them when they say it's an accident. This time, the hospital calls the police.

Thank God. I can go back to the home. Be safe.

I don't want to press charges but I am sent back to the children's home, which is what I want, even though no one asks me. Barry calls and calls. He says he's going to kill himself if I don't go back to him. He knows this threat will work eventually.

I don't want his death hanging over me.

It takes him a few weeks to persuade me that he's changed, that he loves me and will never hurt me again. As they are shutting Beaufort down, the social worker and the children's home agree to let me live with Barry. They release me from care into the arms, and fists, of Barry.

It's okay for a few weeks. I still have to call in once a week to let Social Services know I am okay. Every week the social worker tries to persuade me to go back into care. I tell her Barry cares. He stands next to me as we call from the phone box. He can hear every word the social worker says. He thinks I hesitate when the social worker asks me to come back, so in the phone box he squeezes my arm, reminding me that he's there, that he's listening. At home, because I hesitated about living with him, he busts my nose.

What have I done? What have I done? I want to go back into care. I wish there was a code word between my social worker and me, so I could tell her to come and find me without Barry knowing.

The police are at the door of our flat, they're asking to see me. Barry says I've gone out. He doesn't know when, or if, I'll be back.

Jackie, keep quiet, don't let them hear you. He'll kill you if they find you. Bugger, cramp!

I try and shift my dead leg, squashed in the side of the drawer under the bed with the rest of my small body. Barry's dog is sniffing the drawer in the divan bed where Barry put me to hide. Curled up in the foetal position, hiding from the police when really I want to be found.

Quiet, Jackie, be quiet. He'll kill you.

The door opens. Policeman's shoes.

I'm here. I'm here. I'm a prisoner here. Find me. Save me.

The policeman and his shoes come into the bedroom, he opens the wardrobe, has a search around.

I'm here. I'm here. Over here.

The policeman pats the dog who is sitting next to the divan drawer where I am hiding, guarding me. The policeman says, 'Nothing here.'

No! Look again. I am here, I am here. Don't cry. Barry will kill you.

The policeman turns to leave. He leaves.

Jackie. Aged sixteen.

Even though he spent ages persuading me to live with him, now he's got me, Barry seems to be losing interest in me, except when he thinks I might run off. Today a mate of his is round the house and they're watching a film. I've told him I've to phone the social worker at 3 p.m., before I go and work a night shift at his mum and dad's business.

Before his friend arrives, he has me up against the wall, telling me I'm to come home after the call, before I go to work, and if I take too long he'll find me and kill me.

I wish I had not come back. I wish I had left you to kill yourself.

Now he and his mate are in front of the telly.

'I'm going to call the social worker.'

'Don't take too long.' His voice is friendly, his stare chills me to the bone.

He's gonna kill me, whatever I do. Stay, go, he doesn't care.

I pick up my house keys and his car keys. I call the social worker, she says that I shall soon be seventeen and no longer their responsibility. They can help me until then. She tells me to make a plan. Asks if I can get money. I can't, but I tell her that this morning I've made a plan to escape.

On my way to the phone box I took his car keys. I used them to drop my house keys on the floor of his car.

I go back to the flat after my phone call and his friend lets me in. I tell him I can't find my house keys. I put Barry's car keys back in the bowl. His friend says he's going 'cos Barry is sitting in the bedroom in the dark. I can feel Barry's anger. I tell him I've got to go to work at his mum and dad's business. I tell him I can't find my house keys or car keys, so can he be in when I come home? He sends me on my way with a threat he'll kill me. I believe him.

When I come out of work he isn't at home, where I'd hoped he would be, 'cos I see him, standing over on the other side of the road. I ignore him and start walking. He's in front of me.

'Where are your keys? I can't find them at home. I've been looking and looking.'

'So have I; I couldn't find them.'

'You know, I've had enough of you not doing as you're told. You can fuck off.'

Really? Really?

He starts kicking off in front of his mum and dad's business. Fingers up, swearing, screaming shouting. His mum and dad arrive at work for the start of their working day to be met by their son threatening all sorts in my face.

It's like they've never seen this man, their son, before. They are shocked, don't recognise him. They are trying to calm him down. They can't. I take my chance; I run and hide behind a car on the other side of the street. He breaks free from his parents.

'I'm gonna kill you! Where are you, Jackie? Where are you?'

His mum is crying; her son is a monster, pacing, hunting me down.

She knows he means it. You must've known what he was like?

I look under the car I am hiding behind – there are legs, his legs, looking for me. He turns, moves away down the street. I run, like a soldier under fire, down the side of the cars. At the end of the road, I look back. His mum is watching me; she points Barry in the opposite direction. I turn, nod to her and run.

I run to the train station, explain what's happening, that I've no money. The ticket I am given is free. The next train is in a few minutes. I hide in the station office with the station manager until it arrives and I jump on it. He wishes me good luck. Until I get on the train, I've no real idea where I am going, but the ticket man told me the train is going to London, and he gave me a list of stations it stops at. I can get off anywhere I like. I stay on until the end because I know there is a YWCA next to the station. I go there. They call my social worker. She arrives, says, 'Thank God.'

She asks me if I am okay. Asks me if I am sure that I won't go back. Will I contact him again? She tells me I've an aunt who came forward. She came back from living abroad last month and wants to look after me. She has a good job, is stable, is safe.

'Would you like that?' the social worker asks.

It's the first time that anyone has asked me what I want since for ever. Finally I am safe. My knees buckle at the relief of escaping Barry. My eyes flood with tears. My head nods. I look up. I don't need to speak.

I would like nothing more.

PART FOUR

MOVING ON

Hope. 1991.
I am at my foster home. It's Saturday night and I've just got the kids I am babysitting to sleep. Now it's my time. It's the only time in the week I have to myself. Every week is the same; I look over my savings book and check my diary doesn't clash for the coming week.

It's not enough, not enough. I need money to get a car. I need to pass my driving test. I am shattered, I can't do no more.

I read my week ahead over again: college every day, straight after my extra hours at college there's my job in the factory moulding buckets and spades five evenings a week, Friday and Saturday nights babysitting, and then, to round it all off, working in a pub both days at the weekend.

Gotta do it, 'cos it's all gonna go pear-shaped in the end and I need money to get a car, my own things, be independent.

*   *   *

I open the door to my foster parents' home after college, a quick turnaround before I go and start my job at the factory.

There are two of her kids and four foster kids living in the house, but the house is quiet. It feels strange.

Where is everyone? I'm knackered. They all must be in their rooms.

The telly is on in the front room, where the foster mum is sitting, cup of tea and her dinner on her lap. It smells great. I go into the living room; it's the only room in the house that's really clean. It's cosy, with big sofas that you sink into; it's the room she takes the social workers when they come to visit. I am so tired from working and studying all the time, I could curl up and snooze for a bit. I sit down.

Just for a minute as gotta go to work soon.

She doesn't even say hello.

'What are you doing in here? This is the family's room. You foster kids have your own lounge.'

I stare at her in disbelief.

She's waving her fork at me. I knew there were two living rooms, but didn't know, until now, she actually separated us.

'Go on, your tea is in the oven. It's the pie on the bottom shelf. Don't you go touching the pie on the top shelf, that's for my natural kids, not you foster kids.'

I take both pies out the oven. The word 'natural' spinning round in my head.

I am a freak, I am not natural. I hate that word, natural.

Each of the pies has a slice out of it, so someone must be home. It's a small slice from the foster kids' pie, so it must be Lucy.

Lucy is a skinny kid. She stays in her room all the time. I've been told to keep away from her if I know what's good for me.

The natural family pie is rich in colour, large chunks of steak, thick gravy, vegetables. I know I shouldn't but I taste a small piece and it melts in my mouth, the flavours and smells are amazing.

Crap, she's coming.

I quickly put the natural family's pie back on the top shelf and serve up a piece of the foster kids' pie, the filling looks almost brown/grey.

My foster mum comes into the kitchen. I ask her, 'What's in the pie?'

'Steak.'

'Really?'

'You must be thick if you can't see that's steak. Now, get out my sight. Have you seen that slag Lucy today? She's no good, you keep away from her. Full of lies, she is. Says her granddad fiddled with her. Well, we know that's not true. She's a little liar that one; ruined her family's life. Imagine getting pregnant so young. You don't want to be mixing with the likes of her, a nice girl like you. Now off with you to your own living room.'

I shiver; it's so cold in here. I fidget 'cos the sofa is rock hard. I strain my eyes at the tiny old telly in the corner.

No wonder the other foster kids stay in their rooms. It's beginning to feel like this house is segregated. Like South Africa.

I take a bite.

Yuk, this pie is disgusting. Steak? I don't think so, more like cheap burger pie. I should eat at college and the factory.

As I finish my tea, Lee comes in with his own plate. Sits next to me; the sofa is small so we're close. I can tell he's been affected by everything that's happened to him.

'Seen Abby recently?' I ask.

'Nuh.'

'I have to go to work now, catch ya later?'

He doesn't answer, just stares into space.

I go upstairs to change for work. My foster mum is in her room, the door is open.

There's another fridge in her bedroom! It's got a lock on it.

I am standing on the upstairs landing looking in, my previous suspicions confirmed.

She's just like all the other foster placements, after all. She's got a separate fridge. One for them, one for us.

Though she tries to have us all eat at separate times, I've seen her kids eating food which is brighter and more vibrant than ours. Until now, until a series of things happening all came together, I wasn't sure. Right now both the bedroom and fridge doors are open together. She's just done a bulk shop and, as I am standing in the hallway quiet as a mouse looking through the bedroom door, now I know.

There's even a lock on the fridge door! What's in there? Keep quiet, Hope.

Her head is practically in the fridge so I stretch myself up, move from side to side to see past her large bum, looking at the contents. She's unpacking the bags – yoghurts and cheese. Proper butter. Milk! Steak, fresh chicken.

It all looks fresh. Our fridge downstairs has the basic stuff: margarine, stale bread. She's keeping us separate, even our food.

Keep quiet, Hope. Go back to your room. You have a roof over your head. What's the alternative? Being thrown out of care, going to a hostel. No thanks. As bad as the atmosphere is here, it's better than that. Stay here, study. Work towards starting your law degree. I want to be lawyer to stand up for people's rights in the courts. I must pass my exams.

There's a pile of older food on the floor, she puts it in the empty bags, mutters to herself, 'Right, that can go to the foster kids.'

No wonder all our food goes off so quickly.

I open the door of the house, there is screaming, shouting. Lee is pacing back and forth, head in his hands, saying he doesn't understand. The foster mum is upstairs, I can hear her.

'Lee, what's happening?'

He can't hear me; he's in the place he goes when he's distressed. His frustration at himself for his lack of understanding about what's going on, at being unable to express himself properly, is being played out by him grabbing his hair, rocking back and forth and screaming. He points outside, says something I don't catch, but it sounds like 'she's throwing'.

I can hear my foster mum upstairs. I look out the back. Clothes, his clothes, are being thrown out of the bedroom window. She's screaming that they've been left on the floor and she's told him once if not a hundred times. If he can't clean it up, she'll do it for him.

But he doesn't understand; he can't cope with what happened to him, with people being mean. You said you would be able to cope with him.

Her overweight frame storms downstairs, slamming his bedroom door as she goes past screaming and shouting. She's now outside, picking up all his clothes again, mixing them into a pile of sand that's waiting to go into a cement mixer to build a new extension for more foster kids.

Lee and I go outside; she's in such a mood that I know not to get involved. She turns, picks up the hose and sprays Lee with it. He's knocked out of his trance by the force of the water. She's screaming.

'I told you, I told you to clean up after yourself. This isn't a hotel, you know.'

He lunges at her, and they're fighting, physically, round the garden. Lee shouting, 'Stop. Stop. Stop.'

She manages to get away, runs into the house, shouting that she's calling for the police. He sinks into the sand, next to his clothes and waits for them.

The police believe her when she says it was him who threw his clothes out, that she was trying to stop him and he assaulted her.

They arrest him for assault. The police take him away. He doesn't come back. I hear he gets bail and then he skips parole.

Robert. Aged twenty-two.
'Come on, then, come on.'

There are about thirty Chelsea supporters who appear from nowhere; they're shouting, chanting, ready for the fight under the railway bridge, screaming, braying in front of us. They are deliberately blocking our path, waiting for us to step forward, to be men. Just moments before we turned in under the bridge, five of the twenty or so Leeds supporters who came down for the match and a fight.

I need this fight, it makes me feel alive.

We turn back, but it's too late. Right here, right now, the five of us are surrounded by ten times that many.

Before the match I bumped into Lee, Abby, me ex's little brother. He was outside the grounds, trying to sneak in to watch the match. He said he was looking for me, had run away again. We got him into the match, and I've told him to wait for me by the Boss's car after the game and the fight.

Best way to keep Lee safe, place him near the Boss.

It didn't work out with Abby. I might have thrown that away, but I can still look out for her kid brother.

He can join us, move to Leeds, the Boss is always on the lookout for good people who will do as they're told.

The Boss says he's thinking about it. 'Right now,' he says, 'Lee's not our challenge.' He turns round, points at a group of men, says, 'This lot are.'

All through the match they were taunting us. All through the match they were shouting how they were gonna do us in, and we responded in kind. We lost 1–0 so that makes them stronger, braver than they were before. Now they have us trapped.

Where are the others? They should be here?

Adrenalin is pumping through me veins giving me a high. It's the same every time. The day before a match I choose me clothes carefully, to look hard enough for the fight and yet trendy enough so it don't look like I'm bothered if the clothes get damaged.

Chelsea and Leeds, we fight good, but there are so fuckin' many of them. They are hard, but we are harder.

We will take this fight to them, even though there are ten times the number of them.

The men scream and bray at us, shake the metal fencing at the end of the bridge. Obscenities bounce off the walls, all of them screaming at us to 'Come on!' Trying to measure up the opposition, who's hardest, show us what you've got, who's gonna go for who first. Fists in the air, sticks being hurled about. For a moment I seem to step out of myself, to see this for what it is: 60 or so grown men with jobs, who can afford to have designer clothes on their backs as they go to support their football teams, going into battle. We've wives and kids at home. And yet, here we are, screaming at each other, feeding our addiction to violence, getting beaten up to feed low self-esteem, or beating someone else up to feed an ego. All of us high on chemicals in the head without taking man-made drugs. This is an addiction that comes from having pushed stuff down, and it's all let out on a Saturday afternoon at the football on some poor bugger's head, someone who needs this fight to feel, just as much as the man who put the boot in does. And yet, there's no other feeling like this; the anger, the tension of the week is all released so you don't take it out on the kids or the missus at home. Anger and tension replaced with power.

I'm the man.

Or that's what we tell ourselves to justify this football war. For some, it don't work out like that. For some, they take the addiction home and practice midweek on their wives, girlfriends, kids. Now, according to my rules, they have crossed a line.

I come back to the present in a flash and I spot one of the Chelsea guys and decide he beats his missus. I hate him, and I go for him first.

The rest pile in, it's five against fifty and, even though the other twenty Leeds fans turn up, it's not a fair fight. These guys are armed with logs and baseball bats. It's carnage. Into the stomach, I knock the wind out of the bastard I think beats his wife, and someone rushes into me with a full rugby tackle. I spin, fall, hit the deck. Get up, a couple of punches, take two guys out. Trip over a body. Out of the corner of my eye I can see the black of police uniforms arriving, which means time to go.

If I run low along the wall, I can get out of here.

I move to push myself up against the wall, halfway up and the graffiti next to me reads *Welcome to Hell*. I am ready to crouch and run. I look up, there's an arm above me, I see a glint of light on metal and a man with the sun behind him. I hear metal hit the bone. I look down at my arm.

Fuck – was that a machete?

I'm floating; there are voices and sirens around me. Now I am moving fast. I am on a rocket. Buttons are being pressed. I am alone on the rocket. There's a walkie-talkie. People are trying to reach me on the radio but I can't understand what they're saying and they can't hear me. I move from dark into light and the sounds of familiar voices reach me, but I don't know what they want.

Beep. Beep. Beep. Beep.

It's all white and bright. The beeping is doing me head in. My eyes adjust and there's a woman in a nurse's uniform checking a machine. It's a cliché, but for a moment I wonder if I am dead. I turn my head slightly – someone's even left me flowers.

Stupid fuck. I'm dead.

There's a shooting pain in my arm, which tells me that maybe I'm not. There's a voice, outside my head that I can hardly hear, so I try and focus a bit more on where it's coming from.

Beep. Beep. Beep.

What's that noise?

Turning my head away from the nurse, towards the voice, I see two people, both men – well, man and boy. The Boss and Lee.

The Boss speaks, 'Made a name for yourself there, mister, all grown up. Real proud of you. Part of the brotherhood now, mister.'

I mumble a response. I can feel my head flapping from side to side. I can't control it. 'Brilliant, Boss, that's brilliant. What happened?'

'Machete in the arm. Not all off, but a big slice through. Docs did a miracle sewin' it all back on. Four fucking days you've been out of it, mate. Coma. The lad 'ere, Lee, never left your side. Idolises you, he does. Talked to you all the time, 'e did, so you'd know you's wasn't on yer own. You knew you'd get battered. Unfair fight that was but you stood, you stood your effin' ground. Made a name there for yerself, man. Made a name. Lost four pints of blood, you did. Well done, well fuckin' done.'

The door opens, it's two policeman and their uniforms. The Boss nods at them, stands up. Lee is behind him, turns his back on the policemen, slips away.

The officer speaks, 'You're awake, then?'

Questions, questions, I am too out of it to hear, or answer, properly.

Then me mam barges in, past the policemen, pushing them out the way. Screaming at me, 'What are you doing? How did you get involved in this?'

The police go, come back again later. Lee manages to disappear until the police leave. It's like a revolving door, the police, they aren't giving up – more questions, question after question. Me mam sits at me bedside. The social worker, the residential care worker from Chesterfields visits, brings some grapes. I hate grapes. He speaks with Lee and asks him what he's doing here and why isn't he with his foster parents. Turns to me, asks me what Lee is doing here. Everyone is on at me. Doing me head in. The machines, too. Beep. Beep. Beep. I wish I was still in a coma. I wish I hadn't woken up.

Lee. Aged seventeen.

I step off the bus into the sunshine, remembering to be polite to the driver as my mum always taught me.

Ah, Mum.

'Thanks, driver.'

He smiles in that way country bus drivers do when they know why someone, who's not from round here, gets off the bus in the middle of nowhere. He doesn't reply, just closes the bus doors behind me and drives off. I stand on the grassy verge for a bit, looking out over some fields, back north towards the city of Newcastle. It's the first time I've been here.

Me head is thumpin', both from the kicking I got outside the pub last night, and the booze I drank. Nothing dulls me pain.

At least I didn't get arrested. I'm still on the run from bail; they'd throw the book at me.

Can't fuckin' stand them.

The Boss and his gang are looking after me; as long as I do a bit of running for them with some parcels I'll be okay. My bike works well for that. I just wait, kicking me ball against the wall, until they tell me to get on me bike and take a parcel to one club or another for them. In return I get me a place to stay and I get to go to the football games where the real action is. I love a fight. I need a fight; it's what I do best. Yesterday I made the fight happen by deliberately slagging off this girl in front of her boyfriend. I got a bit of a kickin', though. But I deserved it; I didn't duck too well. Still, not too many sore bits today. As I stand looking over the countryside, the sound of the fight swirls in my head, until the blackbirds in the bushes take over.

Come on, man, get yer head right before you go in. This is the middle of nowhere. Where is this place? Where's that bit of paper?

Reaching into my pocket, I pull out the map that my mum sent me of how to get here. The letter she sent with it was burnt when I got so pissed off with her for getting herself into this situation and I didn't want to see her again. But I kept the map and I thought, as I'm in the area for a few days with the Boss anyway, I may as well go visit. Well, that's what I told the Boss and that's why he gave me the money for the bus and told me to go and see my mum while he did some business in the city with some other bloke. Despite getting a beating yesterday, he told me I did well for someone of my age and then he gave me some other instructions on where to find him later if I want a lift back to Leeds. I've gotta be back by 4 p.m. or I'll have to walk home and it's a long way to Leeds from Newcastle. His advice was to go see my mum, kiss her on the forehead and come back pretty sharp. Now I'm here, I wish I'd longer to see her, to speak to her, 'cos even though she's never been nice to me or my sister, she's still my mum and I want to make sure she's getting the help she needs.

I follow the map drawn by my mum and sent to me care of my sister. I got the letter when I went round to collect some clothes and drop off me washing. My sister and her new boyfriend don't seem to care that I'm never there, but they keep a bed for me and do my washing. It's nice, but she doesn't come with me to see Mum. Abby's getting her own life sorted so, really, she doesn't give a shit what I do about Mum.

Moving from the bus stop marked with an 'X' on the map, I cross the road towards the gate she's drawn and marked with another, bigger 'X'. Even though the way she's drawn the map makes it look like a wide gap and a walk, it's only a few steps from the bus stop to where I'm headed.

Here it is.

The gates are stone, big blocks of granite, showing strength. They are open. The sign announces this is an NHS Psychiatric Residential Care Unit.

How did you end up here, Mum?

Each step along the long path brings me nearer to an old house which, by its size, must've once been a private house. I like to make up stories about objects and people so, as I walk up the drive, I imagine the old days. A rich trading family or, no, a coal mine owner and his family, who got too greedy, invested in some bad stuff, couldn't pay their taxes and, rather than being able to keep the house for generations, had to hand the house over to the government. They then turned it into a hospital where the coal mine owner was the first mental patient. I laugh to myself at my story and wonder if it's true. As I walk it feels like someone is watching me from the trees and I pick up the pace. It all feels a bit eerie.

There's no one outside. Where is everyone? It's a sunny day. This place is deserted.

When I get to the entrance I'm faced with a large glass and wire door that doesn't match the exterior of this old stone mansion. There's a buzz and the door opens. I look left and then right, still seeing no one. I step through the door and it shuts behind me. There's a voice to my right.

'Hi. Can I help you?'

I turn and there's a surprisingly pretty lady behind the desk. I don't know why I am surprised she's pretty, but she's pretty and I'm surprised. Before I can say anything, another woman appears; she, too, is pretty, older than me, but not by much. She's got long, blond hair and is wearing a clean, white T-shirt with no pattern but it's low-cut and showing her boobs. She's got a very short skirt like from the 60s, with no tights or shoes. Every part of her body, except her face, has the evidence of cuts, the whiteness of the T-shirt highlighting them.

'All right?' she says.

'Yeah,' I reply.

'What you lookin' at? Don't you find me attractive? Don't you want me? I can find us a room if you do. Ah, but I don't want you anyway, not really.'

What's going on? I'm seventeen. I know I look older, but what's going on? What is this place?

I turn away from her. To my left, there's an old geezer, his trousers and pants are down round his ankles, but still he's walking along, two steps and he makes to go to take a piss, stops, another two steps and again he makes the motion of going for a piss. He does this left to right of the entrance hall. The girl with the cuts has turned her attention to the old guy and asks him the same question she asked me. He ignores her, too. She doesn't seem bothered. Both of them seem to be in their own private worlds. Both seem to be wanting to do something but realizing, just in time, that they should not do this thing, then after a moment decide to try again. Stop, start, stop.

Nurses pass through the corridor while I stand looking. These two perform, it seems, for me. The nurses say nothing, do nothing, except walk past this strange version of normal.

There's a man with his pants down and a girl with cuts all over her asking a seventeen-year-old and an old man for sex. Why don't you do something? Is this normal to you?

The girl behind the desk asks again if she can help me. I shake my head. I turn around and ask her to let me out.

There's a buzz, the door opens and I run through it back into the sun, down the drive to the bus stop that will take me back home, to Leeds via Newcastle. I'm still breathing heavily when the bus arrives. It's the same driver as before, this time going the other way, and the bus is empty. He looks at me sympathetically and waves me on the bus saying, 'Bad day, Son? Going in there for a visit? Not so good, I'd say.' He smiles. 'On you go, then, this trip is on me, lad. I suggest you sit down and take the countryside in; you'll feel better by the time we get back to town with these views.'

I sit. He's right; we get to the bus station and immediately I spend the bus fare on a few tinnies. My height and large frame, which has been built up by boxing, my Burberry jacket and Pringles shirt, all help make me look a bit older. I might be underage but I always seem to be able to get booze in the shops, especially near bus stations. They don't care. No one cares.

Sitting on the wall at the meeting point for the Boss, I know I've an hour to kill. I can do these four cans of cider in that time, no problem. Try and take a bit of the pain away.

Maybe the Boss will give me a toke when I get back to Leeds. Maybe that will help dull the pain, block out the memories. What happened today? Why has my mum managed to get locked up in there?

I've the last swig from this can, then drop it on the ground, open the second can and take a sip. A policeman walks past and doesn't give me a second glance. No one gives a shit. No one except the Boss. He's dead on time and, as I haven't opened the fourth and last can of cider, I stuff it inside my jacket, so the Boss won't see.

I sit in the front with the Boss's driver. There's a mean-looking, shaved-headed, bald guy who I haven't seen before next to the Boss in the back who grunts hello.

'How's your mum, Lee?'

I look out the window and lie about seeing her.

'Good, thanks, Boss; she'll recover soon.'

A strong hand squeezes my shoulder.

'That's good, boy, that's good. She's in the right place. This here is Bruiser, he's coming to work for me for a bit. Now you know your mum is being looked after, you can work with him for a bit, too. He'll show you the ropes.'

They all laugh at the Boss saying that, like ropes means something. The three of them seem pleased with themselves. As we drive from Newcastle back to the ganglands of Leeds, I stare out of the car window, wanting the countryside to make me feel like it did when I was on the bus. Calm, happy. I think about the bus driver, trying to remember if I said thank you.

On this journey I see the bus driver is wrong about the countryside making you feel better. I guess it all depends on where the countryside is taking you, or what it's taking you from. The Boss and the crew in the car are laughing and joking about how someone's head looked after it got kicked in. They tell me I should've seen it. I look at the countryside zooming past, turning into city, and it doesn't feel the same as it did on the bus. I guess that's 'cos countryside doesn't exist where we're going.

Hope. 1992.

I've passed my driving test and I have a new job, doing my foster mum's accounts. I am sitting at the table in the living room doing them. It's the only time I'm allowed in the living room, so I take my time. Claiming for petrol journeys I know never happened.

There was an incident a while back with Lucy and the new foster boy. I was working at the factory. It was serious, but I'm not sure anyone believed her.

The police couldn't have believed her, as they didn't arrest the boy, and now it's all a bit weird, because, although it was agreed with the police and the social workers that all the men in the house will stay at a caravan in Essex, they ain't, they're staying here.

Lucy doesn't feel safe at all and locks her door. Even before the incident she was like a tiny bird, nervous, especially around men. Now she seems to have become even smaller. She only comes out of her room when she knows no one is in the house, or at least no men are in the house. Sometimes I hear her at night, like a mouse, moving around, restless, unable to sleep, despite her locked door, living in fear.

Of what?

My foster mum hates her, always did, but even more so now. Lucy hates me, as I've sided with my foster mum. I look at the expenses for them, working out their mileage to and from the caravan in Essex. All lies. Thieves.

When Lucy finally turns eighteen and moves out, she closes the door without a goodbye to anyone.

I'm in the living room with my foster mum. As the men will now be able to move back in officially, I am doing the last set of fiddling expenses, relating to that.

I'm sure she'll find another fiddle.

My foster mum watches Lucy leaving through the net curtains. Lucy struggles down the path with her things all in black bags. Without a word my foster mum sits down again on the sofa. I hand her the books and the forms to claim money they haven't spent.

'Thank you, Hope. Now, don't you forget that if anyone finds out we've been doing a bit of creative accounting, you'll never be a lawyer. The social work people may be funding you to carry on with your education, but don't you forget where your bread is buttered, young lady. We both know that a condition of you getting the money for your education is that you come here in the holidays. You go telling anyone about these extra claims and you won't have a place to stay, and you'll ruin your career before it begins.'

Shit, I didn't think of that. I am implicated, too. I'm trapped. She's trapped me. I don't want to come home here, even if that's a condition of my funding. I'm not sure I want to go to university anyway. Now I have my car, I can do anything.

'Come on, let's have a race.'

My mate's car is pretty flash, but I bought mine with me own money. We're racing down the high street; I am beating her in my new car with its wheel arch alloy wheels.

I love it.

My foster dad did me a favour, sold it to me for a good price. It drives well although the alignment is a bit out. Still, me and my beautiful new car are beating the flash car.

Ha ha! All flash no power.

I look in the rear-view mirror.

She's well behind.

Slow to turn a corner. Whack. I bounce forward, back.

Shit.

The person in the other car doesn't look amused. There's a policeman on the corner. It was just a little bump, but my car looks even more squint at the front now. My mate drives past, pretending she's not with me.

The policeman is stern, serious.

'You know your car has what's called crabbed?'

'What's that?'

'The crash has made it fold up at the front.'

The other policeman is looking under my car. He comes up, nods, confirming something to his colleague.

What? What's going on?

'It's a cut and shut all right.'

I must look confused.

'Two cars welded together.'

I'm in trouble now.

Don't tell them where you got it from.

I tell them that I am a ward of court, that I am in care.

The police back off.

Always works. I know how they think – too much trouble to interview this one, send her back to the foster family.

On my return home, my foster mum denies it all.

I hate you, I hate you. You put my life at risk. I don't want to be here. I don't care what you do about me fiddling your accounts. I hate you. I don't want to be a lawyer anyway. I want to be a mum.

I've tried education and work, but it is all too much. I want to be a Mum.

Lee. Aged eighteen.

Back in Leeds, the Boss gets me to run packages and work with Bruiser debt collecting.

He's just given me another package to deliver; I collect it from a warehouse outside town. When I came out, I puked into an old oil barrel.

The Boss is in there with a bunch of real gangsters with Newcastle accents. I left them in there with some poor sod

in a chair who owes money. Beyond scared he is, with a
bunch of bad guys that the Boss is now involved with.
Blood on the floor there was, and it didn't belong to the
guy on the chair, so this is gonna be bad. He knows, I
know. I left, he didn't.

*I don't like this. I need this. I can't deal with this. I need a
drink. A score, I need a score.*

I thought I was hard, I thought I was bad, but these
guys . . . these guys are something else. Pliers, electrics, a
chair.

*This ain't good, Lee, not good. You thought you were hard, a
gangster. Not this, though, not this. These guys are gangsters,
I'm just a prick who beats some people up now and again. I don't
even beat them up these days, just threaten them with action.
That's worse, the thought of it, than the feeling it.*

*Nice to their wives, I am. And if they've a cat or a dog, I pet it,
looking into the human's eyes, menacing like, while stroking
their pet. But I don't really hurt them, not these days. Too much
shittin' of pants for my liking. The thought of what I might do is
worse. But this, this is different. Fuck, what am I into? I brought
this guy here for them, like a package. Gotta do as the Boss says.
Gotta get out of here, gotta get this stuff out of my head. Gotta go
somewhere else.*

I reach into my pocket, take a half bottle out. A swig, the
bitterness of the cheap vodka no longer making me wince.
It's not enough, not enough.

*Need to find Bruiser, Bruiser will help me out, help me
forget all this shit spinnin' in my head. Bruiser, gotta find
Bruiser. He ain't in there, 'cos the Boss has his new crew from
Newcastle.*

I rub the inside of my arm again.

Hardening up there, should still be able to find a vein. If not, might need to inject into my arse. Bruiser, Bruiser. I need to find Bruiser. Need to get rid of all this stuff attacking my head.

I take a few steps forward, the grey-brown warehouses and deserted grounds make me stop, turn back, think.

That man, I left that man in there. That man. Nothing I can do, can't do nothing, got my own problems. All this stuff needs to go from my head.

I walk over to the car and, with one of the fastest three-point turns and skid marks on the ground, I am out of there, focused on finding Bruiser.

I find him at home, feeling sorry for himself 'cos the Boss is going big time and forgetting us. The Boss is angry 'cos we're using and you should deal, or use, but not both. The Boss has told Bruiser he, we, are turning into liabilities.

There's some stupid programme on the telly about a policeman in Yorkshire in the 1960s. Bruiser is so pissed off with it that he's just kicking the telly in. I am sitting on the sofa watching him bounce around and the sparks that come out of the telly with each kick are wild. I am preparing lines of coke for us, ready for when he's finished.

Bruiser is in the kind of mood when he'd do anything to anyone. I'm glad he likes me and that every day he grabs the back of my neck, pulls me in, face to face, and tells me, 'I'd never hurt you, lad. You know that, don't ya?'

I nod as much as I can with the big Bruiser holding my neck, nose to nose, spitting the words in my face. He's become a big brother to me, looks out for me, and lets me have what I need to forget the shit that went on before. We take some coke to keep us alert and feel the confidence of kings and to stop the blackness, until the effect of the coke starts to wear off and we feel shit again. Then we know we're almost ready for the next hit.

Need something stronger this time.

I laugh 'cos, as I make the next hit up, Bruiser hits out and sends another kick towards the telly. Trying to stop the feeling of coming down from where we've been, Bruiser releases the wild man in him. With no one else around to kick, 'cos he wouldn't hurt me, it's the telly that gets it. There's bits of glass and sparks of electricity everywhere, jumping out at him as he jumps back and forth like he did on that casual's stomach earlier today. Kick. Kick. Kick. I feel for a vein.

It's dark now, except for the light on the landing of the flats, which glows orange over Bruiser's sleeping hulk.

How long have we been awake? Must be over twenty-four hours. Good for him to sleep.

I look over at his heavy body, draped over his half of the sofa, next to me. He's like a sleeping bear with a beer can in his hand. His chest is rising up and down, he's snoring. My eyes are heavy, but my brain won't shut up. I pick up the remote control and press buttons; it doesn't work, so I lift it up to point it more directly at the telly. Still nothing happens. I try and focus, turn my head to look at the screen. The telly is on its side, the screen is in pieces on the floor. Out loud I say, 'The telly has a hole in it.'

I reach out to thump Bruiser on his arm, to find out what's happened, but I'm high, so there's no power in my arm, and my hand just flops onto his sleeping shoulder and then my brain takes over.

Bruiser has ruined the telly. I wanted to watch that, it's unfair. Why did he do that? Ruins my night, that does. How come he did that? Everyone is out to get me; life is so unfair, not just the telly, right back to when I was little. Fuckin' mother, beat me, treated me like shit. Only good thing in life is my sister Abby and she's off making her own life now. Doesn't care no more. She called me yesterday, but what's the point in calling her back? She doesn't want me hanging around. She doesn't care, she pretends, but not really. I know she doesn't really care. Only friend I have is Bruiser, and the only way I can forget the crap is through the drugs and, even then, the coke doesn't seem to be working no more. I'm gonna be dead by the time I'm twenty-five anyway, I know it. I know it. Me dead and no one will care. Who looks out for me? Bruiser? Not really, he just wants me around because no one else will speak to him outside of football days. No one else speaks to me. Just us two. I hate my life. My mother, everyone has ruined my life. Ruined it. Fuckers, all out to get me, all out to make it so hard. The booze is even against me, it no longer dulls the pain of people not caring. No one cares. People go and leave me. There was that girl, last week, what was her name? I really liked her. She was rude to me, went off and got someone else. Said I was too young, but I am a man. I hang out with Bruiser and the Boss. We showed her. Me and Bruiser. She had to go to A&E. That's when the Boss sent us off to think about things. Robert doesn't care. He's off, trying to get himself clean. What's he gone and done that for? Good on him, but he doesn't want anything to do with me now. Fucker. Ruined my life, he did, leaving me. My life is mapped out. Twenty-five years old, I'll be dead by then, you'll see. Ruined my life she did, my mother. She needs to be dead. Ruined my life she did. What's the point? It's all shit, no one cares, no one looks out for you. I wonder how I'll die. No one will care, but I wonder how it will happen.

Robert. Aged twenty-three.

I am standing on the landing of the high-rise, leaning on the barrier, looking down to the street, waiting for my daughter and her mum. She's six months old, my daughter, and I love her more than . . . more than . . . Her mum I love, too, but I can't deal with feeling such love for one person, let alone two.

Love, what is love except to be challenged and destroyed?

She's making me wait, too, my daughter's mum. I've to stand outside their flat for half an hour like a big Jessie who's been stood up. Me and my thoughts. People walking along the outside corridor wondering if I'm waiting to kick off like I used to when I lived here. They don't look me in the eye, but they say hello 'cos they're scared of me.

Me scare them? I don't remember doing nothing to scare them. Anyway, it's good now; the Boss understood I wanted to do the best for my kid. Let me go, provided I go into rehab.

I worry that she ain't coming. Did I scare her, too? I don't remember. I stand and stare at the bus stop, waiting, like I did as a child waiting for Mum. From outside her flat on the fifth floor of the high rise I can see the bus coming. I hope. I hope. She gets off, struggling with the pram; my heart does something funny on seeing her and the pram.

Me family.

The lift is broken, so I think about going to help her. But as she's late, I don't. This makes her even later. More for me to put on her; more time for me to get angry.

By the time she gets up five flights of stairs with my beautiful girl in the pram, I feel such a git for not helping. But I can't help myself. As soon as she turns the corner, I'm on her, accusing her, I don't even say hello to her or my daughter. Instead: 'Where have you been? You're late. Am I not friggin' important enough for you to come on time? No respect? You know I hate people being late. Where have you been? Is your time more important than mine? Well? Well?'

The baby starts crying. Her mum just walks past me with the pram, a face like she knows I made the decision not to help her to punish her. She opens the door, doesn't say a word to me. Puts down her keys, her bag, pulls some shopping from the pram, unhooks our daughter and quietly, without anger, takes my baby out of the pram and hands her to me. My hands are shaking. I hold her; I want her mum to hold me.

God, you are beautiful. Just hug me, just hold me. Walk away, then. You're late. I need a drink to cope with this. I've been trying to get clean on me own, but it's not working.

The baby is feeling my face. I love that feeling of a baby, my baby, putting her hands on my face, feeling my ears. My ex speaks. She's so calm, which means she's angry. Really angry. She never raises her voice when she's this angry.

She says she saw me watching her get off the bus and is disappointed that I didn't come to help her as the lift was broken. I am not to deny knowing this as I would've had to walk up the stairs to get here, too. That she saw me flick a fag over the side of the high-rise, turn my back to wait, to work myself up and not to help. She tells me she's disappointed but that I am not to say a word until she's finished. That I don't love her and the baby enough to laugh and help; that I would rather get angry and shout. She tells me she loved me and, for that, and for my daughter, she wants me to be around, but it's hard. She tells me while it's too late for me and her, my daughter loves me but she won't for long if I carry on being a prick and not a dad. She tells me I don't know what normal is, that I try and destroy everything. That I am an addict to booze and she suspects drugs, and is this what I want my daughter to learn? Is this the father I want to be? Would I allow my daughter to be treated by a man in the way I am treating her? That I distance myself from her. That I need to sort myself out. I hear her and with every softly spoken word I feel smaller and smaller, like a child.

I stand. I hand her daughter back to her. I feel weak, stupid, vulnerable. I feel hot, stressed. I remove my jacket for something to do. Place it on the back of a chair.

Hold me, please. Tell me it's going to be okay. Ask me if I want to talk about it.

No, put the front on, be hard.

I stand, turn to face her back. Pick my jacket up again.

'I'll go, then, if you don't want me here.'

'No, Robert, you aren't listening to me.'

She takes my jacket off me, hands the baby back to me. The baby reaches up again to put her hands on my face. Soft hands, pat, pat, pat.

'You stay, get to know your daughter, think about what I've said. I just need some air. I'm the one who's going. I won't be long. I'll be down by the canal, for a walk. Just for an hour . . .'

She must see the panic on my face.

She smiles and carries on, 'Half an hour, maybe. Robert, you'll be fine. For the sake of your daughter, for the sake of you having a good life where you smile and we get on, for the sake of her, think about it. What life will she have with a dad like you? Involved in all sorts, putting stuff into your body that shouldn't be there. Think about what you want to do. There's a bottle on the side.'

I freeze.

She's offering me a drink?

She smiles, laughs, her voice happy, 'In the steriliser . . . for her. Oh, you are a git!'

Laughing, she picks up her bag and walks out.

I hold my baby at arm's length, then draw her in, holding her close. She smells of baby. She wriggles, so I find a toy with lots of colours and shapes that go inside a box when you find the right-sized gap.

The baby and I play for a bit. I watch her exploring the shapes and the different patterns on her toys. She tries to put a square peg through a round hole. It doesn't fit. We get it right eventually. I teach her something and my chest fills with pride. Then she's touching the shapes on my face, again. I wonder if I smell of booze, of fags. I am disappointed in myself.

I give her a bottle when I think she needs it and she falls asleep in my arms. I sit there too scared to move. Tears don't come, but I feel like crying.

The door opens. The baby is still asleep on my chest and, since she trusted me enough to fall asleep on me, the only part of my body I've moved is my brain. Her mum walks in, places her bag gently on the chair. I don't want to move. I want to hold the baby like this forever. She lifts the baby from me, takes her through to her room. I follow and stand at the bedroom door, leaning on the frame, arms crossed. I watch her and her mother's love. I feel something that I want to feel more of. It's nice, but I don't know. I'm scared of it, scared of loving, of being loved. I don't know if I can. I don't know if I am capable. What if I'm like my own dad? That's all I know. I don't know this, this kindness, this love, it ain't normal.

Is this normal?

She walks over to me, is up on her tip toes, kisses my forehead, puts a hand on my arm, and squeezes gently before she walks past me into the kitchen.

I know what I have to do.

I pick up my jacket and, without putting it on, I say nothing. I leave, closing the door quietly behind me.

Whatever it takes, I am going to get clean.

Hope. 1992.

My last set of foster parents are being investigated. Social Services finally believe Lucy and, although it will be some time before they're struck off, I feel better 'cos they interview me and they believed me, too. My new foster home is crazy, but this time in a good way. We've a half-blind pot-bellied pig who comes into the kitchen, millions of cats, dogs, mad geese, horses etc. It's chaos. The foster dad is just like my dad, in build and height; he even drinks like my dad, all day and evening. Him and the foster mum are the kindest people I know.

Life is good, even if I've spent the last two years just going to college and working, today I turn eighteen so I leave care. I get my own flat and last week I found out that I am pregnant. It means I won't start my law degree, but that can wait. I've a big grin following me around, as I am going to be a mum. A good mum.

Hope. 1993.

I am awake in my new flat. I'm lying on the bed but I can still see the cracks in the ceiling and the unpainted walls. In the dark, a feeling overtakes me that rises from my stomach, an ever-expanding lump, pulling at my chest, it feels tight, heavy, sore. My eyes want to burst from my thumping head, which seems to be pushing in on itself. It's because I am scared. The clock says it's three o'clock in the morning. I've no reason to disbelieve it, except I'm not asleep. I want to be asleep, but instead my own thoughts invade me and pummel the inside of my head.

Today, it's ten years since I went into care. I know it's now time for me to be in my own flat, but I feel so alone. No one wants me, everyone gets rid of me. All those people, my new family, the people who brought me up, all gone, just because I turned eighteen. I hate living alone. I've never lived alone.

What do I do? I don't know how to live, except in the care system. My flat is a mess, the landlord is taking the piss, there's no heating, a load of repairs to do. I'm pregnant. I'm going to have to learn how to be a single mum.

I need to move again. I will have to call my old residential key worker, Glen. He'll come with Alex, who was the housekeeper at Beaufort. They'll help me move. They'll help me move me to a new place. This is stupid. I've got to find somewhere better. It's already been three places in six months. I need to find somewhere to settle for the baby.

I am totally lost. It's really painful being me.

I turn over to try and sleep. I see the clock turn four in the morning and with it a pain in my lower body that makes me yell out loud.

Shit, that's painful. Oh no, it's the middle of the night, don't come now, baby. I'm on my own. Who do I phone? Breathe, Hope, Breathe. Contractions. Are these contractions? They must be. The baby, the baby is coming.

My daughter is born. She's pure beautiful. I hold her in my arms. I love her so much, I want to eat her.

Precious. Precious.

Who wants to be a lawyer anyway, when you can have this? This is what I'm good at. Looking out for people. Looking after people.

My daughter. You will have a lovely life. I'll never do anything to hurt you.

A nurse comes in. 'You're the one that was in care.'

It's a statement that makes me shiver.

What's that got to do with anything?

'You have to stay in for a few days.'

'Why?'

She's so matter-of-fact, I freeze. 'Because you do. You have to stay in hospital to prove you are capable of looking after a baby.'

What!? But I love my baby.

I wake up and there is a woman next to my baby, stony-faced, checking her. The questions start. Questions, questions. 'How is her feeding?' 'Is she sleeping well?'

Hope, be positive, be strong, tell her how things are. The baby is doing great. The nice nurse says we are doing fine and not to worry. Why doesn't this woman with all these questions smile? Why aren't you smiling at the baby? Why aren't you being kind to me? Do you want me to fail?

Someone always seems to appear when I change her nappy, feed her, clothe her, bath her, soothe her, comfort her and get her to stop crying. At first it seems natural, but as they watch me being a mum, marking me, doubt creeps in.

You're making me feel small. You're making me feel like I can't do this. Hope, say nothing to them, they will just turn it against ya.

I want to cry at every possible moment. But only cry when I'm alone.

They will not, cannot take the joy of my baby away from me. But you're checking my every move, my fitness as a mother. It seems like you don't want me to enjoy my baby. I love her.

I look up from feeding her. There is a woman lurking over me. Day and night it seems that nurses check if I am doing this or that right. Every day I'm here I feel smaller and smaller. Doubts start to creep in.

What if I can't do this? What if they are right?

A week after my baby is born I am told I can take her home. Alex comes to the hospital to help me. I walk out through the hospital doors, and I feel released. I can breathe again. I look down at my beautiful girl, her tiny hand moves, she stretches her fingers out as if she is reaching for me. I place my finger between hers and five tiny fingers wrap themselves around mine. It melts my heart.

She's so beautiful. My world. You will always be laughing and loved. This is the start of my life.

Hope. 1998.
We've a house. I'm so happy. When I watch my daughter and my son, who is three and a half, sleeping, my thoughts are positive.

Even though we are on our own now, we can start to live our life, right?

Alone at night, my head starts killing me with my flashbacks and feelings.

I hate myself but I've to get on and be as good a mum as I can be. I don't know how to be a mum. What am I going to do? I left school with a handful of exams. I tried getting more exams, but left college to have my daughter. Two kids now. Alone again. I feel empty. Oh, I can't have them being mad at me. I don't want them to be sad. I want them to know they are loved.

'Kids, come here, Mummy wants a cuddle. I love you both very much. You are very special to me.'

I love cuddles with my kids, they're precious.

The kids are asleep, they're safe and their room is as warm as I can get it with the electric heater. I haven't eaten all day.

So my kids can.

I sit in the living room wrapped up in my duvet, worrying about them. There's no telly as there's no spare money for me to watch it. I hold a book from the library, but I haven't the energy to read it. My thoughts are busy as the nighttime kicks in.

I am alone. I don't know what to do. I've an eviction notice from the council. My housing benefit has been stopped. I didn't fill in the form. I can't turn out like my parents. I can't. I've no money. I have to survive on my own, no one to fall back on. I am alone. I am letting my kids down.

The lady from Home-Start is coming tomorrow, maybe she can help me.

Maybe I should go and see Mum and Dad.

* * *

Hamilton Road looks exactly the same.

I'm amazed my mum and dad still live here.

They better not be drinking. Not in front of my two babies, I told them.

I go to the bathroom, at least there's toilet paper now. I go back to the kitchen. My mum has a whisky, she looks at me.

'What? Just a little drink to celebrate?'

'What did I say, Mum? Come on, kids, we're going.'

The next time I go to Hamilton Road, I'm on my own.

'Where are the kids? Have they been taken off you? Don't want to tell us they're in care? You can tell us, we never told your grandma, but you can tell us.'

'They aren't in care. I was just in the area, thought I'd pop in and say hi. I want to bring the kids on Saturday, but no drinking, right?'

The next time and every other time we go back to see them after that, my parents try hard. I am proud of them. The kitchen and living room are clean, they buy sweets and toys for the kids.

They are trying to be decent grandparents.

But, oh, Dad, you are getting old.

The kids laugh with them and love them. Apart from that first time, my parents do not misbehave in front of the kids. Not once.

Hope. 1999.

There's a knock on my door. My daughter is at school. My son and I are getting ready for him to start preschool next week. I'll be moving from being a volunteer at Citizens' Advice into a paid job with them. Last night we celebrated with cake and Smarties.

The man on my doorstep introduces himself as being from Social Services. I stand, stunned, unable to move.

Shit, what have I done? Who reported me? Maybe it's the Home-Start worker who reported me. But she has been coming for over a year. She says I'm doing okay.

I'm crying even before I let him through the door. My son is running around being boisterous.

'Shhh, love, shhh. Go and play with some toys, there's a good boy.'

He doesn't. I smile at the social worker, make him a cup of tea.

'We've received an allegation. From a neighbour. We understand that you are going out at night and leaving your children alone.'

What? NO! I would never leave my kids.

'Please, Ms Daniels, we are just following up, you know we have to. We've been to your daughter's school.'

What? Oh no! What did they say?

'We received a glowing report. They tell us that you volunteer at the playgroup where your son goes, and that you go into the school to hear the kids read.'

Oh, okay. Please don't take my kids.

'We've also spoken to your health visitor; she, too, gave you a glowing report. Home-Start say that you have been working with them for over a year and are now managing well, and that your kids are happy and loved. That you volunteer at the CAB, too, and that you just got yourself a paid job. Congratulations.'

'Thank you.'

'There's one thing we need to check, though . . .'

Here we go, this is the thing, the thing that will mean they take my kids away. Don't take my kids away, I'll die. I don't mean to do anything bad.

The seriousness of the situation means my tears turn to hysteria. He's lovely and calms me down. So I can tell him.

'The thing is, right, my kids, they go to their dad every other weekend. I ain't got no keys, always loose 'em. I don't know why. Never have. Never needed them as a kid. Never had 'em in care. So, the nights I drop the kids off with their dad, I sometimes go out, or visit a friend 'cos I can't stand being in the house on my own. Never have got used to it, since, you know, being in care. When I come home and I've to get back in my house, the only way to do it is to climb in the kitchen window.

'Only at night, though. During day times, when the kids are with me, I just risk it and leave the door on the latch. My parents do the same, always have, still do, and they live in Hackney. No one's ever gone into their house uninvited when the door was on the latch!

'Is that why the neighbours think I leave my kids alone, at home, 'cos I climb in the window? Do they think the kids are inside? What kind of person thinks like that?'

Please believe me, it's the truth. You have to believe me. Am I going to lose my kids?

As he's taking notes, I carry on, 'Look, just 'cos I was in care, you're not taking my babies from me. You can't; I've done nothing wrong. The reports, you said they're all good. Please, you can't take my kids.'

He smiles, 'I've no reason to disbelieve you, Hope. Can I just have a look around the house so I can finish off my report?'

Love my house. Wait until you see what I've done with the kids' rooms.

I smile. 'As long as you take your shoes off before going into the kids' rooms.'

My daughter's room is a princess room and my son, who is following me around like he's going to lose me, his room is decorated with everything Thomas the Tank Engine. I tell the social worker that all the decoration was bought and paid off with Provident loans. I am proud of myself and my decorating.

He puts me at ease and we talk most of the day about what I've learnt since leaving care. All the while, my son runs around, playing. He never stops. The social worker asks how I'm getting on with my son.

'Fine, I think.'

He says, 'I think your son is very hyperactive and I'd like to send you to a practical parenting group; and for your son to have an assessment with a paediatrician. How does that sound?'

I trust you, I can tell you. I know that you are trying to help. You believe me. You don't want to take my kids away. You have listened to me.

'You know, I've no idea what expected behaviour is for my son. I think, with my upbringing, my sense of normality is far off-key . . .'

'Hope, don't give yourself such a hard time. You are doing really well. You will love the practical parenting course, I know it; maybe you will meet some other mums, too, and not be on your own all the time . . .'

I smile. 'I've got to get my daughter from school.'

He tells me my kids are a credit to me.

I am crying when he leaves. I am happy.

Hope. 1999.

The phone rings, I see from the caller ID that it's Abby. I am really pleased to hear from her; I heard that she recently married and has bought a house in Spain. She's a teaching assistant now, and I bet a really good one.

It will be great to catch up, haven't seen her in ages.

The minute I hear her voice, I know something is wrong.

'Abby, what is it?'

'It's Lee. He's dead. A drug overdose. Heroin. Been in a coma for days. He didn't make it, Hope; he couldn't fight his demons. No one could help him. I didn't even know it had got that bad. Truth be told, I haven't seen him for a bit. He always said he was busy. He hid his pain so well.'

My stomach feels turned inside out.

'Oh, Abby, I am so sorry.'

When we've finished chatting, I put down the phone. My legs can't hold me up, they give way. I am on the floor, washing it with my tears.

Hope. 2007.

I wake up with another hangover. No memory of the night before.

I shake my husband awake.

'It stops now.'

'What does?'

'My drinking. I want to show my kids a better way. I'm going to try and stop drinking. Right now. It's gone too far.'

He hugs me. 'At last,' he whispers. 'At last.'

That afternoon, I go to a local meeting. I walk in focused on the present. There's a man, tall, well built next to the tea table. He turns just as I recognise him.

'Robert? Is that you?

He nods, I can see he can't quite place me.

'I'm Hope Daniels, we had a friend in common, Abby, at one point, too, remember her? You in recovery, then?'

'Yeah, a long time now, Hope.'

'Am so proud of ya, Robert . . . Serendipity, eh?'

Debbie. Aged thirty-two.
The school bell rings.

'Come on, kids, go to your next class quietly, please. Put your homework jotters over there. Not long now 'til your exams.'

The class files out of the room – the same room that I sat in learning as much as I could when I was a kid. One of the boys, Jon, tries to sneak past me. I've been watching him for a while. I'm concerned.

'Jon, come here, please. Sit down.'

I sit across from him, at the same height so I'm not looking down on him.

'You didn't hand in any homework.'

He's looking at his shoes, they are worn through. Winter is coming. I noticed this morning, he's no coat.

'No, Miss.'

'Can you explain why?'

'No, Miss.'

I take a deep breath.

'Look at me, please, Jon.'

He does. There are many families with not much money round here, but Jon is different. His eyes are hollow, dark, dull. His skin is pale, cheeks sunken.

He's given up. I know he's been in care before, but he's now back at home. What's going on?

'Jon, I can help. I need to tell you a secret. Only the Head knows, okay?'

He looks petrified. He nods.

I raise my sleeve. On my arm there's a blue blob of a tattoo, a mark of honour of all I've come through. A tattoo I gave myself on the same day as Jackie and Hope got theirs. It was a flower, but it's faded now. I can tell Jon knows what it means. He stares and stares, then in a small voice starts to talk, to tell me his story, of things that he's never told anyone, of things that have taken his childhood.

I listen. I call Social Services. As we wait I tell him he's very brave. I tell him he'll be safe now. That he deserves a childhood that's better.

He tells me that my tattoo is shit, but he's glad that I have it.

Me too. Me too.

Hope. 2011.

It's there, an invitation from Jackie on Facebook to a care leavers' reunion in June this year. There are over sixty people going already. Social workers, residential care workers and care leavers alike, all who passed through the system in London at one point in their care lives during the 1980s.

Wow! How great is this? I'll be able to see my lovely social workers again.

My thoughts are soon infected by self-doubt and self-loathing which, even in my thirties, I carry with me.

Why did they invite me? None of them like me. They thought, and probably still think, I'm a shit.

I've had a text from Jackie asking me why I haven't replied yet. I told her I will and ask about her two kids. As she's one of the organisers, she's able to tell me who else is going. To encourage me, she follows up the text with two emails – one with recent photos of her kids attached, they are all laughing and smiling, and the second telling me that some of my old social workers are definitely going to be there.

They threw me out. The system ensured they cut me off and it broke my heart losing them. It's not normal to cut someone off when they've lived with you for so long. And yet they try to do that, they did. Feelings dragged up again. I've been in recovery a few years now. Well proud. I've done what my parents couldn't. Beaten alcohol addiction. One day at a time.

Is it too soon? Crap. I want to go. Can I go? But they must think I'm an idiot. Thick. Disgusting. Maybe if I go I can put a few ghosts to rest. I can always see how I feel on the day. Try and finally deal with the feelings of loss at being kicked out of the very system that saved me. My sponsor in recovery says I have to deal with this if I want to stay in recovery. Relapse is too easy when you don't deal with stuff. The pain is still raw. I loved, love, 'my' staff.

I stare at the page for a long time. My daughter comes in, is looking over my shoulder.

'What's that, Mum?'

'A reunion, for kids in care.'

'If you don't press that button and go tell them how great a mum you are, I'll press it for you.'

She smiles beautifully as she reaches out to press 'yes' to say I am attending. But I get there before her. I'm going. An unexpected feeling of calm takes over me.

'Thanks, my lovely; you're just what I needed.'

Even though I stop off on the way to the reunion to see my first Home-Start worker, the one who showed me how to be a mum and who has been a constant in my life, along with my old social worker, from when the kids were small, I arrive at the reunion early.

I love seeing them. Catching up, telling them about the kids.

There's a bench just down the hill from the reunion. From here I can see what used to be Beaufort Community Home with Education.

They closed it down six months after they chucked me out.

I repeat the name in my head time and again. Stare at the new houses that replace what was my home. Advice from my childhood, from Glen, my key worker, rings in my ears. Ethics and morals I pass on to my own kids. Glen's voice in my head is as clear as day, because I repeat what he taught me so often:

'Never ring in sick to work unless you cannot get out of bed, or it's catching!'

I never do.

'Always tell the truth to your boss.'

I do. I have.

'Never do anything that feels wrong in your stomach.'

*Took me a while to learn that one! But when tummy says no,
I think of you and all you did for me, Glen.*

I feel a small smile on my face. My first proper family
home. Until they changed it. I frown at the memory of
being moved upstairs, away from my staff.

*It matters who is in charge. By moving me upstairs, they took
away my family, they took away my life. Downstairs I knew they
loved me, they really, really looked out for me, and after me. I
loved the praise and hated to disappoint anyone – that's how I
knew I loved them, too. That's how I became settled. I studied.
Worked hard. My life was the happiest ever at that time.*

Other memories flood into my head.

*The live-in staff would take me out to family things, games of
rounders, cricket matches . . . They reassured me, told me time
and again, that I was just as special as the other kids. That every
child is special.*

I come back to the present, look over at the village park. I
smile.

*It felt like I had a family. Those kids with real mums and dads
were the odd ones out in my world.*

Another memory kicks in.

Girls coming home, carrying TVs from their parents. I am
sad. Alex, the housekeeper, buys me a TV. It's black and white
and 'not as snazzy as the other girls', but I love it so bad!

Alex applies by letter to the Principal to foster me.

That letter isn't in my files.

The staff hear about the application, tell me about it. I
discuss it with Alex on a day that she takes me out for
dinner with Glen, her boyfriend. Nothing's ever done
about it.

Why couldn't they foster me?

I laugh at how we all had dummies and blankies for a while. Regression they call it nowadays; the start of rebuilding, learning how to be a child.

The staff downstairs, they totally built me up from a very sad little girl into someone who felt loved. And then the Principal moved me.

That hurt me. You were my family. You were my security. Why did it happen? Even though you were taken away, even though I was sent away, in my head, you never left me. Glen, Alex, all the lovely staff. They may have thrown me out, but you never left me, because I kept you close. I wouldn't, couldn't, ever let you go.

A tear falls. I am so sad for that fifteen-year-old girl who was moved upstairs to different staff. A new Principal came in, moved me. I hate her. Jackie told me she's not been invited to the reunion.

It was like having my family torn from me. You didn't even let me go downstairs to see them. I was barred. How could you? A young girl. How did you expect me to cope with the loss? You wonder why I went off the rails again? That one decision meant lost years of my life. I gave up on education. Became a secret drinker. You tore away everything the staff and I had worked for. Knocked me over. Broke me.

I raise my hands to my face. Wipe away the tears with the palms of my hands, top to bottom. Deep breath. Breathe out. I hear Glen's voice in my head, 'Come on, girl. Hope, move up.'

He's not in my head. He's here.

I hug and hold on to Glen for all the years I haven't seen him. I hold him, we hug each other, for all the days that have passed that his words of wisdom were in my head, but he wasn't there.

It was like you had died. I was barred from seeing you.

We sit, we speak. I tell him of my life; I tell him how I've tried to live my life by what he taught me. We both repeat the words at the same time:

'If you do something you can't justify to yourself, then you are on the wrong path.'

He smiles, 'I'm glad you remember.'

'It's been tough, but it's working out okay now. I've a lovely husband, two kids . . .'

It all comes tumbling out. I tell him about how I am a project manager at Citizens' Advice, how they supported me, worked with me throughout my career. I tell him about the book I've written, *Hackney Child*. How it's helped me with recovery. How the reaction I've had from it means I am now proud of being a care-leaver, of the skills I have, of what I have to offer. I tell him about my lecturing. How there's so much I still don't understand, how he can still help me.

'Why did they put me upstairs? Ban me from being downstairs.'

'They thought we were getting too close. That you were getting too attached.'

'But you were my new family. How was I expected to feel? She threw me out.'

'Yes, we know now that the Principal was put in place with the objective to close down the home. At the time, we knew she didn't care for the kids; at first, we couldn't work out why. There were thirty-eight of you when she joined. In the end there was none. Took her nine months.'

We are both quiet, looking at the posh estate that used to be Beaufort.

After a while, Glen laughs.

'You could be one stroppy little madam.'

We are sitting on the bench, he nudges me shoulder to shoulder.

'When you arrived, I didn't think you would last long with us; you were a runner all right. I thought you would be back in Secure, quick as a flash. A yo-yo. Running away, that's normal, all part of the settling-in period. But you proved us all wrong. You, you settled in quickly. But you let us know what you liked and didn't like all right. Sulky one, you were. You didn't like getting told off by people you liked. If you didn't like the person who was tellin' you off, you grumbled. If you liked them, you sulked. A right stroppy madam. Going around, hurt, defensive. Three days of not talking to the staff. Yup, if memory serves, I think that was your record!'

'Really? That bad? You must've all hated me.'

I know they loved me.

Glen laughs, 'Not at all, Hope. Not at all. In fact, I was speaking with Alex the other day. She can't come, but would love to meet up. We were saying how all the staff used to seek you out on bad days to chat to you and get a cuddle off you. You were the one that would make *us* feel better. Especially during that time when the men were hanging around . . . All of us staff were scared then.'

His voice trails off, becomes stronger again. 'You settled in, luckily, though. Weekends you were happier staying at school than going home. We arranged it so your brother could come down. How's he doing?'

'He's wicked, thanks. We're still in touch. He's doing well.'

'It was all about trust for you two. Especially you. You wanted a family so badly – foster me this, foster me that. When you got your head round it not happening, you selected your own group, your own family. Then you settled, really settled. All the kids settled there, eventually. I remember one girl, terribly abused she'd been. She was terrified her abusers would find her. She couldn't sleep, so I got her out of bed, I asked her to help me with the lock-up. She came round with me, turned every key. Checked every door. Broke the rules, I did, but, you know, a few days after, she settled down. Trusted us to keep her safe. Away from the bad people she was used to. Felt that she belonged, she told me. It was a magical moment, Hope.

'A lot of people didn't like risks like that but, for you, once you'd settled, once every kid settled, and you all did there, your behaviour was no different to that of other teenage kids. You all laughed. You especially, and you, Hope Daniels, you could talk. A lot! You were selective about who you would talk to all right, but once you decided that person was okay, then, in your mind, they were okay.

'We must've done something right, though, treating kids and staff as individuals. Here you are, looking splendid. Life sorted. You troubled us, though, especially after you were moved upstairs . . . If you ran away once, you ran away a hundred times. We found you in squats, the police found you wandering the streets; days and days of worry. It was the same time as when the girls were getting involved with some bad men who were selecting girls for their clients. They stood outside the station, watching you all get off the train, picking girls out; using you all. And then those guys would bring them, pretending to be worried for their safety. As worried as I was for you, I was always glad you never got brought home in a Mercedes.

'It was heartbreaking. Debbie told us she'd been asked to do something that didn't sit right in her tummy. I was so proud my words had got through. I was so scared about what was going on, how the girls were being drawn in. We knew who they were, the police had warned us.'

I wasn't picked. A blessing. Why wasn't I picked?

'So we had to move five girls in one go. After we did that, this guy, a big shot in London crime life, had enough front to come to Beaufort looking for one of the girls. He put himself up as someone who cared, who knew her. Brought his madam with him, too. Concerned citizens, my arse.'

'What did you do?'

'Called the police, said you ain't gonna believe this . . . Truth is stranger than fiction. The girls, as far as I know, were moved all round the country. I heard they were all safe, but those kind of men would have just found others. They are clever in the way they can make a vulnerable girl feel like she's wanted, when the reality is they are using the girls to make money. I always say, pick your battles, and that was one I chose. I wish I'd fought harder to keep you downstairs.'

'It's okay; I knew you had as much choice as I did, which was none. That new Principal, though, what was she on?'

'She had an agenda. She came in and the laughing stopped. We weren't allowed to cuddle you kids no more.

She stopped girls at the last minute from going home, when they had been looking forward to it all week. Tough love she called it. I call it emotional torture. She was sadistic, I reckon. Working you kids up all week, watching you all pack, only to tell you you weren't going anywhere. We weren't allowed to socialise with you kids or take you to our families, or out on fun days. She set out to destroy that place. She was a hatchet woman, I think, sent in to close Beaufort down. No doubt in my mind. You, you were the manifestation of all that hidden agenda stuff that was going on. Here's a kid, you, who had done all that was expected of you. We got through to you, you were doing GCSEs, planning to be a lawyer, you had ambition, you were happy. You had made yourself a little family. It was working.'

'Then it all changed, Glen. They took it all away from me.'

Glen leans forward. His elbows are on his knees. He looks at the ground for a moment, then turns his head round to me. Looks me straight in the eye.

'That was a clinical decision, Hope. Purely clinical. The fact that you were close to people downstairs, the fact that you embraced Beaufort, you embraced me and my pontificating. Any closeness, she didn't want, she wanted to destroy. I'll say it again, she was sent in to close us down. She needed to be disruptive. She also changed our conditions, our way of working, put barriers up. Didn't want anyone to be emotionally connected to Beaufort. She had one focus; shut the place down. She did her job well, I'll give her that.'

Glen leans back on the bench before carrying on. 'You know, she threw the letter Alex wrote asking to foster you in the bin. She stopped it. Ever since I left that place, you never left me. Nagging away in my head.'

We both smile, both so terribly sad for the teenage girls, for me, whose family was taken away.

'But, you know what, Glen? I've found you now. You can nag me in person from now on, and not just in my head . . . You know, it's lucky we were both early.'

'I knew you would be,' Glen smiles.

I stand up, brush myself down. 'Come on, there are lots of other people that will want to see you again.'

We walk together, up to the reunion. Glen turns to me. 'So, you broke the cycle, then?'

We both smile. Glen carries on. 'Did you say you had two kids of your own, eh?'

'And a granddaughter that I love so much I could eat her, and a gorgeous husband, and . . . a book.'

'So, you haven't lost your ability to talk a bit, then?'

Oh, I've missed you, Glen.

EPILOGUE

Hope. 2012.

The outside of Huddersfield University, Department of Social Work is scary; its beige and black walls tower above me. On the drive up here, I was so excited. I kept laughing to myself.

Lecturing to social workers – how cool is that? Me. Wow.

Now I don't feel so clever. Now I'm pacing back and forth in front of the building. My mind is blank of everything I've prepared and only full of doubts.

I'm shittin' it. What do they want to know from me? Why should any of these masters degree students take notice of what I've to say? What do I know that they don't already know?

I put my hands out in front of me, they're shaking. I try and hold them steady. My hands carry on shaking of their own accord.

Stop shaking. Hope, pull yourself together. Come on, girl; they wouldn't have invited you here if they didn't want you to speak. To share. What will they learn from me? Won't I just be teaching grannies to suck eggs? What are they going to learn from me? I don't want to do this, I want to go home.

Inside the lecture theatre there are about sixty faces looking back at me. Rows of people, of all ages, staring back at me. The lecture room is full of pens, some poised, others wiggling as notes are scribbled in response to the senior lecturer. She's presenting a lecture on the lessons learnt by the authorities as a result of serious case reviews.

I would have loved her as my social worker. Would she have taken me home? Loved me? What am I meant to be talking about? That's it. Serious case reviews. Teenagers. Girls in care. What do I know?

I've read this report already, out of interest and in preparation for today, but it's only when the lecturer is doing her summary that I hear the implications, understand the connection.

She's saying, 'Social workers felt it was a lifestyle choice to have sex with so many older men.'

What, how and why did they think that? These are children, damaged, fragile, in care; I can't believe the social workers thought this was a 'lifestyle choice'. Why did they not protect them? Want to protect them? Why did they have to believe so little of them?

My heart hurts.

The lecturer goes on. Now she's highlighting a particular case that I remember from the Rochdale report. The report calls her 'Suzie'. I focus on the words of the lecturer:

'Summarising the report, therefore, at fifteen years old Suzie was already showing signs that she was a troubled and vulnerable young person. She confides in two different agencies and, on these two occasions, tells them that she is the victim of serious sexual assaults by a number of adults, linked to takeaway premises. The police do follow up and investigate. However, the possibility that she's being sexually exploited isn't initially recognised. The initial professional focus is on providing support services for Suzie and on assisting her parents to set boundaries to keep her safe. As it turns out, these safeguards have little impact on Suzie's circumstances: she remains at risk of sexual harm, compounded by her abuse of alcohol and possibly drugs.'

I feel myself start to shake. I feel sick.

Oh my God, she could be describing me. But this review, it's not about me. But that is what happened to me. No, no, no. How come I haven't made the connection before? They were men in their thirties, they took us out, took us to parties. I was fifteen. I thought they were just being nice but, no, he just wanted to come on to me, wanted to use me. Oh my God, have I blocked it out? I ran away. No, no, no. Nothing happened. I got away. I was so lucky. Then why do I feel so sick at the thought of these men? Did this happen to me? All this time, I thought the fact that they chased us was my fault.

He built us up, 'You're so special.' Told us he'd saved us from being beaten by his wife's brother. He told us, 'Don't worry, I'll protect ya. I'm the one that saved ya.' Built our trust, then betrayed it. 'Don't worry about staying out, no one will miss ya. But I'll miss ya, if ya not here. You owe me 'cos I saved ya from a beatin'.'

Looking down my top. Dirty old man.

I believed, really believed, that those two blokes spent time with me 'cos they liked me. I thought they made me feel sick 'cos

*all men made me feel sick. Well, apart from my men social work-
ers. They were different. Those men, one of them married a young
girl from care, then moved on to me. But I thought they'd saved
me that night from violence. They told me I was beautiful. But
they were so much older than me . . .*

*Bastard. For twenty years I've believed it was my fault he came
on to me. Disgusted at myself. Never for a second did I think this
guy had targeted girls in care, me, my friends. He must've targeted
his own wife. Married her, for fuck's sake. Marrying her doesn't
make it better. She was fifteen when she started seeing him, then he
married her as soon as she left care. And then he moved on to me.
Why hadn't I made the connection? Oh shit.*

In the break I go outside to clear my head. On my way out,
I grab a copy of the Rochdale report so if anyone tries to
interrupt me, I can pretend I'm reading, preparing for my
own lecture.

My head is being pulled forward with the weight of
what I've just worked out. I sit down on a bench, close my
eyes. Rub my forehead and my brain feels full. I try to
rationalise what has just happened.

*After all these years. All these years and I never realised. All
those wasted years, when I carried that disgust about myself
around with me. I blamed myself for that old man trying to cheat
on his wife with me. I was fifteen, we all were. Fuck. He targeted
us, us girls in care.*

It was not my fault.

I look down at the report in my hands, read through the
summary again. This thing that happened to those girls in
Rochdale. A lifestyle choice?

Really?

No – we were just scared and trapped and he made out like he was the only person around who could help us. There was nothing we could do. What were we meant to do? The man says he loves you, and you accept it, 'cos you don't know what love is. You believe this is love. You don't know what's normal, let alone love. Instinct tells ya something ain't right, but not until you realise that what he wants from you is more than you want to give. But you're trapped. You don't know what love should be, but you know this isn't love either. Sitting there, as he strokes your arm for the first time, you know it's just a dirty old man wanting stuff he shouldn't he asking for from a fifteen-year-old girl. Those poor girls.

Die, you dirty old man. Die, you dirty old man.

Back at the front of the lecture theatre, I stand to speak and, at the same time, take a deep breath and I begin.

On my way home, I think about how best to share what I've learnt today. I formulate a new lecture in my head:

'Listening to the previous lecture, I realised that what happened in Rochdale to those girls . . . I realised, for the first time, that a similar thing happened to me and friends of mine. It's taken me twenty years to work this out and, as I've only just realised what danger my friends and I faced, how were social workers, with partial information and surrounded by secrets and lies that the perpetrator had spun, meant to realise? How are you meant to deal with this?

'You could have a child who may or may not believe that what's happening to her is wrong. I didn't know it was wrong when it was happening to me. The child's life may be so chaotic that she's no time to think, cannot work it out. Or she may have worked it out but doesn't know how to get out of the situation. This is where you can help, by showing that you do care.

'From the moment I walked into that police station at nine years old with my younger brothers, and throughout my time in care, people have been looking out for me. Telling me I matter. Because, however much we want home to be the place to grow up, sometimes, care is better than home . . .'

POSTSCRIPT

REFLECTIONS FROM HOPE

Letter **1.**
Found in April 2000. A half-finished letter in the Social Services files.

Dear Mum

Just seen my psychiatrist, he told me you were sober when he saw you. Shame you couldn't manage that for us.

I told him I was ashamed of you.

Why? he said. You know why, don't you?

You make me feel sick – why, don't you stop all those disgusting men pawing you and buying you – and why the fuck did you do all those things in front of me – you are rotten. Right, pure rotten.

Don't you care that I'm locked up? I'm thirteen – don't that bother ya? The doctor bloke said you never even mentioned it – I should be at home with a mum and dad, not locked up in a kid's prison – for what? Drinking so bad that I can't control myself – wonder where I learnt that from, eh?

You should not have been allowed to be my mum – but you was – you should go to prison for making me feel so disgusting.

Taken up again when writing *Tainted Love* – July 2013.

Dear Mum

I don't regret the words above, but I'm happy and relieved it wasn't sent to you.

I look back on your life as my mum and see a life of such sadness that you don't deserve harsh words from me.

You haven't got much time left in this world – and whilst I choose not to have you in my life today, active addiction and all, I have got something to say.

I loved you, love you today, and forgive you.

Lots of love

Hope xx

Letter 2.
A blog, 2013.

Dear all

When I left care, I was a huge melting pot of emotions – negative feelings – about myself. I absolutely despised myself. A horrible, unlovable, ugly, nasty, spiteful person, I believed I was.

It really, really hurt when I thought of my childhood with my parents and, as I was back in contact with them, I internalised my feelings for them, and my lost childhood, and tried the best I could to make a life for my children.

After all – my parents were all I had now – all of those loving social workers who had been so integral to my life had gone.

But you can't really just shove these feelings and emotions away – they come out sideways, whether you like it or not.

Mine came out in the way of self-hatred, and manifested them-selves in an alcohol addiction.

When I agreed to enter treatment for my addiction, I knew that to stay sober I would have to deal with the ghosts of my past, but had absolutely no idea how. I mean, this pain and fear had been part of my life forever. Who was I without it?

My identity was totally skewed – I had no idea what my char-acter assets were – I could and would reel off character defects like a restaurant menu.

But how could I let go of the pain of my childhood, and the loss I felt from being 'evicted' from the Care System?

A wonderful Recovery Worker spent many hours with me, sharing with me the power of forgiveness. 'Forgiveness!' I was enraged. 'Why would I want to let these people who had hurt me so bad off the hook?'

'But you are not, you are allowing yourself to live,' said my Recovery Worker.

So I tried it – and this is how:

1) Your feelings are legitimate. You are deceiving yourself not to accept that someone did not hurt you when, in fact, they did. Badly.

2) There is no such thing as revenge. It simply does not exist. You can hurt someone even worse than they hurt you, yet it will never 'even the score'. There is a saying, 'Acid does more damage to the vessel it is stored in than to what it is poured on.'

3) Forgiveness is not what you feel. It is what you do with those feelings. If someone runs over a loved one with a car, it is going to take a while for you to get over the anger. Yet you can forgive the person more quickly. How? Because the action part of forgiveness is the 'laying down of weapons'. What are weapons? Getting even, yelling, name-calling, being passive aggressive,

and the like. Anything I do purposely to hurt someone is a weapon. I may have to lay down my weapons ten times in ten minutes. It is something I am in control of, as opposed to controlling the way I feel. You cannot always control your feelings, but you can control your actions.

4) Forgiveness means to grieve. It is acknowledging that we've been hurt. Whatever was done to you, you let it go. Let it die. There is no way to get even, it will only haunt you. Let yourself grieve whatever was done to you, that you might be free of that injury. Forgiving them will enable you to be free. By letting it go you choose not to get even, either through thought or deed. Once you are able to do this, you will cease to be haunted by what was done to you.

I share this with all my young people in the care system, and my care-leavers who are struggling with the same internal pain that I had – it's the most amazing thing in the world to be told by them, 'I get it now, and I ain't letting them rob me of my life no more!'

Life can and will be amazing post-childhood trauma and the care system, if you want it to be, as the success of those in this book show.

Love Hope

(letters as originally written by Hope)

AUTHORS' NOTES

From Hope

Since the writing and publication of *Hackney Child*, my life has changed beyond recognition. I am no longer ashamed of myself. I finally see myself as a child in my early years, a concept I could not grasp before. My children are happy and settled and, to my absolute joy, my daughter has started her own journey towards becoming a social worker. Another new beginning to our family life, free from abuse.

I never imagined that the response to my story would be so positive. The emotional healing from my childhood that started with recovery, and continues to this day, is simply magical. I've been inundated with requests from social work practitioners who feel I have something to give back to the system. I now feel the same. Thank you.

Oh my, I have so many beautiful people, who have shown the utmost of humanity to thank, that I can't possibly name you all.

I have to thank my mum and dad. Mum and Dad, you finally let go of us, allowed us to live a life away from the very people who loved us but couldn't parent us. Thank you.

A massive thank you to my co-writer, Morag Livingstone, who contributed so much to both *Hackney Child* and this book. Also to all my friends who feature in this book – we're together again, eh!

Thanks to my babies and husband, Dan. You are my world, I love, love, love you all. Enough said.

Thank you to all the many, many social workers, Ann and Jeff in particular, who we came into contact with – you had a hard task taking on our family but boy did you deliver – I hope you are proud of yourselves and of me.

To my beautiful, beautiful staff in the children's homes and the second secure unit. My favourite staff, my key workers Jimbo, John, Daud, June, Elizabeth, Jeremy, Richard, Mrs Gilby, Mr X (cannot remember your surname, but can still feel the hugs you gave me in the lock-up), and the list could go on – you all worked so hard with and for me, and you still can't get rid of me, and never will ☺

Thank you to the legend by the name of Sir Martin Narey – I would never have had the confidence to have got so far without your stewardship – shame for me that you didn't choose to foster, and foster me – maybe not for you and your sanity though, eh!

Thank you to all those social workers who showed us that there was another way of living – we're all testament to your skills and dedication.

I will finish with the most loving, inspiring and compassionate woman I have ever met – Ruth Neville. You embody the qualities that are essential in every social worker – the love you have shown me over the last two years will never leave me – you are a very, very special lady – love you lots.

From Morag
To Rebecca Winfield, our enthusiastic agent, Kerri Sharp, our detailed and experienced editor, and Jo Roberts-Miller for your valuable structural and editorial advice, along with all the wonderful team at Simon & Schuster; thank you all for your belief in us and for working so hard to make dreams come true. To my own family, dear friends and to those who taught me about how to best utilise words to form a story, thank you.

Being careful not to identify those in the book, we want to thank from the bottom of our hearts those who searched deep to share their stories. We think it only fair to say thank you for their openness and to bring the reader up to date with their success. Below is a composite of the present-day situation of the people whose real-life stories we have introduced throughout this book; all have, despite major challenges, made successes of their lives.

Between them they have fourteen children, none of whom are in care, or need to be.

There is a teacher's assistant

A school teacher

A PRU worker

A project manager of a food bank

One went to university

One is a successful artist

Another owns two homes, in the UK and abroad

All are in recovery from their childhoods and all are happy, as is Hope – you are an inspiration. Thank you.

If you would like to contact Hope,
please do so via the following:

https://www.facebook.com/hackneychild
hackneychild@gmail.co.uk